I0605675

THE LIBYAN PHARAOHS OF EGYPT

THE LIBYAN PHARAOHS OF EGYPT

THEIR LIVES AND AFTERLIVES

AIDAN DODSON

The American University in Cairo Press
Cairo New York

First published in 2025 by
The American University in Cairo Press
113 Sharia Kasr el Aini, Cairo, Egypt
420 Lexington Avenue, Suite 1644, New York, NY 10170
www.aucpress.com

ISBN 978 1 649 03310 9

Library of Congress Cataloging-in-Publication Data

Names: Dodson, Aidan, 1962- author.
Title: The Libyan pharaohs of Egypt : their lives and afterlives / Aidan Dodson.
Identifiers: LCCN 2025007379 | ISBN 9781649033109 (hardback) | ISBN 9781649033116 (adobe pdf)
Subjects: LCSH: Libyans--Egypt--History--To 1500. | Egypt--History--Third Intermediate Period, ca. 1071-ca. 650 B.C. | Egypt--Kings and rulers.
Classification: LCC DT90 .D629 2025

1 2 3 4 5 29 28 27 26 25

Designed by Sally Boylan
Printed in China

To the memories of
Robert K. Ritner
(1953–2021)
&
Kenneth A. Kitchen
(1932–2025)

Contents

Preface

During the tenth through seventh centuries BC, Egypt was ruled by kings whose backgrounds would have—at best—perplexed an Egyptian of earlier centuries. In its hierarchy of peoples, the Egyptians placed themselves above all others, reserving particular scorn for immediate neighbors in northeastern Africa: the Nubians in the south, and the Libyans to the west. Yet at the beginning of the seventh century, Egypt's paramount ruler was a Nubian, with regional thrones occupied by kings of Libyan descent—including a line who had once been the undisputed pharaohs of the whole of Egypt. Other regional worthies held unashamedly Libyan titles that had once been by definition those of foes of Egypt.

This situation was ultimately an outcome of a series of events that went back into the thirteenth century, but had crystallized early in the twelfth, when the so-called "Late Bronze Age Collapse" had upended the known world. Although Egypt had repelled invasion, her economy was impacted by the dislocation of world trade. This led to civil and political disorder and the assassination of at least one king, further facilitating incursions by Libyan elements from the west. By the first part of the eleventh century, the country had split into northern and southern portions, with Libyan names beginning to appear among the ruling family. Before the end of the century, the pharaonic throne would be occupied by a man of paternal Libyan descent, with the family firmly ensconced as the royal line of Egypt by the middle of the following century.

They were initially successful, with the first successful military incursion into Palestine in many years, and renewed trade links with the Levant. However, this was followed in the early ninth century by apparent troubles, a short revival, and then a disintegration of the country into a series of independent or quasi-independent polities. One of the principal examples, the Thebaid, then fell into a decades-long civil war, and a few decades later was absorbed into the burgeoning kingdom of Kush, which had evolved in Nubia in the wake of the collapse of Egyptian hegemony there early in the eleventh century. Nubian domination then expanded northward, to the Mediterranean, although the local Libyan dynasts continued to rule under Kushite suzerainty until Assyrian invasions in the later seventh century led to the sweeping away of some four centuries of political tradition in favor of a renewed unitary state.

While a significant amount of data survives from this era—nowadays dubbed the Third Intermediate Period—much of it is distinctly equivocal, with more than one interpretation possible. This extends to questioning the very independent existence of the owners of certain sets of pharaonic names, a problem exacerbated by the repeated reuse of a limited number of prenomina, leaving identification to parsing the subtleties of the profusion of epithets that some kings incorporated into their cartouches. As a result, Egyptologists have produced over the years a variety of assessments of the chronology, structure, and dynamics of the period. It is therefore impossible to speak of a "consensus" except in the most general terms.

Accordingly, and perhaps even more so than in my books in this series on Nefertiti and Tutankhamun(!), the picture presented here is very much my personal "working hypothesis." Nevertheless, as always, I have endeavored to indicate other points of view, and to explore the historiography of the period in some detail in chapter 6. One strand of historiographic debate has embraced elaborate attempts at reconciling the complex history and competing royal lines of the second part of the period covered with the breakdown and lists surviving from the work of the third-century BC historian Manetho. This has been particularly true over the definition of the Twenty-third Dynasty or Dynasties, which has usually generated more heat and smoke than light. Accordingly, my historical narrative of events during the eighth century BC avoids the use of that particular dynastic number, and simply defines the various royal groupings geographically.

As always, thanks are due to various people for their help during the writing of this book, in particular Lonneke Delpeut, Salima Ikram, Eva Lange-Athinodorou, Ian Mladjov, and Peter van der Veen, as well as one of the anonymous reviewers of the manuscript. I am also indebted to my army of proofreaders: Ali Ball, Victoria Baylis-Jones, Reg Clark, Vanessa Foott, Sid and Mary Kitchel, Esme McNamara, and, as always, the Hilton sisters, Anne and my wife Dyan. Residual errors and infelicities remain, of course, my sole responsibility.

This book is dedicated to the memories of two men: Rob Ritner, of the University of Chicago, whose book *The Libyan Anarchy*[1] is an indispensable and fundamental source and tool for anyone working on the Third Intermediate Period; and my old teacher, Ken Kitchen, of the University of Liverpool, a pioneer of the modern study of the period, who died while this book was in production.

Abbreviations and Conventions

Aberdeen	Marischal Museum, University of Aberdeen, UK
Ashmolean	Ashmolean Museum, Oxford, UK
Athens	Ethnikó Archaiologikó Mouseío, Athens, Greece.
BD	Book of the Dead Chapter.
Berlin ÄM	Ägyptisches Museum und Papyrussamlung, Berlin, Germany.
Berlin VA	Vorderasiatisches Museum, Berlin, Germany.
BM	British Museum, London, UK.
Brooklyn	Brooklyn Museum, New York, USA.
Budapest	Szépmúvészeti Museum, Budapest, Hungary.
Cairo	Egyptian Museum, Cairo, Egypt.
Durham	Oriental Museum, University of Durham, UK.
Fitzwilliam	Fitzwilliam Museum, Cambridge, UK.
Florence	Museo Archeologico, Florence, Italy.
GEM	Grand Egyptian Museum, Cairo, Egypt.
Geneva	Musée d'Art et d'Histoire, Geneva, Switzerland.
Gulbenkian	Museu Calouste Gulbenkian, Lisbon, Portugal.
Hamburg	Museum für Völkerkunde, Hamburg, Germany.
Heidelberg	Sammlung des Ägyptologischen Instituts, Universität Heidelberg, Germany.
Hermitage	State Hermitage Museum, St. Petersburg, Russia.
IFAO	Institut français d'archéologie orientale, Cairo, Egypt.
Jerusalem	Rockefeller Archæological Museum, Jerusalem.
Louvre	Musée du Louvre, Paris, France.

Manchester	Manchester Museum, Manchester, UK.
MFA	Museum of Fine Arts, Boston, MA, USA.
MMA	Metropolitan Museum of Art, New York, USA.
NMS	National Museums Scotland, Edinburgh.
NRT	Tanis royal cemetery tomb number.
p	Papyrus
Petrie	Petrie Museum of Egyptian and Sudanese Archaeology, University College London, UK.
Pushkin	State Pushkin Museum of Fine Arts, Moscow, Russia.
RMO	Rijksmuseum van Oudheden, Leiden, Netherlands.
Strasbourg	Institut d'égyptologie, Université de Strasbourg, France.
Stockholm	Medelhavsmuseet, Stockholm, Sweden.
Swansea	Egypt Centre, Swansea University, UK.
TT	Theban Tomb number.
Turin	Museo Egizio, Turin, Italy.
UPMAA	University of Pennsylvania Museum of Archaeology and Anthropology, Philadelphia, PA, USA.
Vatican	Musei Gregoriano Egizio, Vatican City.
Vienna	Kunsthistorisches Museum, Vienna, Austria.
*	biography of individual available in Bierbrier 2019.

Ancient Egyptian dates are given in terms of the king's regnal year, and the months and days of the three Egyptian seasons (*3ḫt, prt, and šmw*). So "Year 23, IV *prt* 5" means "23rd regnal year, 4th month of the *prt*-season, day 5."

Under Egyptological convention, kingly and high-priestly homonyms are distinguished by upper-case roman numerals (e.g., Osorkon III), while lesser individuals are distinguished by upper-case letters (e.g., Osorkon F) or lower-case Roman numerals (e.g., Pamiu i). The ordinals for kings named Shoshenq are as agreed at the Leiden conference on the period in 2007.[1]

In transcriptions and translations, restorations/lacunae/interpolations are enclosed by square brackets and glosses by parentheses; ⌜…⌝ indicates that the reading of the enclosed material is uncertain.

Introduction

Archaeologically, the term "Libya" has come to be used to refer to the area beyond the chain of oases that runs between two hundred and five hundred kilometers west of the Nile, as far as Cyrenaica.[1] The term derives ultimately from the Egyptian word "Libu" (*rbw/lbw*: the sounds *r* and *l* were for a long time not distinguished in writing), found from the time of Rameses II onward. This term referred to people, rather than territory, and is one of a range of terms used by the Egyptians for groups coming from the area in question. There is a lack of consistency in the way specific terms are used, which may reflect a lack of understanding by the Egyptians of the subtleties involved, or/and some fluidity within the Libyan populations themselves.

The earliest terms found referring to Libyan groups are Tjehenu (*ṯḥnw*, probably current at the beginning of the fourth millennium BC) and Tjemehu (*ṯmḥmw*, current by the Sixth Dynasty). While both were apparently to be found close to Egyptian territory, the two seem to have been formally distinct. However, they may have essentially merged in practice by the Middle Kingdom, when the Story of Sinuhe speaks of a campaign by Senwosret I that went to "Tjehenu-land," but returned with "Tjemehu" prisoners. By the New Kingdom, further Libyan groups had entered the Egyptian lexicon. As well as the Libu, there were now also the Mashwesh (*mšwš*, often abbreviated to Ma [*mꜥ*]), and a number of others that only occur once in Egyptian texts, most commonly in the account of the Libyan campaign of Rameses III (see below).

As for the nature of these groups, they are generally seen as having been at least semi-nomadic, with significant herds of animals, but also practicing some agriculture. Such conclusions have been drawn from Egyptian references, and also assuming cultural and economic parallels with groups inhabiting the area in more recent times. The groups seem to have had stratified societies led by what the Egyptians referred to as "Chiefs" (*wrw*), a term later used by the Libyans themselves in Egypt. Members of these groups

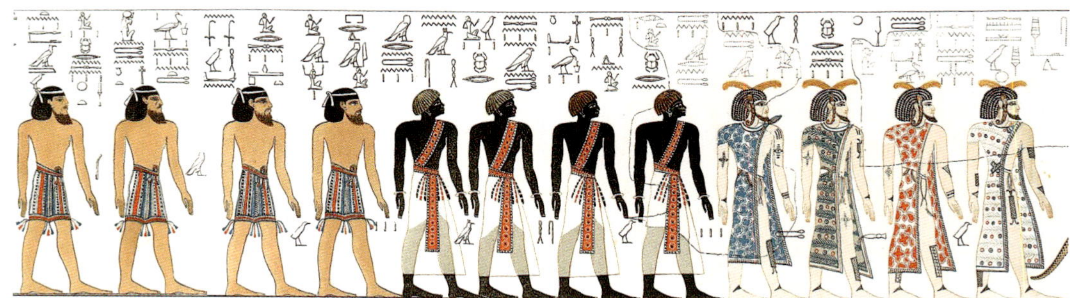

FIGURE 1 Syrians, Nubians, and Libyans (right), as shown in the Book of Gates; tomb of Sethy I in the Valley of the Kings (KV17).

seem to have lived not only in their likely heartland of Cyrenaica, but also further east along the Mediterranean coast. They were also to be found in at least the western part of the Nile Delta, as well as in the wider Western Desert and its oases.

Recorded interactions between the Egyptians and Libyan groups go back to the dawn of Egyptian history, with representations of defeated Tjehenu in Old Kingdom royal mortuary temples, and the Tjehemu noted as foes of the king of the Nubian polity of Yam during the reign of Pepy II. Campaigns against Libyans are mentioned by a number of later kings, but trade items are also recorded. Like other foreigners, Libyans had by the New Kingdom achieved a standard "look" in Egyptian art (fig. 1). However, after the time of Rameses III they are generally shown after the manner of Egyptians, although the ostrich feather in the hair that had long been part of conventional representations of Libyans continued to be used on occasion, in particular during the late ninth to the eighth centuries BC (cf. figs. 64, 66, 68a, b).

A change in relationships seems to occur around the beginning of the Nineteenth Dynasty, with a prominent depiction of a campaign into Libya placed on the walls of Karnak by Sethy I (fig. 2), and a chain of fortresses established to the west of the Delta under Rameses II, which stretched through El-Alamein out to Zawiyet Umm el-Rakham. However, more Libyans came to settle in the oases, and in Year 5 of Merenptah a full-scale invasion was attempted.[2] This attack was in coalition with elements of the so-called "Sea Peoples"—groups apparently displaced from the Balkans and Aegean region. These men were perhaps being employed by the Libyans as mercenaries, or they might have been simply making common cause in coveting Egyptian territory. The combination initially made good progress, and were only finally stopped at "Perire," likely in the southern part of the western Delta.[3] These events were recorded in Merenptah's Great Karnak Inscription and associated reliefs in the *Cour de la Cachette* in the temple of Amun-Re at Karnak.

FIGURE 2 Top: the Libyan war of Sethy I, as shown at Karnak. Bottom: episodes from the first and second Libyan wars of Rameses III, as depicted at Medinet Habu.

Ironically, the defeat of the invaders meant that prisoners came into Egypt as a labor force (and were later employed as soldiers), and thus actually bolstered the Libyan presence in Egypt, particularly in the Delta, but also in the Nile valley. The threat from Libyans outside Egypt nevertheless continued. Rameses III had to repel two incursions in force.[4] One came in Year 5 and another in Year 11, both by a coalition of members of the Mashwesh, Libu, and Seped Libyan tribes. Between these two attempts, Rameses had had to deal with a further invasion attempt, this time by a larger group of the Libyans' old allies, the Sea Peoples. They had rampaged through much of the Levant, contributing to the collapse of a number of long-standing states, and widespread dislocation of peoples and polities. Now, Egypt was effectively the "last man standing" of the Late Bronze Age states along the shores of the eastern Mediterranean.[5]

While Rameses III was successful in stopping the Sea Peoples and the Libyan invasion, prisoners from all three campaigns ended up in Egypt and, although initially settled in menial roles around the country, their descendants became part of the broader population. In the case of the Libyans, many doubtless came to marry into families from earlier waves of immigration, thereby reinforcing the communities who looked to the west for their traditions and outlook. These would soon be playing important roles in the Egyptian state, with some making alliances with old Egyptian families. These were doubtless the seeds from which later sprang the Libyan pharaohs.

In parallel with these settled Libyans, their compatriots resident in the Western Desert continued to be thorns in the flesh of those living on the western margins of Egypt during the latter part of the Twentieth Dynasty. Raids on even the Theban necropolis and its inhabitants are recorded from the time of Rameses VI onward. These incursions became more intensive during the civil troubles that emerged during the reign of Rameses IX (see page 7), with major incidents attested in Years 10, 11, 13, and 15 at the royal tomb-workmen's village of Deir el-Medina.[6] During Year 3 of his successor, Rameses X, construction activity at the royal tomb was only undertaken on one working day in five, and there are a number of cases where rations were not delivered on time. On III *prt* 6, 9, 11, 12, 18, 21, and 24 the Deir el-Medina crew were recorded as "inactive because of the foreigners." Ultimately, the threat from these intruders contributed to the transfer of the workmen's community from its historic village of Deir el-Medina to within the fortified walls of the temple complex at Medinet Habu.

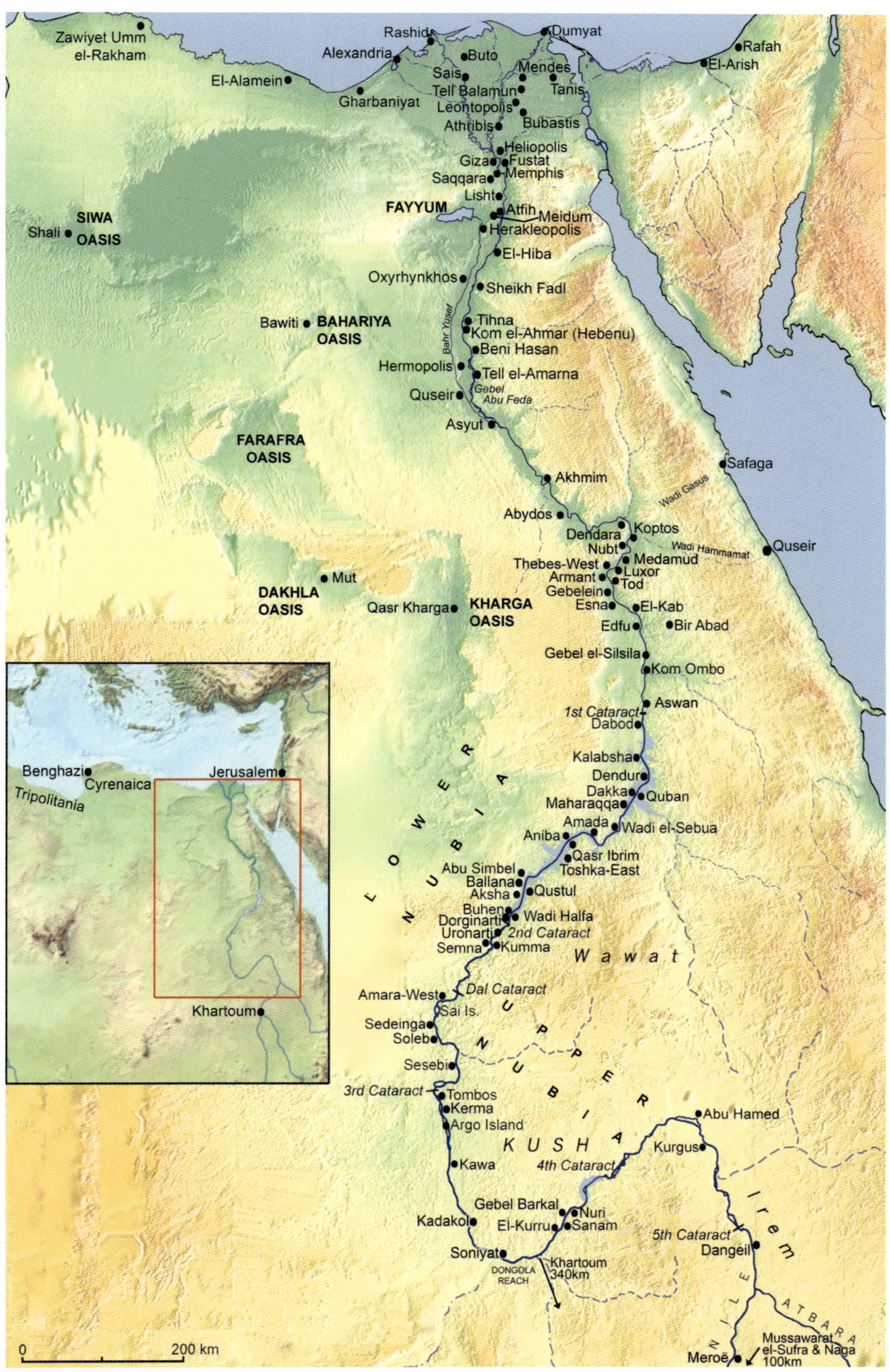

FIGURE 3 Map of Egypt and Nubia.

1 Post-Imperial Egypt and the Advent of the Libyan Pharaohs

While Rameses III had successfully defended Egypt from invasion, his reign ended in economic troubles and his own assassination.[1] The former may have been, at least in part, the result of the international dislocation caused by the Late Bronze Age Collapse of Aegean and Levantine polities that had accompanied the advance of the Sea Peoples. But in a culture that held the divine king to be omnipotent and omniprescient, the pharaoh's position would clearly have been weakened by events within and without Egypt.

The assassination plot had been intended to place a junior son on the throne, but was unsuccessful in this aim, and Rameses IV, apparently the nominated heir, successfully became king. However, he and his immediate successors had short reigns, and on two occasions a king was succeeded by an uncle. Then, although the reign of Rameses IX lasted nearly two decades, Egypt was wracked by troubles. These ranged from the raids out of the Libyan desert, through extensive graft and pilfering within temples, and tomb robbery in the Theban necropolis. These and other events culminated in the violent "suppression" of the High Priest of Amun at Karnak, Amenhotep G (fig. 4), around the end of the reign.[2] It is also possible that Rameses IX had to share the throne with another king, ruling in the north, from around his Year 7. This man, Rameses XI, would eventually become the king of all Egypt, after the deaths of Rameses IX and his short-lived successor, Rameses X.[3] The "suppression" of Amenhotep G may have coincided with the reign of Rameses X, and the concomitant civil war ("the War of the High Priest") is a potential explanation for the king's premature death.

The reuniting of national power under Rameses XI following the demise of Rameses X seems to have been followed by a serious attempt at resolving the ongoing disputes.

FIGURE 4 The High Priest Amenhotep G before Rameses IX, showing him on the same scale as the king; Karnak.

FIGURE 5 Another example of the equivalency in size, and in this case status as well, between a High Priest and a king: Herihor and Rameses XI in the temple of Khonsu at Karnak.

Part of this was behind the eleventh Rameses' inauguration of an unprecedented new dating era known as the "Renaissance" (*wḥm-mswt*), starting from Rameses XI's Year 19. The Renaissance then ran in parallel with the rest of his reign—at the end of which the country once again began to fall apart.

At the heart of Egypt's problems seem to have been power struggles for control of the key offices of High Priest of Amun at Karnak and the Viceroyalty of Kush.[4] At Thebes, Amenhotep G's probable successor, Herihor, was displaced from his office by a certain Piankh, who also assumed the viceroyalty, around Year 7 of the Renaissance. Piankh then launched a military campaign into Nubia, which some have seen as an operation against a former viceroy, Panehsy, who had earlier been instrumental in ending the "suppression" of Amenhotep G.

The status of Piankh's regime remains unclear: was he a supporter or disruptor of the status quo?[5] Nevertheless, it came to an abrupt end around Year 11 of the Renaissance. The cause of the demise of Piankh's regime remains obscure, but both Herihor and Panehsy now resumed their former offices. A year or two later, Herihor took the viceroyalty as well, perhaps on the death of Panehsy. However, it is unclear how much of Nubia now remained under Egyptian control, and Herihor is the last known person to have held the viceroyalty in a substantive way.[6] Herihor's standing at this point in time is demonstrated by his representations in the hypostyle hall of the temple of Khonsu. Here he is shown alternating with Rameses XI in offering scenes, depicted on the same scale as the king, implying an equality of status (fig. 5). Such a thing would have been unheard-of in most earlier times, but parallels representations of the High Priest Amenhotep G from a few years earlier (fig. 4).

Tanis and Thebes

On the death of Rameses XI, apparently without a direct heir, there was a major reconfiguration of the Egyptian state.[7] In the north, the city of Tanis became the seat of the first king of a new Twenty-first Dynasty. Tanis (San el-Hagar) seems to have been a long-established settlement, but had long been very much in the shadow of the great royal residence city of Per-Rameses (Qantir), some twenty kilometers to the southwest. However, the silting up of the Nile branch upon which Per-Rameses was sited led to its decline, with Tanis taking over its role as both a regional and a national center. Over the coming decades, Per-Rameses's buildings would be dismantled and the material incorporated into new structures at Tanis (figs. 6, 7)—and at certain other Delta sites as well.[8]

The new king at Tanis was Nesibanebdjedet I (Greek Smendes), by his name a native of Mendes (Tell Ruba; Banedbdjedet was the god of that city), but who is attested as resident at Tanis during Year 5 of the Renaissance, along with his wife Tentamun, the couple being dubbed "the pillars whom Amun has set up for the north of his land."[9] Their

FIGURE 6 Tanis. Top and middle: the approach to the temple of Amun, with the tomb of Shoshenq III visible on the right. Bottom left: recumbent reused statue of Rameses II. Bottom right: the East Temple, with reused Old Kingdom columns.

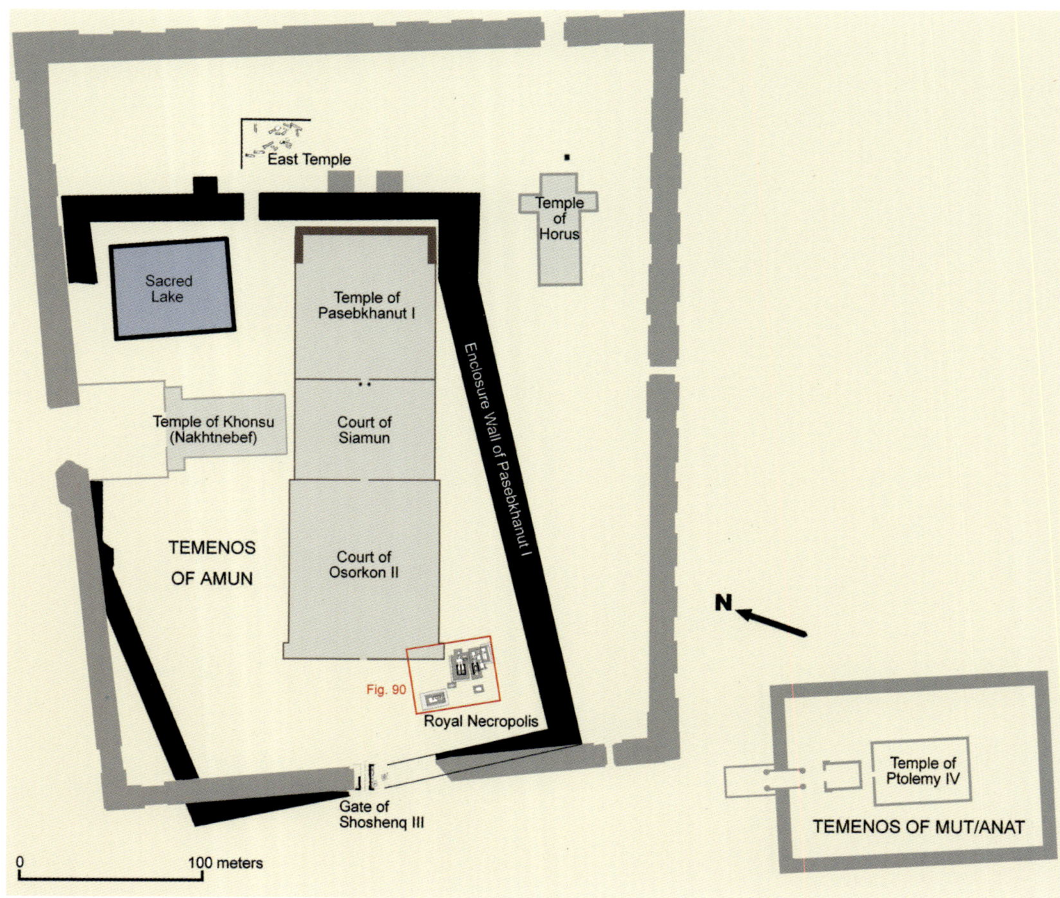

FIGURE 7 The temple area at Tanis.

affiliations remain unclear, but a working hypothesis is that Tentamun was a daughter of Rameses XI, and Nesibanebdjedet was a son of Amenhotep G, and also a brother-in law of Herihor (see family tree, fig. 18).

It was probably at the same time that Herihor was elevated to pharaonic status at Thebes.[10] Curiously, his prenomen was simply "High Priest of Amun" (Hemnetjertepyenamun), but the slightly later king Pasebkhanut I used this as an alternate prenomen, and within the peristyle court at the Khonsu temple Herihor is depicted as a full pharaoh (fig. 8). Given his apparent connections with Nesibanbdjedet, this division of kingship seems likely to have been agreed between the two men, and there are no signs of conflict in Egypt at this time. Among the icons Herihor employed in his monumental work was that of a procession of the king's children, something previously introduced into the repertoire by Rameses II and used extensively by him, and subsequently employed by Rameses III in his Medinet Habu temple.

Herihor's procession comprises nineteen sons and nineteen daughters, headed by his wife Nedjmet (fig. 9). It is highly unlikely that she can have been the mother of all of these children.[11] A clue to the background of at least one of the other mothers is to be found in the fact that, while most have typical Egyptian names of the period, six—Masaharta (i), Masaqaharta, [...]na, Wasuna, Osorkon (i), and Madeneb—not only have Libyan names, but these are determined with the sign 𓌙, denoting a foreign name. Since nothing survives to imply Herihor was anything other than an Egyptian, this appearance of Libyan names among his offspring would seem best explained through his marriage to a woman of Libyan heritage.

FIGURE 8 Herihor as king, as shown in the Khonsu temple at Karnak.

The question of when one can first regard Egypt as coming under something that could be called "Libyan rule"—or at least "Libyan-influenced rule"—has been a key question in the historiography of the period.[12] There is no question that, from the latter part of the tenth century through the first part of the seventh century, many key individuals in the Egyptian state not only had Libyan names, but also used Libyan titles alongside, and sometimes in preference to, Egyptian ones. Furthermore, an explanation, in whole or part, for the breakup of Egypt into multiple polities from the ninth century onward can be found in what seems to have been the Libyan tradition of coequal tribal leaders, in which a king might not have a claim to be anything more than a "first among equals" (see pages 54–55, 96–98).

Whether this can be projected back into the eleventh century as a basis for the collapse of the New Kingdom and the existence of a split kingship at the beginning of the Twenty-first Dynasty[13] is a more problematic proposition. A key issue is that during the eleventh and early tenth centuries Libyan names only surface occasionally among the ruling elements; there is no sign of Libyan titles among them until after the advent of the Libyan-named King Osorkon the Elder during the second decade of the tenth century (pages 19–21). Accordingly, while not denying the presence of an increasingly powerful and influential Libyan stratum in Egyptian society during the eleventh century (and before), it does not seem necessary to seek an explanation for the events of that century in overt "Libyan" activity. Rather, one might posit that Libyans took advantage of a much more complex set of conflicts and rivalries between primarily Egyptian vested interests in the wake of the economic and social woes that followed in the fallout from the Late Bronze Age Collapse.

FIGURE 9 The children of Herihor, as depicted in the Khonsu temple, with those bearing Libyan names highlighted.

Libyans thus allied themselves with those who had emerged as pharaohs and pontiffs following the death of Rameses XI, and it is probable that it is through the resulting intermarriage that they came by stages to emerge as pharaohs themselves around a century later.

This scenario of Egyptian worthies marrying Libyan wives would also help explain the appearance of a Libyan name in the family of another sometime holder of the office of High Priest of Amun. The latter was Panedjem I, a son of Herihor's former rival, Piankh, who seems to have succeeded Herihor as High Priest when he was elevated to kingship. Given Panedjem's background, and the fact that Herihor had many sons, one wonders how Panedjem came by the office. Perhaps some "deal" was done following Piankh's demise to secure Herihor's return to the pontificate in exchange for the office eventually returning to the family of Piankh?

Panedjem I had two wives whose names are known. One was Henttawy A, daughter of Tentamun, and thus granddaughter of Rameses XI and stepdaughter of Nesibanebdjedet I. She had at least three children, the later King Pasebkhanut I, the latter's sister-wife Mutnedjmet, and the future God's Wife of Amun, Maatkare A. His other known wife was Isetemkheb A, who had previously been married to an unknown man, with whom she had a daughter [...]hetepi. By Panedjem, she had the future High Priest Menkheperre. The mothers of the other two known children of Panedjem I, both future High Priests, Masaharta A and Djedkhonsiufankh I, are unknown. However, the fact that the Libyan name Masaharta once again appears in the record would suggest that his mother was of Libyan background.

While it is thus clear that the ruling family had significant Libyan connections, purely Egyptian names continued to dominate the naming of children within the royal/pontifical family. This strongly suggests that this family cannot yet be characterized as "Libyan," as has been asserted by some scholars, and that conclusions based on that characterization should be treated with care.[14]

Another interesting, and very much "Egyptian," factor among the names of the children of Panedjem I is the naming of two of them for the prenomina of kings Thutmose III (Menkheperre) and Hatshepsut (Maatkare) of the Eighteenth Dynasty. This is likely to be linked with the fact that Panedjem appropriated one of the coffins of Thutmose I, extensively reworking it for his own burial.[15] This suggests a real interest in the Thutmosid period, now four centuries in the past, on the part of Panedjem.

Panedjem I served as High Priest for a decade and a half, first in parallel with Herihor reigning as king, and then perhaps with the shadowy King Amenemnesut, potentially a son of Herihor, who is in any case known to have still been a king fifteen years later (cf. page 190 n23).[16] Toward the end of his time as pontiff, Panedjem began to adopt royal regalia, albeit while still using purely High Priestly titles (fig. 11). Then, around Year 16 of Nesibanebdjedet I, Panedjem became a fully fledged king in Thebes.[17]

With Panedjem's elevation, his son Masaharta became the new High Priest, and as such the first Libyan-named individual

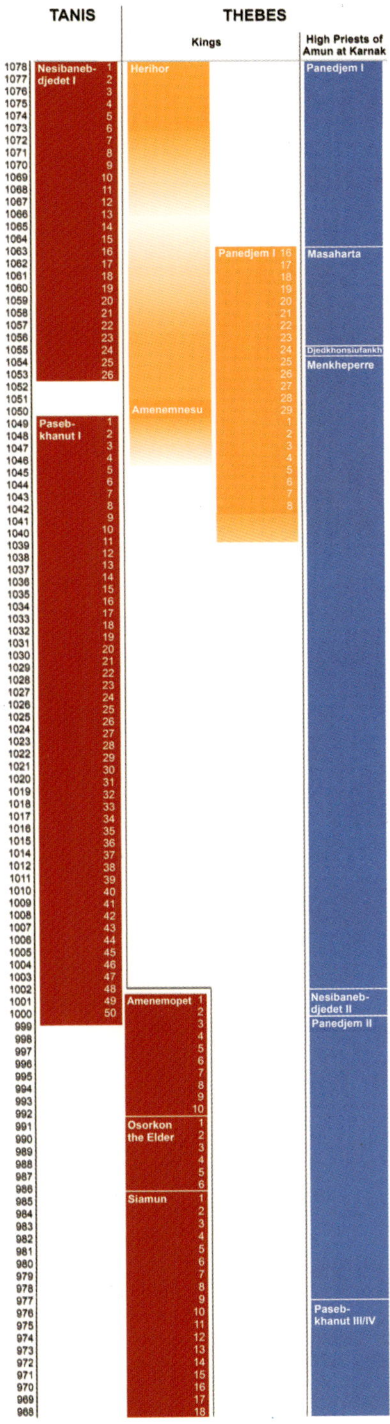

FIGURE 10 Chronology: eleventh to tenth centuries BC.

FIGURE 11 Panudjem I as High Priest (top left, Luxor temple), "crowned High Priest" (left and top right, Karnak and Cairo CG42191), and as king on his Book of the Dead papyrus (from TT320, Cairo JE11488).

FIGURE 12 Gateway of Masaharta at Karnak.

to hold high office in Egypt (fig. 12). However, his tenure lasted less than a decade, his demise possibly following an illness at El-Hiba, the northern headquarters of the High Priests at Karnak,[18] whose authority by now extended throughout Upper Egypt.[19] He seems then to have been followed in office briefly by his brother Djedkhonsiufankh I,[20] and then by their sibling Menkheperre. A stela erected at Karnak by the latter indicates that when he came into office he was confronted by opposition (fig. 13).[21] Details are not clear, but it seems probable that the death of Masaharta was accompanied by some kind of civil conflict, which might even have ended the life of Djedkhonsiufankh. Menkheperre states that he restored order and recalled exiles from the western desert oases, presumably as part of a settlement with opposition elements.

These events took place in a Year 25 that can only be that of Nesibanebdjedet I.[22] But that king's reign was nearly over, and the next Tanite king proved to be yet another son of Panedjem I—Pasebkhanut I. So, with Panedjem I still king at Thebes, Menkheperre as High Priest there, and Pasebkhanut I king at Tanis, the whole country was in the control of a tight family group. Pasebkhanut I was at least nominally the senior, in that it was his regnal years that were employed as a national dating era, succeeding those of Nesibanebdjedet I.

Both the new Tanite king and Menkheperre seem to have been younger sons of Panedjem I, as both would remain in power for half a century. At his accession, Pasebkhanut

FIGURE 13 The Banishment Stela of Menkheperre (Louvre C256).

shared kingship with not only his father, but also the obscure Amenemnesut,[23] but in the course of time he became Egypt's sole king. This would last until shortly before his death, when he took a certain Amenemopet as his co-regent. The new king's origins are unknown, although it is quite possible that he was a son of Pasebkhanut. Amenemopet would then reign for a decade, being (re?)buried in the tomb of his predecessor at Tanis (NRT-III, page 125).

The First Libyan Pharaoh: Osorkon the Elder

Nothing is known of the family of Amenemopet, other than that his successor was not his son. Rather, Amenemopet was followed on the throne by a man named Osorkon, who was of solidly Libyan paternal ancestry, going back five generations. On his mother's side he was descended from [...]hetepti, a maternal half-sister of the High Priest Menkheperre (see just below). This genealogical information is all provided by much later texts left by his collateral descendants Pasenhor (fig. 75)[24] and Ankhefenkhonsu (fig. 14), as contemporary data are scanty.

The latter comprise a single inscribed block of unknown origins, an entry in the Karnak Priestly Annals (long-term records of priestly inductions),[25] dating to his Year 2,[26] a faience seal (fig. 15a–c), and a group of blocks from Atfih.[27] These all belong to a King Akheperre-setepenre/amun Osorkon-meryamun:[28]

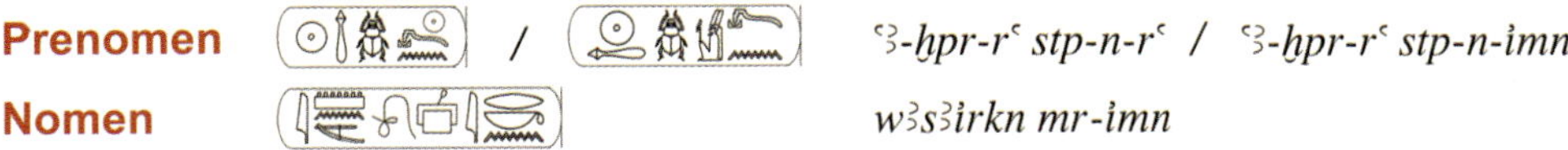

Today, he is generally referred to as Osorkon the Elder, the use of this epithet, rather than an ordinal, being because he was discovered by Egyptology some time after the designation of the later Osorkons had become fixed.[29]

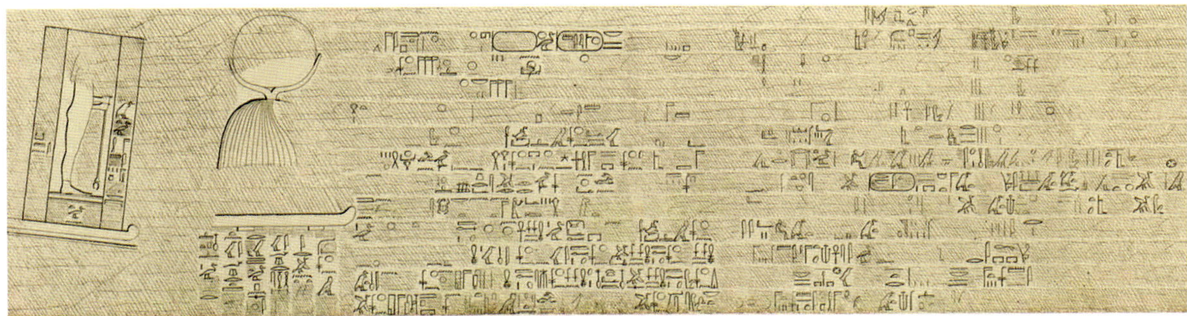

FIGURE 14 Text from the roof of the Khonsu temple, recording the induction of a priest named Ankhefenkhonsu in Year 7 of Takelot III. It includes a genealogy for the inductee that includes Osorkon the Elder, and confirms his place in history.

FIGURE 15 a. Block with cartouches of Osorkon the Elder (RMO F1972/9.1). b. Fragment of Karnak Priestly Annals mentioning Osorkon the Elder (3a). c. Finger ring naming Osorkon the Elder (RMO AO 10a). d. Fragment of Karnak Priestly Annals mentioning Shoshenq I as Chief of the Ma (4b).

As would be the case throughout the Third Intermediate Period, and in contrast to most kings of the New Kingdom and earlier periods, Osorkon's prenomen was unoriginal, and would be used again by later kings. Its core, Akheperre, had been used by Pasebkhanut I only one reign earlier, along with the epithet -setepenamun, a combination found on two of Osorkon's known monuments. However, in the Karnak Priestly Annals, the name appears with the epithet -setepenre, perhaps for clarity and to avoid confusion with entries from Pasebkhanut I's reign. The king's nomen employed the simple meryamun epithet, common since the middle of the New Kingdom. It is, however, found without it in his posthumous mention in the Ankhefenkhonsu genealogy, reflecting the simplification of royal cartouches at the time it was written (cf. pages 107–109).

As revealed by this text, complemented by that of Pasenhor, Osorkon was a son of the Great Chief (of the Ma—a contraction of the name of the Mashwesh tribe [page 1; cf. page 167])[30] Shoshenq A. The latter's father Paihuty, grandfather Mawasun, and great-grandfather Nebneshi had also borne the same title. Nebneshi's father, however, is simply referred to as "the Libyan" *(tḥn)*. Shoshenq's mother, Mehytemweskhet, was allegedly the seventh-generation descendant of Menkheperre's half-sister (fig. 18), although this number of generations seems distinctly excessive, and it is possible that some degree of corruption might have slipped into Ankhefenkhonsu's genealogy (which dates to some two centuries after Osorkon's time).[31]

It may have been through Mehytemweskhet that Osorkon gained some claim to the throne, since the surviving names in her ancestry are all Egyptian. However, the fact that the author of the genealogy highlighted the half-sibling relationship of his ancestress [...]hetepti with Menkheperre suggests that he was the only major figure even close to Mehytemweskhet's line.

Of course, the fact that our information on the genealogy comes from two private individuals, interested only in their own direct bloodlines, means that we have only a fraction of the whole story. It may be that the basis for Osorkon's regality came from some marriage by one of the pre-Shoshenq A Chiefs of the Ma. It is of course possible that he seized the throne, but there is no substantive evidence for this, and Osorkon the Elder's advent seems not to have disturbed the status quo at Thebes while, as already noted, priestly inductions were dated to his regnal years.

The only regnal year known for Osorkon the Elder is the Year 2 in the Karnak Priestly Annals, the only evidence for its overall length being the six years allocated to him in the third-century BC chronicle of Manetho (for which see pages 159–60). No trace of any funerary equipment has ever come to light, so it is unknown whether he was buried in the royal necropolis at Tanis, with his immediate predecessors and successors, or elsewhere.

Siamun, Pasebkhanut II, and the Theban High Priesthood

Osorkon was succeeded by a man named Siamun. We know nothing of his origins, so it is purely a matter of speculation whether he was an Egyptian, as his name might indicate, a Libyan who had adopted an Egyptian name, or someone of mixed ancestry. His highest known regnal year is his seventeenth, which suggests that the nine years given to him by Manetho (page 159) was an error for nineteen. At some point during Siamun's reign, Osorkon the Elder's brother, the Chief of the Ma Nimlot A, undertook some military activities, possibly in Lower Nubia, but the stela, from Karnak, that includes this information is in poor condition.[32]

FIGURE 16 Statuette of Thutmose III, rededicated to Pasebkhanut II by Shoshenq I (from Karnak; Cairo CG42192).

Siamun's reign saw the death of the High Priest Panedjem II. A son of Menkheperre, he had come to office during the reign of Amenemopet, after the brief pontificate of his brother Nesibanebdjedet II, who had succeeded their father, Menkheperre, just before the death of Pasebkhanut I. Panedjem was followed in office by his son Pasebkhanut, but at this point matters become complicated, because, as king, Siamun was also succeeded by a Pasebkhanut. The two Pasebkhanuts have often been regarded as the same person, but the temple of Sethy I at Abydos contains a graffito which seems best interpreted as indicating that at the time it was written, Egypt's king and the High Priest of Amun at Karnak were *both* named Pasebkhanut. On this basis one would distinguish a King Pasebkhanut II and a High Priest Pasebkhanut III.[33]

If Pasebkhanut II was indeed a different person from the High Priest of the name, nothing is known of his origins.[34] Few events can be attributed to his reign, aside from three entries in the Karnak Priestly Annals,[35] and a stela instituting a statue cult for Nimlot A at Abydos.[36] This was undertaken by the king at the petition of Nimlot's son, the Chief of the Ma Shoshenq B,[37] and it may have been in the wake of this that Pasebkhanut II's daughter, Maatkare B, married Shoshenq's son, Osorkon (see page 41).

FIGURE 17 Text mentioning Shoshenq I and Pasebkhanut II in tomb TTA18 at Dra Abu'l-Naga, Thebes-West, as copied by Gardner Wilkinson during the 1820s. The precise location of the tomb is presently unknown, but is in the general area marked.

The length of Pasebkhanut II's reign is unclear, but probably extended over some two decades.[38] Both he and Siamun were interred in the antechamber of the tomb of Pasebkhanut I at Tanis, although their bodies and coffins were utterly decayed when found (page 127), and the burials could be identified only by the presence of their shabtis in the room.[39] Pasebkhanut's interment was presumably carried out by Shoshenq B, as the legal mechanism for his accession as pharaoh—much as had been the case with Ay succeeding Tutankhamun nearly four centuries earlier.

That the definitive transition between the dynasties was peaceful is suggested not only by the marriage between Pasebkhanut II's daughter and Shoshenq's son, but also by a statue that was dedicated, after Shoshenq became king, to the late King Pasebkhanut, in which the now–Shoshenq I calls that king "his father" (fig. 16).[40] A further link between the kings is to be found in a text in the now lost tomb TTA18, which seems to be part of a biographical inscription spanning the dynastic transition, and naming both kings (fig. 17).[41] TTA18, belonging to a Priest and Document-Scribe of Amun, named Amenemopet, is one of the tiny number of decorated private tomb-chapels known from the Third Intermediate Period.

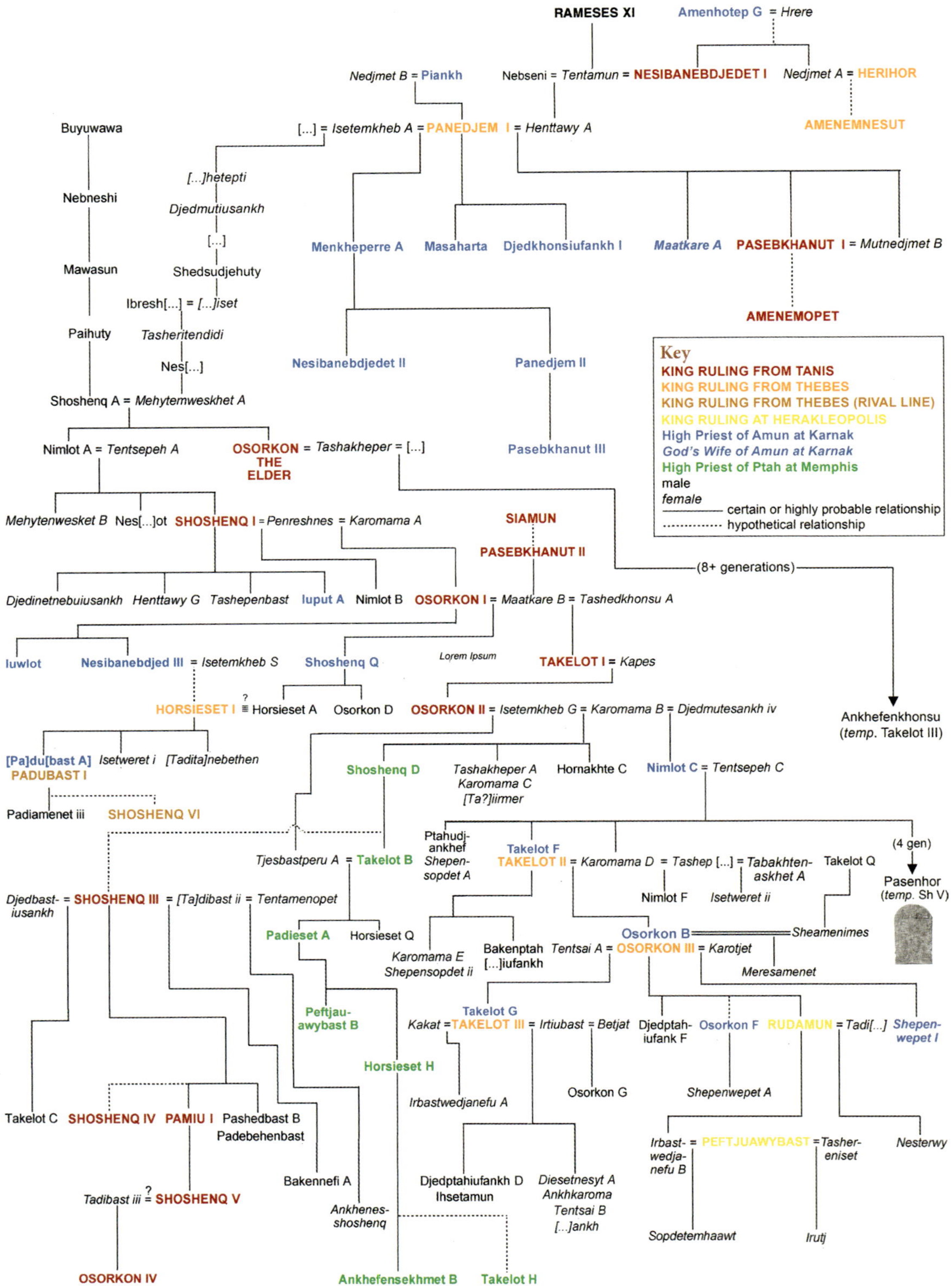

FIGURE 18 Family tree of the Libyan pharaohs.

2 Heyday

Shoshenq I

As already noted, the man who would become Shoshenq I was a son of Nimlot A, and as such the nephew of Osorkon the Elder. Manetho states that his dynasty came from Bubastis (Tell Basta) in the southwest Delta, but apart from the fact that two of his descendants did significant work there, we have no verification of this from contemporary sources.[1]

The mechanics of his accession to the throne are not wholly clear, as among the Karnak Priestly Annals is one that dates a priest's induction to "Year 2 . . . of the Great Chief of the Ma, Shashaq" (fig. 15d).[2] Although this has generally been dated to the first years of Shoshenq I's independent reign,[3] one remains uncomfortable with the idea that a crowned pharaoh of Egypt could be so gratuitously insulted through being referred to by his previous title in the heart of the state temple at Karnak. The implicit view that this was because he might have been seen as an "upstart foreigner" seems unlikely—his uncle Osorkon the Elder had already been a pharaoh and had been referred to as such in the same set of annals.

Rather, the dateline might suggest a period of corule with Pasebkhanut II, during which Shoshenq began to count a dating era, but did not yet take pharaonic titles, with Shoshenq granted control of the Thebaid. Conceivably, this could have followed the demise of the High Priest Pasebkhanut III, with the High Priesthood itself simultaneously bestowed on Shoshenq's son, Iuput A.[4] It is possible that Shoshenq transitioned to a full co-regency with Pasebkhanut II before the latter's death, since this could explain two attestations of the otherwise unknown prenomen [hieroglyphic cartouche], Tutkheperre-[...], alongside the nomen Shoshenq-meryamun (fig. 19).[5] This prenomen could be seen to

FIGURE 19 Block at Bubastis naming a Tutkheperre Shoshenq.

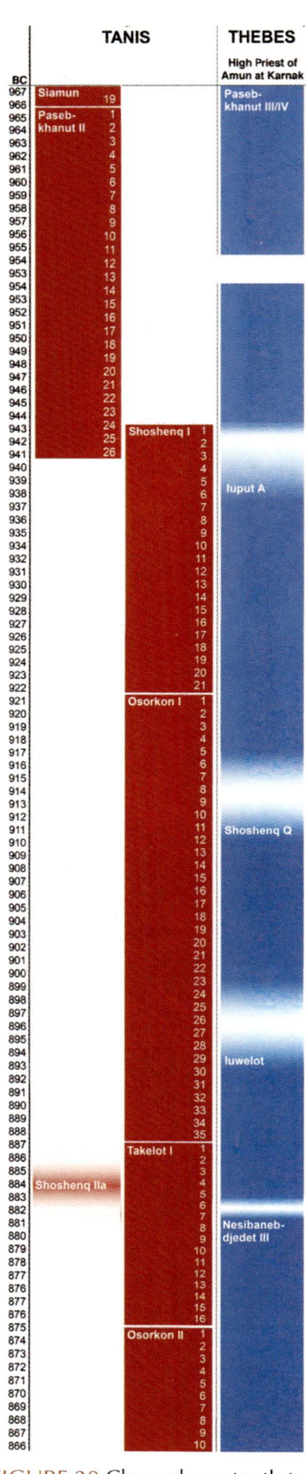

FIGURE 20 Chronology: tenth to ninth centuries BC.

FIGURE 21 Left: relief showing Shoshenq I with his wife Karomama A (NMS A.1967.2). Right: cartonnage mummy case and coffin of Henttawy G, daughter of Shoshenq I (Louvre Abu Dhabi LAD 2014.023.001).

be a play on Tyetkheperre, the prenomen of Pasebkhanut II—both *twt* and *tỉt* mean "image"—and thus might support their being used by co-rulers as a "matched pair."

In any case, no later than Year 5, Shoshenq I's titulary had stabilized as follows:

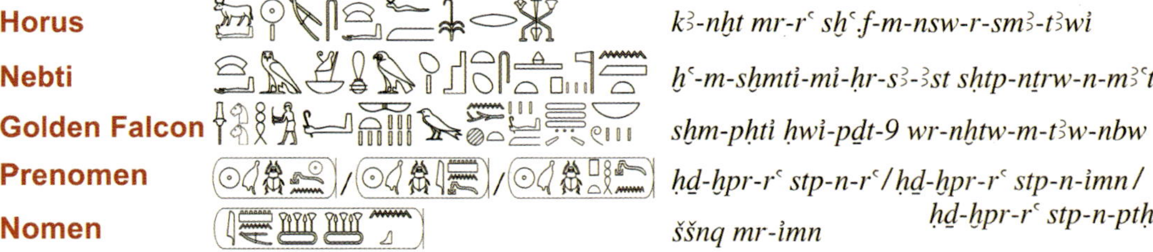

The king's prenomen ("The dazzling one is a manifestation of Re") had previously been used by Nesibanebdjedet, another dynastic founder. It might thus have been chosen to indicate a new beginning—or as a statement that Shoshenq was a continuity of the previous line, rather than an upstart. A range of "chosen" *(stp)* epithets were employed, with "by Amun" and "by Ptah" found alongside the usual "by Re." The Horus name, "Strong bull, beloved of Re, who has caused (him) to appear as king to unite the Two Lands," could be seen as a statement of renewal, but the Nebti and Golden Falcon names are more generic, although not actually copying any earlier pharaoh. The former reads "Who has appeared in the Double Crown like Horus son-of-Isis, and has satisfied the gods with Maat," the latter "Powerful of might, who has struck down the Nine Bows, great of victories in all lands." The king's personal name is invariably accompanied by the epithet "beloved of Amun," as had so many royal names since the end of the Eighteenth Dynasty.

Two wives of Shoshenq I are definitely known.[6] Karomama A (fig. 21 left) is named as the mother of the future Osorkon I on a contemporary block from Saft el-Henna (page 41), and in the genealogy of Pasenhor. Another son, Nimlot B (later Army Leader of the Entire Army),[7] was borne by Penreshnes, daughter of an unnamed Chief of the Ma.[8] The maternity of Shoshenq I's other known children is, however, uncertain. These were the aforementioned Iuput A and three daughters, Tashepenbast,[9] Djedinetnebuiusankh,[10] and Henttawy G (fig. 21 right).[11] It is interesting that while the two known boys were given Libyan names, the girls all had Egyptian ones, Henttawy being a name particularly associated with the High Priestly family of the Twenty-first Dynasty.

The general impression one gains of the reign of Shoshenq I is that the king's objective was to reform and revitalize Egypt. The former aspect may be seen in the way that the High Priesthood of Amun ceased to be a hereditary office running in parallel with that of kingship. Rather than choosing any further scion of the family of Panedjem I, Shoshenq appointed his own son Iuput (fig. 22). This practice of each king appointing a son endured until the reign of Osorkon II, and even then it was not a case of a High Priest being directly followed by his son, but only after a gap (see page 65). Like the earlier High Priests, however, Iuput combined his priestly title with the military ones of Generalissimo and Army Leader. In contrast, at Memphis, the Twenty-first Dynasty pontifical line continued in charge of the Ptah cult, and would do so for several further generations.[12]

Further new blood seems also to have been brought into the senior priesthood, as the office of Fourth Priest was granted to Nesy, who also had the Libyan title of Chief of the Mahasun; he was then followed in the function by his son Nesankhefmaat.[13] In contrast, the offices of Second and Third Priest remained in the hands of a likely son-in-law of Panedjem II, Djedptahiufankh A, until at least the end of the first decade of the reign.[14] This man, and his probable wife, Nesitanebetashru A, were buried in tomb TT320, south of Deir el-Bahari (the so-called "Royal Cache"). Probably originally the tomb of Queen Ahmes-Nefertiry of the Eighteenth Dynasty, this sepulcher had been appropriated during the Twenty-first Dynasty for the reburials of kings of the New Kingdom and members of the high-priestly family, along with primary burials of Panedjem II and his immediate family.[15] Following the interments of the bodies of Nesitanebetashru, probably Panedjem's daughter, and Djedptahiufankh, likely her husband, possibly early in the second decade of Shoshenq I's reign, the very last reburials of ancient royalty were placed in TT320, after which it remained undisturbed until the nineteenth century AD.

Builder king

A significant amount of building work was undertaken during Shoshenq I's reign. While questions of preservation make it difficult to be certain, the lack of new construction at Karnak since the middle of the Twentieth Dynasty (work at the Khonsu temple seems to have been decoration only) seems a reasonable indicator of overall levels of building activity in Egypt as a whole. From the Twenty-first Dynasty, all we seem to have are the first phase of the temple of Amun at Tanis, by Pasebkhanut I,[16] a doorway at Memphis,[17] and the small temple of Isis Mistress of the Pyramids at Giza by the same king[18] (with continuation by Amenemopet),[19] and some minor works by Siamun at Tanis and Memphis.[20]

In contrast, from the reign of Shoshenq I can be identified architectural fragments and usurped sculpture at Tanis, Bubastis, Tell el-Maskhuta, Athribis (Tell Atrib), and Heliopolis.[21] A considerable amount of work is evidenced at Memphis, including probably the erection of a large gate.[22] This included new embalming facilities for the sacred Apis bull (fig. 23), although nothing of Shoshenq I's time has been identified at the necropolis of the bulls, the Serapeum at Saqqara. On the other hand, a block from a chapel of the king has been found at Saqqara, indicating some royal interest there.[23] Just

FIGURE 22 Pilaster in the Bubastite Portal at Karnak (fig. 28), showing Shoshenq I being suckled by Hathor, with the High Priest Iuput standing behind him.

FIGURE 23 The Apis Embalming House at Memphis.

south of the Fayyum, Prince Nimlot B decreed an enhanced offering regime for the god Heryshef at Herakleopolis (Ihnasiya el-Medina)[24] while, on the opposite side of the Nile, at El-Hiba, a new temple was begun in the name of the king (fig. 24).[25]

It is at Thebes, however, where the most extensive work of Shoshenq I survives. He was in particular responsible for laying out a new peristyle court in front of Pylon II at Karnak, which had hitherto been the principal frontage of the temple (figs. 25, 26). The courtyard already contained the bark-shrine of Sethy II and the bark-temple of Rameses

FIGURE 24 El-Hiba, as viewed from the Nile, and its temple, with fragments of its decoration by Shoshenq I. Top: smiting scene from the original façade, later obscured by a (probably) Thirtieth Dynasty pronaos. Bottom: scenes from around an external corner (Heidelberg University 1970-8.9, 562-4, 562-1).

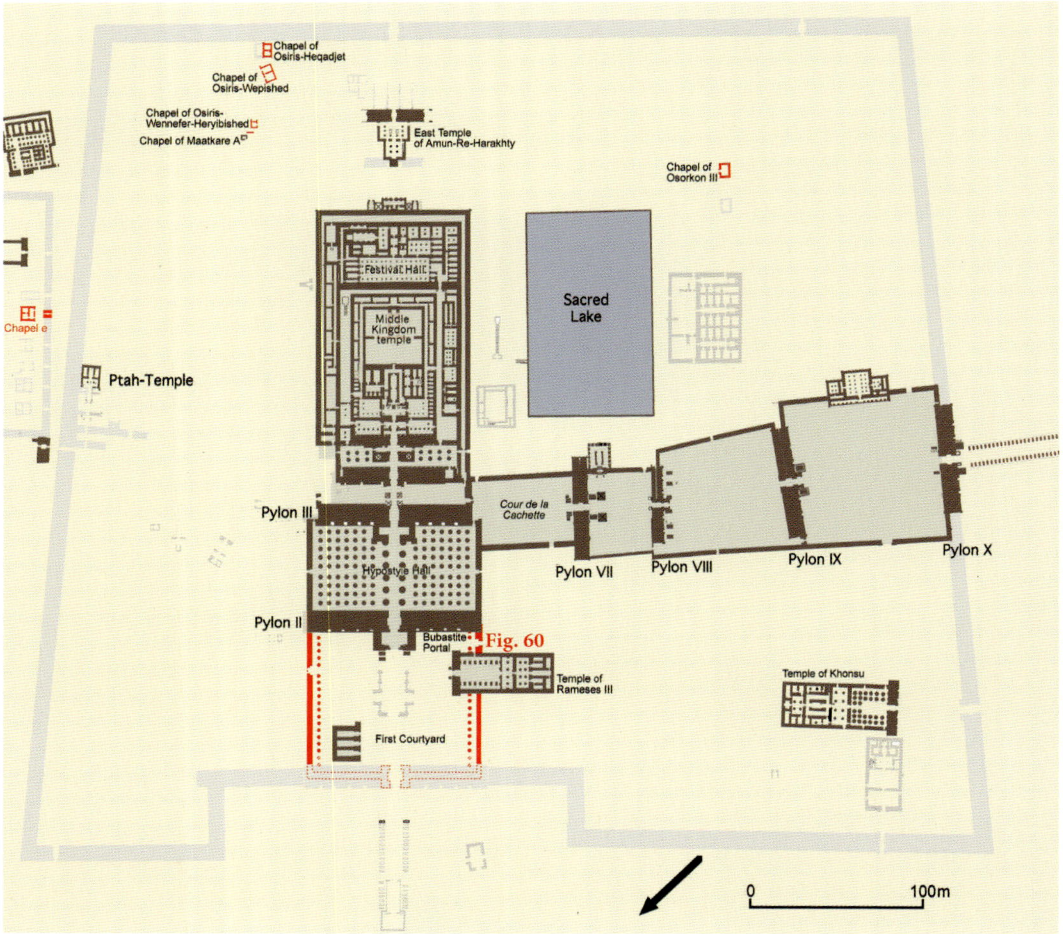

FIGURE 25 Plan of the temenos of Amun-Re at Karnak, with elements dating to the Libyan Period shown in red.

III, the latter's presence meaning that the south wall of the new court was interrupted by the Rameses III temple. It is unclear what form the western part of the court took, as Pylon I was erected in this location three centuries later. When this was done, the westernmost columns of Shoshenq's scheme were replaced by new ones (which, like the pylon, were never completed). It is, however, likely that Shoshenq planned some kind of monumental gateway, or even a pylon, for this location.

The provision of the stone for this part of the court was the subject of a decree of II *šmw*, Year 21, preserved on stela 100 at the Gebel el-Silsila sandstone quarries (fig. 27).[26] This ordered the Overseer of Works Horemsaf to extract stone there for the construction at Karnak of "very great pylon-towers . . . to make a festival court . . . surround(ed) with statues and a colonnade." It seems likely that Year 21 was the last of the reign, as Manetho states that Shoshenq's reign lasted twenty-one years, and no later-dated documents are known. Since other parts of the court were already under decoration at the king's death, they cannot have been begun this late, and must have been subject to earlier batches of stone, records of which have not been preserved. In support of this is the fact that the decree singles out the pylon, which would logically be the last thing to be built.

The decoration actually undertaken before the king's death was restricted to the southeastern gateway, which joined the temple of Rameses III to Pylon II (fig. 28c, d), and as a stand-alone element was probably the first part of the project to be constructed.

FIGURE 26 The First Court at Karnak, constructed by Shoshenq I in front of Horemheb's Pylon II. The colonnaded kiosk in the center was added by Taharqa of the Twenty-fifth Dynasty.

FIGURE 27 The sandstone quarries at Silsila-West, with the stelae of Shoshenq I (inset) and Rameses V.

Known as the "Bubastite Portal" (on the basis of Manetho's statement that the dynasty came from Bubastis: see page 159), the wall joining it to Pylon II was adorned with a scene of the king smiting enemies (fig. 29), while the pilasters received depictions of the king with deities, on occasion accompanied by the High Priest Iuput A (fig. 22).[27] Some of these are contiguous with scenes depicting the next king, Osorkon I (fig. 36), suggesting that they were being carved when Shoshenq I died, the work being continued under his successor. However, no further decoration was carried out anywhere else in the court, leaving vast areas of unadorned stone, both within the colonnades and on the exterior (fig. 28a, b). A series of texts were added to the interior of the Bubastite Portal during the late ninth century BC (figs. 59, 60).

FIGURE 28 a. The northern entrance to Shoshenq I's First Court at Karnak. b. Southern colonnade of First Court. c. South Wall of the Hypostyle Hall, with the Bubastite Portal of Shoshenq I at the left-hand end. d. The Bubastite Portal from the north. e. Shoshenq I suckled by Mut. f. Fragments of a cornice of Shoshenq I.

Also at Karnak, a notation of the maximum inundation level reached in Year 6 of Shoshenq I is recorded on the podium on the river wall (fig. 39[1]). This is the earliest of a long series of such notations, which are important sources for the history of Thebes during the latter part of the Third Intermediate Period.[28]

War and peace in the Levant

The smiting scene on the exterior of the Portal (fig. 29)[29] is fairly conventional, following New Kingdom patterns, with the king carrying out the act before Amun, below whom are name rings, representing towns and locales conquered by the pharaoh in question. These places are entirely Palestinian, and show that Shoshenq I was the first ruler of Egypt since the first half of the Twentieth Dynasty known to have campaigned in the southern Levant (fig. 83). The exact itinerary has been much discussed,[30] but the overall record has generally been linked with a passage in the Old Testament:

> And it came to pass in the fifth year of king Rehoboam that Shishak king of Egypt came up against Jerusalem: and he took away the treasures of the house of the Lord.[31]

Since the earliest days of Egyptology (pages 163–64), it has been generally accepted that "Shishak" was simply a rendering of "Shoshe(n)q" (the *n* often being omitted in Egyptian sources). This has been combined with an assumption that the campaign recorded in the Bible and the one recorded at Karnak were one and the same. However, Jerusalem is not actually mentioned in the Karnak texts. This omission has been explained in various ways: at one extreme, that the name lay among those now unreadable; at the other, that Shishak was not Shoshenq I after all (pages 180–81). The problem with taking the Karnak campaign as identical with the biblical one is that Jerusalem does not easily fit into the itinerary that can be deduced from the readable name rings. However, there are grave difficulties in identifying a credible alternative to Shoshenq as the Egyptian king involved in the Bible narrative.[32]

An alternative view is that the omission of Jerusalem from the Bubastite Portal tableau simply indicates that the particular campaign commemorated—explicitly called the king's "first [campaign of vi]ctory"—did not include Jerusalem. There seems no reason to exclude the possibility that there could then have been a subsequent campaign that *did* include Jerusalem in its itinerary. This would have been commemorated in a subsequent phase of decoration at Karnak—which was never carried through owing to Shoshenq's death.[33]

Probably to be attributed to the "Portal" campaign is a fragment of a stela (fig. 30 left) found at Megiddo (Tell el-Mutesellim, one of the cities listed).[34] There also survives

FIGURE 29 The victory tableau of Shoshenq I, on the south face of the Bubastite Portal, showing the king smiting enemies before Amun, with a list of conquered locales behind and below him. The figure of the kings seems to have originally been modeled in plaster in raised relief; this has fallen away, leaving just a few ghostly outlines, reinforced in blue in this image.

a fragmentary account of a border skirmish that culminated in a successful battle on the shore of the Bitter Lakes (fig. 31).[35]

There is no need to assume that the carving of the smiting tableau close to the end of the reign implies that the campaign was carried out late in the reign. It may simply have been that it was not until the new courtyard was built (perhaps with tribute extracted during this and other military operations) that there was anywhere at Karnak to place a commemorative relief. Then, the earliest campaign was memorialized in the first part of the court to be ready (the Bubastite Portal), with later activities (including the Jerusalem campaign) to be placed elsewhere—perhaps on the continuation of the exterior wall beyond the Rameses III temple, or adjacent to the northern gateway (fig. 28a). Here, Shoshenq's new walling was contiguous with the battle reliefs of Sethy I on the north wall of the Hypostyle Hall, just as the Bubastite Portal tableau was juxtaposed with campaign reliefs of Rameses II on the south wall of the Hypostyle Hall.[36] On this basis,

FIGURE 30 a. Fragment of stela of Shoshenq I from Megiddo (Jerusalem I.3554). b. Fragment of statuette of Shoshenq I, with added Phoenician text by Abibaal, King of Byblos; from Byblos (Berlin VA3361).

Shoshenq I's military activities in Palestine, including at least two campaigns, cannot be precisely placed within his reign.

Shoshenq's synchronism with Rehoboam of Judah is a key "hook" in constructing an absolute chronology (i.e., one expressed in terms of years BC) of the first part of the Third Intermediate Period. This is because it is the only point prior to the late seventh century at which Egyptian history can be linked into the secure absolute chronology of Assyria, which exists from the late tenth century onward.[37] Rehoboam can be dated via synchronisms between the regnal years of Shalmaneser III of Assyria and those of Kings Ahab and Jehu of Israel. Biblical data links these Israelite reigns with those of their Judean contemporaries, allowing back-calculation to determine Rehoboam's dates as king. His accession has accordingly generally been placed between 937 and 926 BC,[38] placing Rehoboam's Year 5 between 932 and 921.

Assuming that Shoshenq I's Jerusalem campaign took place during the second decade of his reign, his accession would, on this basis, lie between c. 945 and c. 935 BC. Within these constraints, a record of a festival in Year 5 of Shoshenq I[39] has been interpreted as providing a lunar date whose only acceptable resolution between 950 and 930 is 939—thus narrowing Shoshenq I's accession to 944/3.[40]

Victory scenes—without any surviving indication of the location of the event being commemorated—are to be found at the temple at El-Hiba (fig. 24a),[41] with a probable reference to one of Shoshenq I's campaigns on the mummy cartonnage of the Priest of Amun-Re and Royal Scribe Hor "[who followed] the king on his journey in the lands of

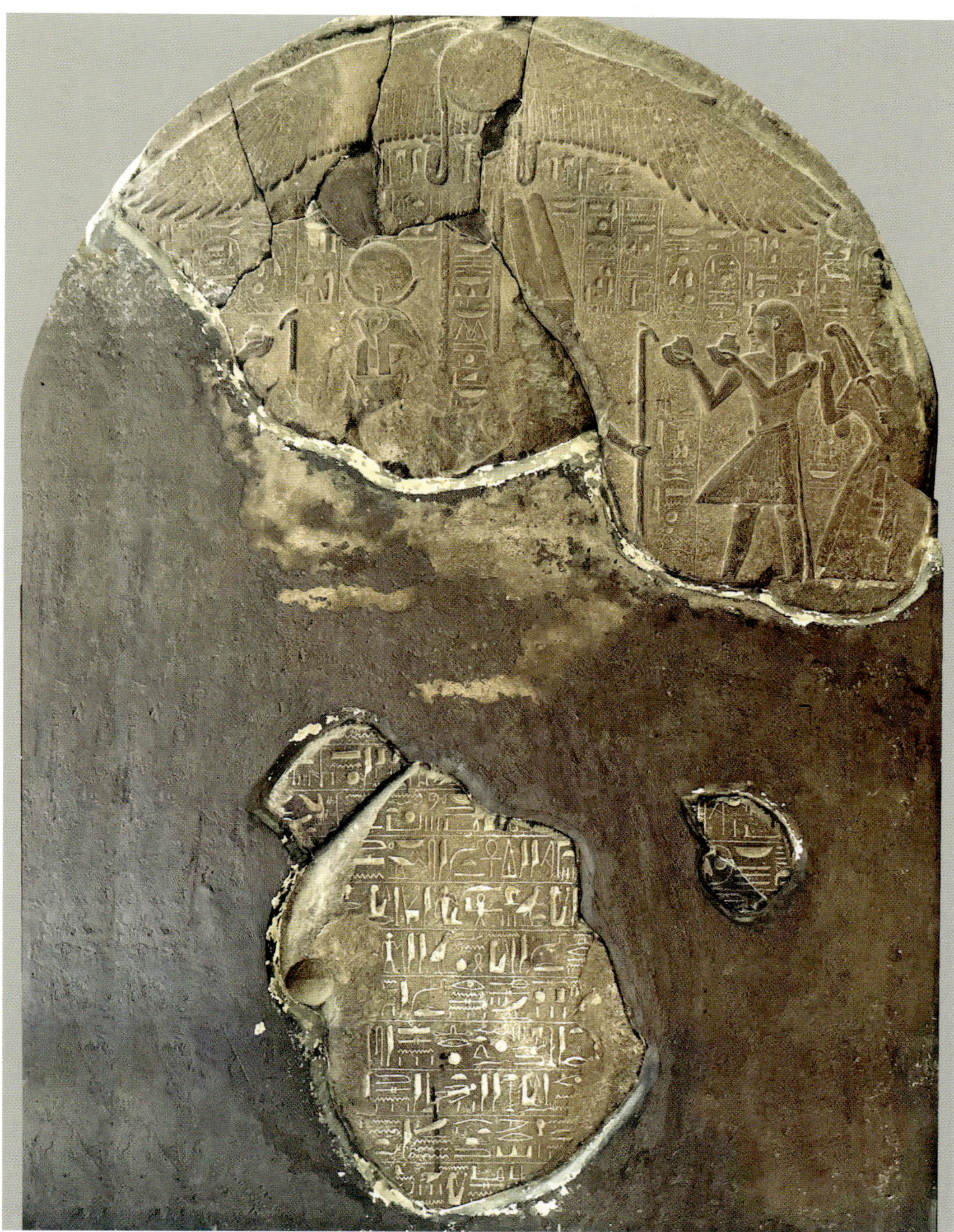

FIGURE 31 Stela of Shoshenq I from Karnak, concerning a skirmish on the border of Palestine. The High Priest Iuput is shown behind his father on the lunette (Cairo JE59635).

FIGURE 32 Cartonnage mummy case of Hor; from the Ramesseum (Fitzwilliam E.8.1896).

Retjenu (Syria-Palestine)" (fig. 32).[42] That Shoshenq's engagement in Palestine involved more than simple raids is suggested by a study of cultural material from the area, pointing to a prolonged and significant Egyptian involvement during early Iron Age IIA times.[43]

Egypt's re-engagement with the Levant is also to be seen further north, at Byblos. This port city had long been a key commercial hub, in particular for the export of high-quality timber. This was important for Egypt, as native woods were unsuitable for large-scale structural purposes, and cedar was being brought in from at least the Early Dynastic Period. Egyptian material has been found at Byblos dating to the end of that same period, with significant amounts through the Middle and New Kingdoms.[44] Indeed, it has been alleged that the city was virtually an Egyptian colony for some of this time. However, by the end of the New Kingdom, Egypt's position had greatly deteriorated, and an emissary of Herihor, Wenamun, was faced with major problems when attempting to procure cedar for a new bark of Amun during the Renaissance era.[45] That the situation improved under Shoshenq I is suggested by the presence of a statuette of the king—and stone images of some of his successors (figs. 30b, 33)—at Byblos.[46]

The data surviving from Shoshenq I's reign all indicates a desire by the king to imitate his New Kingdom predecessors both at home and abroad. One can only speculate how far his ambitions and actions might have been linked with his personal background and a desire to demonstrate that, although of Libyan ancestry, and with a Libyan name, he was a fully fledged pharaoh of Egypt. Nevertheless, his activities certainly seem to have lifted the country from the doldrums of the previous century or more, and one wonders what more he could have achieved had he lived longer. The fact that ambitious building plans were in train on his death suggests that this was unexpected. It is unclear where Shoshenq I was buried (see pages 125–27), but his funeral will have been carried out by his son Osorkon, who would occupy the Egyptian throne for some three decades.

Osorkon I

The later king Osorkon I is probably referred to in his earlier life on a block from Saft el-Henna, naming him a Priest of Sopdu, Generalissimo and Leader of the Archers of Pharaoh, [Oso]rkon, son of Shoshenq and Karomama.[47] As king, he adopted the following titulary:

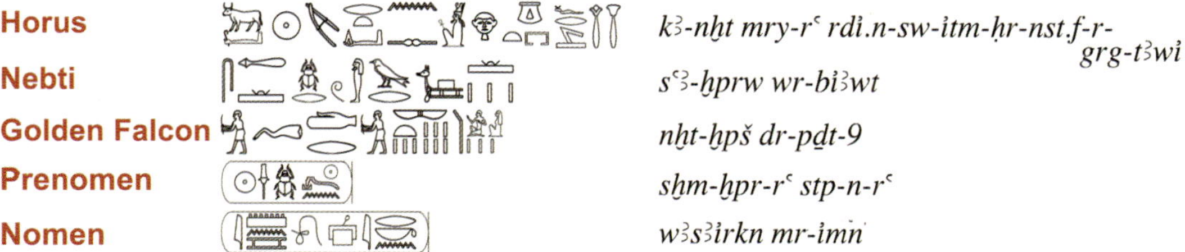

These names are quite original, in contrast to so many royal titularies of the Third Intermediate Period. Although the first part of the Horus name, "Strong bull, beloved of Re," copied Shoshenq I and other earlier kings, the rest, "whom Atum has put on his throne to establish the Two Lands," was new, as was the Nebti name, "The one who has magnified his manifestations is one great of marvels." However, the first part of the Golden Falcon name, "The strong of arm who has repelled the Nine Bows, the sovereign who has seized all lands," had previously been used by Sethy II of the Nineteenth Dynasty. The prenomen had never been used before—nor would it ever be employed by any later king. Both features are highly unusual among royal names of the Third Intermediate Period.

Before his accession, Osorkon had married Maatkare B, daughter of Pasebkhanut II. She had, like a number of other ladies of the dynasty, been the subject of a property decree at Karnak, in this case carved on Pylon VII at Karnak.[48] The couple had a son, Shoshenq Q (see below), but Maatkare seems to have died before Osorkon's accession, since she is mentioned on two of Shoshenq's statues (fig. 34a, b) only as a King's Daughter and a Priestess of Hathor, never as a queen.

None of Osorkon I's monuments mention any queen, but the Pasenhor genealogy states that the mother of Osorkon's son and successor, Takelot I, was named Tashedkhonsu, and a shabti belonging to a woman of that name was found in the burial chamber of Takelot I.[49] Unfortunately, it is not clear whether Tashedkhonsu's title on this piece is "King's Wife" or "King's Mother." Apart from Shoshenq and Takelot, Osorkon I had two other sons, Iuwlot and Nesibanebdjedet (III, interestingly, an Egyptian name), but neither of their mothers is named on their surviving monuments.

The latter two, and Shoshenq, all served as High Priests of Amun at Karnak. The first to do so was Shoshenq, who followed his uncle Iuput A in office. He adopted a

FIGURE 33 Left: part of a statue of Osorkon I, with Phoenician text of Ebibaal, King of Byblos; from temple esplanade, Byblos (Louvre AO9502). Right: sphinx of Osorkon I (Vienna ÄS52).

particularly high profile, writing his name in a cartouche with the epithet "–meryamun," just like a king, and creating or appropriating three statues at Karnak (fig. 34).[50] Also at Karnak is a record of his conducting a priestly induction in an unknown year.[51] From his use of a cartouche—unique for a prince of the Third Intermediate Period[52]—it seems clear that Shoshenq anticipated his own accession as king. However, this was not to be, and it is clear from the monuments of his descendants that he was never more than High Priest (cf. pages 51–52).[53] Likewise, none of his children ever became kings. All of Shoshenq's known sons were ordinary Priests of Amun (fig. 35; cf. page 61). Instead of becoming pharaoh, Shoshenq died before his father, and was followed as High Priest by his brother Iuwlot. It would be Takelot who eventually became king.

Little is known of the events of the reign of Osorkon I, with no military activity attested in Egyptian sources, although a follow-up to Shoshenq I's Palestinian exploits is suggested by an Old Testament account of a battle between King Asa of Judah and "Zerah the Kushite"—presumably a Nubian general in the service of an Egyptian king—which resulted in the defeat of Zerah and his pursuit as far as Gerar.[54] This event has been dated to c. 897 BC on the basis of biblical data,[55] which would fall in the mid-20s of Osorkon I's reign. In any case, continued links with Byblos seem to be indicated by the

FIGURE 34 a. Statue of the personification of the inundation (Hapi), dedicated by Shoshenq Q, who is shown on the side of the back pillar (BM EA8). b. Late Eighteenth/early Nineteenth Dynasty statuette usurped by Shoshenq Q (Cairo CG42194). c. Statuette of Shoshenq Q offering a figure of Amun (Cairo CG42193).

FIGURE 35 Statuette of the god Bes, dedicated by Shoshenq Q, on behalf of his son Horsieset A (Durham N313).

FIGURE 36 Representations of Osorkon I in the Bubastite Portal at Karnak.

discovery of a statue of the king there (fig. 33 left).[56]

Building work during the reign of Osorkon I included some continuation of Shoshenq I's great project at Karnak, with some reliefs added to the Bubastite Portal (fig. 36). An isolated block and the remains of a text in the Khonsu temple are datable to Osorkon I's reign,[57] as are, potentially, repairs to a chapel of Thoth and Amun to the south of the Sacred Lake.[58] The Nile flood of Year 12 was also recorded at Karnak (fig. 39).

As far as the immediate subordinates to Osorkon's sons in the clergy of Amun were concerned, it is unclear who was Second Priest, although he might have been the Bakenamun known to have flourished under either Osorkon I or II.[59] The order of the successors of Djedptahiufankh A in the office of Third Priest is unclear, but Djedthutiufankh A/i (an uncle-by-marriage of Shoshenq Q) seems to have served during the latter part of Osorkon I's reign.[60] Djedthutiufankh's father, Ameneminet i, may have directly preceded him in office.[61] Djedthutiufankh appears to have been succeeded as Third Priest around the end of Osorkon I's reign by Djedkhonsiufankh Q, son of Nespaneferhor B.[62] Nesankhefmaat was succeeded as Fourth Priest by Pashedbast A (like his grandfather, a

FIGURE 37 The remains of the temple at Bubastis, and a block of Osorkon I at the site.

Great Chief of the Mehes),[63] and was probably followed directly by Djedkhonsiufankh A, a son-in-law of Iuput A.[64] A number of more junior officials are known from the Priestly Annals and inscribed pieces of sculpture.[65]

Other religious institutions that received attention during the reign of Osorkon I included one at Kahun,[66] Shoshenq I's temple at El-Hiba, where decoration was continued.[67] Extensive work, including the erection of a hypostyle hall and a gateway, was carried out at the temple of Bastet at Bubastis (fig. 37), an Atum sanctuary also being

FIGURE 38 A semi-hieratic stela recording an order by Osorkon I to the High Priest at Heliopolis, Djedptahiufankh B, to make a donation of fields in the region of Heliopolis for the benefit of the God's Father and Mayor of Heliopolis, Hori (MMA 10.176.42).

built there.[68] Further activity is attested at Atfih and Memphis.[69] At the latter city, the High Priesthood continued to be passed down the long-established line.[70] Although no building work is attested at Heliopolis, the High Priest there, Djedptahiufankh B, is known from a donation stela of Year 6 (fig. 38).

Manetho gives fifteen years for the length of Osorkon's reign, but the presence of a Year 33 dateline on linen from a mummy[71] whose trappings included an object bearing Osorkon I's name, together with the number of Third and Fourth Priests of Amun during the period, has led to a view that Manetho's figure might be an error for "35" years.[72] Nothing whatsoever is known about the king's burial arrangements (see pages 125–27).

Takelot I—and Times of Troubles?

The later genealogy of Pasenhor shows that Osorkon I's son, Takelot I, ruled between Osorkon and Takelot's own son, Osorkon II. However, contemporary documents barely register Takelot I's existence, with regnal years given without mentioning the king to whom they belonged. This phenomenon had previously been seen during the Twenty-first Dynasty, the Renaissance having seemingly encouraged the idea of "dating eras," not necessarily solidly attached to the king to whom they belonged. The apparent return to such a system during the time of Takelot I suggests a—for the time being, temporary—diminution of the standing of the pharaoh, and it is possible that another king may have flourished for a while alongside Takelot (pages 51–52). Indeed, even the prenomen of Takelot I was uncertain until the 1980s (see page 204 n72), and even now the only known parts of his titulary are his prenomen (borrowed from Shoshenq I and Nesibanebdjedet I), and nomen:

Prenomen *ḥḏ-ḫpr-rꜥ*

Nomen *tỉklt mr-ỉmn*

That times may have been hard is suggested by the Nile-level records of the period (fig. 39)—one of those sources of this period which give only a regnal year, without any mention of a king.[73] The flood of Year 5 (fig. 39[16]) was of average height, but another one early in the era (fig. 39[20]: date lost, but under the High Priest Iuwlot, and so pre–Year 8) was some 30 centimeters higher. However, that of Year 8 (fig. 39[17]) was some 90 centimeters below that peak, and the one of Year 14 was some 20 centimeters lower still. Another post–Year 8 level (fig. 39[19], under the High Priest Nesibanebdjedet III) was a full 1.5 meters below the peak, and is by far the lowest Nile level recorded at Karnak.

Such wide variations in the Inundation[74] will clearly have caused problems with agriculture, the lowest floods potentially leading to insufficient water for adequate crop-growing in some areas. Such issues would provide a good backdrop for economic and political

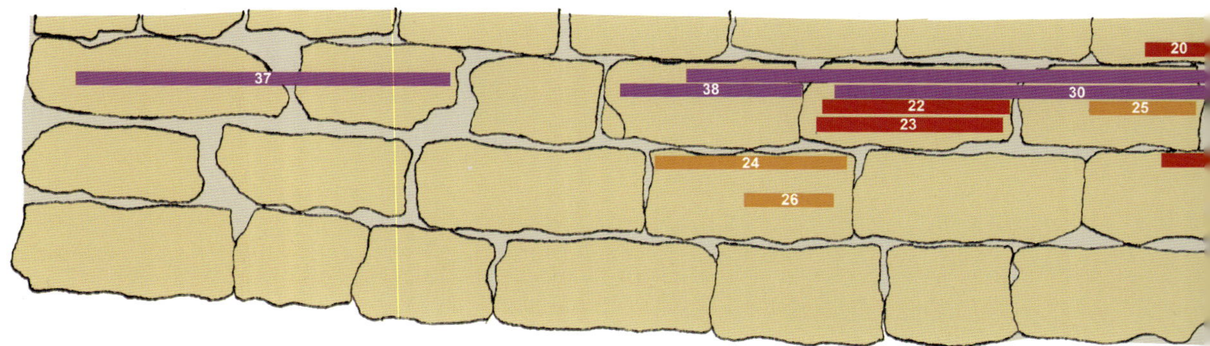

FIGURE 39 The podium on the former waterfront at Karnak, and the tenth- through seventh-century BC records of heights reached by the Nile inundation inscribed on it.

1. Shoshenq I, Year 6
2. Osorkon I, Year 12
3. Shoshenq IV (?), Year 5
4. Takelot III, Year 6
5. Osorkon III, Year 3
6. Osorkon III, Year 5
7. Osorkon III, Year 6
8. Osorkon II, Year 12
9. Osorkon II, Year 12 (correction?)
10. Usermaatre [...], Year 5/6/13/14?
11. Osorkon II, Year 21
12. Osorkon II, Year 22
13. Osorkon III, Year 28 = Takelot III, Year 5
14. Osorkon II, Year 29
15. Lost
16. (Takelot I), Year 5, HPA Iuwlot
17. (Takelot I), Year 8, HPA Nesibanebdjedet III
18. (Takelot I), Year 14, HPA Nesibanebdjedet III
19. (Takelot I), Year [...], HPA Nesibanebdjedet III

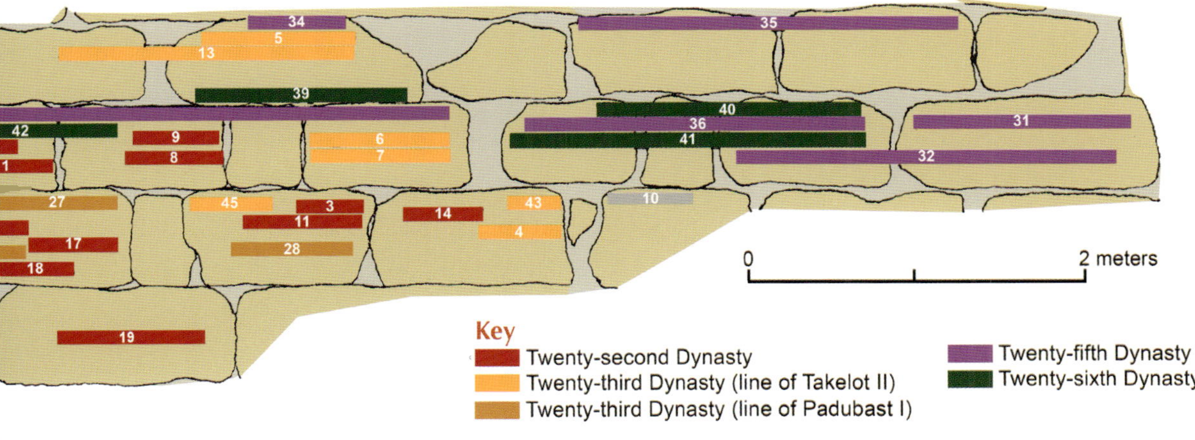

). (Takelot I), Year [...], HPA [Iuwlot]
. (Takelot I), Year [...], HPA [Iuwlot]
. Shoshenq III, Year 39, HPA Osorkon B
. Shoshenq III, Year 6, HPA Horsieset B
. (Shoshenq III), Year 12
= Padubast I, Year 5, HPA Horsieset B
. Shoshenq VI, Year 6, HPA Takelot E
. Padubast I, Year 16 = Iuput I, Year 2
. Padubast I, Year 19, HPA Horsieset B
. Padubast I, Year 18, HPA [...]

29. Padubast I, Year 23, HPA Takelot E
30. Shabaka, Year 2
31. Shabaka, Year [...]
32. Shabaka, Year [...]
33. Shabataka, Year 3
34. Taharqa, Year 6
35. Taharqa, Year 6
36. Taharqa, Year 7
37. Taharqa, Year 8
38. Taharqa, Year 9

39. Psamtik I, Year 10
40. Psamtik I, Year 11
41. Psamtik I, Year 17
42. Psamtik I, Year 19
43. Rudamun?, Year 3
44. Lost. Year x+6, HPA [...]
45. [...]-meryamun, Year 17, 18 or 25.

FIGURE 40 The High Priest of Amun Iuwlot, son of Osorkon I, shown on a stela that records the assignment of land and resources to him; from First Court, Karnak (Cairo JE31882).

FIGURE 41 Stela recording a donation of land under Takelot I, who is shown at the top (Copenhagen, Nationalmuseet 332).

trouble. In such circumstances, the standing of the pharaoh might have been undermined, and the importance of local authorities elevated. Such a situation is certainly hinted at by the Nile-level records, which only name the contemporary High Priest—and highlight the fact that both pontiffs involved were the sons of the previous king, Osorkon I.

Iuwlot had taken office during his father's reign, and is known from a number of items, including an offering stand, two stone baboons,[75] and a pair of stelae. One of the latter probably derives from Iuwlot's (unknown) tomb,[76] while the other recounts an oracle confirming the allocation of resources to his son Khaemwaset (Q) (fig. 40).[77] Iuwlot's daughter, Djedisetiuesankh (i), seems to have married the Third Priest of Amun Padimut ii-Patjenfy.[78]

The Nile-level texts show that sometime between Years 5 and 8 Iuwlot was replaced as High Priest by his brother Nesibanebdjedet III. This shows that there was still a resistance to reinstating dynasties of High Priests, as Iuwlot was survived by at least two sons, the aforementioned Khaemwaset and one Wasakawasa.[79] It is interesting to see that one son of Iuwlot was given a Libyan name, and the other a classic Egyptian one.[80] Nesibanebdjedet III would serve into the reign of Osorkon II.

Elsewhere in Egypt, a new High Priest of Ptah at Memphis followed Osorkon A, a scion of the long-established line there, in office: on a block from the temple area at the Saqqara Serapeum the new man, Merenptah (Q), is named alongside the cartouches of Takelot I.[81] It is possible that a bull was buried in the Serapeum galleries themselves in Year 14, but this remains uncertain.[82] Also found at Saqqara was a fragment of a fan bearing the king's name.[83] Other than items from his burial (see pages 135–38), the only other known documents bearing Takelot I's names are three stelae (fig. 41), probably from Bubastis.[84]

Shoshenq IIa

The problems of understanding the period following Osorkon I are exacerbated by the discovery in 1939 at Tanis (see pages 175–77) of a mummy in a coffin (fig. 42) that bore the following royal names:

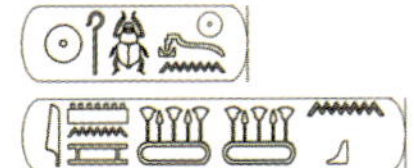

Prenomen *ḥqꜣ-ḫpr-rꜥ stp-n-rꜥ*

Nomen *ššnq mr-ỉmn*

This titulary is not found anywhere else, and various ideas have been put forward as to how the person currently known to scholarship as "Shoshenq IIa" should be fitted into history and genealogy. His broad date can be inferred from the form of his names and material found on the body. The latter includes a bracelet of Shoshenq I, showing that Shoshenq IIa cannot be any earlier than the beginning of the Twenty-second Dynasty. As to his names, kings from Osorkon II onward incorporated epithets into their nomina, over and above the simple "meryamun" that was used by the earlier kings of the dynasty (see page 54). Shoshenq IIa therefore must have reigned prior to the accession of Osorkon II.

Working within these constraints, the most popular option was for a long time that Shoshenq IIa might be

FIGURE 42 Lid of the silver coffin of Shoshenq IIa (Cairo JE72154).

identical with Prince and High Priest Shoshenq Q, gaining his royal titulary by serving briefly as Osorkon I's co-regent. However, in no case do any of Shoshenq Q's known descendants call him a king: for them he is always just a prince and High Priest (albeit one so distinguished as to employ a cartouche). It seems inconceivable that anyone of this period would miss an opportunity to highlight their descent from a pharaoh, no matter how ephemeral.[85] Another idea has been that the body is actually that of Shoshenq I, who for some reason had been given a new prenomen for his afterlife.[86] However, such a change is without any parallels, and particularly unlikely, given that Shoshenq I's canopic chest (fig. 91) bears his regular prenomen, Hedjkheperre.[87]

One possibility is that Shoshenq IIa ruled alongside Takelot I,[88] the presence of an additional king being perhaps one reason for the lack of any royal name in datelines of the period occupied by Takelot's reign. Given the lapse of royal authority hinted at in the Nile-level texts, it may have been taken as an opportunity to ratchet up the "Libyan-ness" of Egypt by admitting the possibility of dividing the kingship in a rather different way from the simple geographical north/south splits seen during the late twelfth/eleventh centuries. This could then be seen as heralding the patchwork of pharaonic and other authorities that would mature during the ninth century and endure into the seventh century. However, nothing can be suggested about how such potential parallel reigns might have functioned. Even the geographical location of Shoshenq IIa is uncertain since, although his body was found at Tanis, it was clearly a reburial, and could have been brought from some distance (see page 125).

One thing that is certainly known about Shoshenq IIa is that he died as a mature individual from an infected head injury.

> An area of the frontal bone about 8 cm. in width and 6 cm. antero-posteriorly ha[d] been affected by some agent which has so damaged the surface that the pericranium has been eroded away and the subjacent bone is blackened and cracked. The condition suggests burning, but whatever the cause of the wound may have been it certainly destroyed the scalp and reached the bone. Septic infection from the wound passed beneath the scalp and the whole surface of the skull within the limits of attachment of the epicranial aponeurosis [the middle (third) layer of the scalp] is finely pitted due to the ensuing periostitis. But the trouble has also spread through the bone to the inner aspect of the skull which is likewise blackened and cracked in the region of the fossae on either side of the middle line of the frontal bone. The rest of the cranial cavity is quite normal in appearance. There is no sign of healing so the disease was still active at the time of death and its spread to the inner surface may very well have resulted in meningitis.[89]

It has also been postulated that two other Kings Shoshenq might be placed in this period.[90] However, their existence as separate kings is questionable: "Shoshenq IIb," with the prenomen Tutkheperre, has been suggested above as having been an initial royal incarnation of Shoshenq I (pages 25–26), while "Shoshenq IIc" (Maatkheperre) seems more likely to be a corrupt writing of the prenomen of Shoshenq I.[91]

Osorkon II: End of an Era

Among the few things that we know for certain about Takelot I is that the Pasenhor genealogy states he had a wife named Kapes, and that they had a son named Osorkon, who became king. This is confirmed by a text in the burial chamber that Osorkon provided for Takelot in his own tomb (NRT-I) at Tanis (see page 135), where the younger king is called "a son benefiting the one who sired him." The second Osorkon II assumed the following titulary:

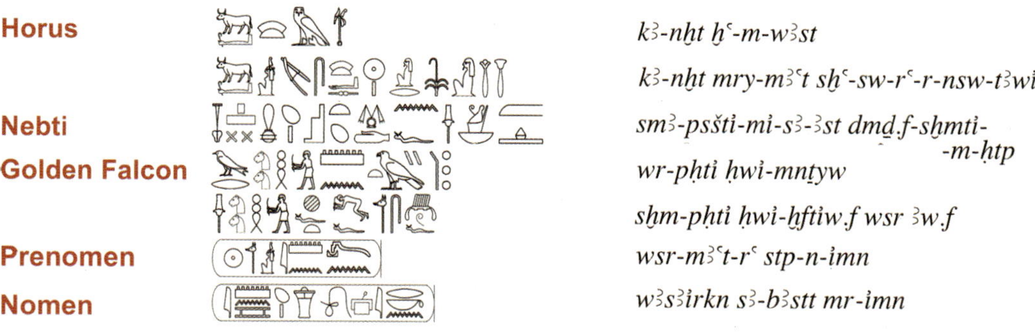

The king's alternate "core" Horus names had long histories. *K3-nḫt mry-m3‘t* ("Strong bull, beloved of Maat"), which is only found at Karnak, had been used by Thutmose I, Sethy I, Rameses II, Amenmeses, Tawosret, and Siamun. The epithet used with it by Osorkon II ("whom Re has caused to appear as King of the Two Lands")[92] had, intriguingly, previously been employed only by the Nineteenth Dynasty southern rebel king Amenmeses. The more usual *k3-nḫt ḫ‘-m-w3st* ("Strong bull, appearing in Thebes") was unequivocally Theban, and had been employed by Thutmose III, Sethy I, Rameses IX, and Panedjem I.

The unique "core" Nebti name employed by Osorkon II read "Who has united the two portions like the son of Isis, who has assembled the two crowns in peace," citing the god Horus, the patron of the Egyptian monarchy, with some variants adding additional phrases at the end. Osorkon's usual Golden Falcon name, "Great of strength, who has smitten the Bedouin," was also a new one, with a Tanite statue providing a variant "Powerful of strength, who has smitten his enemies, and is rich in splendor." A small number of other variant Golden Falcon names also exist for the king.

FIGURE 43 Statue of Osorkon II holding his "manifesto" text; from Tanis (UPMAA E16199 + Cairo CG881 + CG1040). This piece may have been made under Sethy I of the Nineteenth Dynasty, and later reworked.

Osorkon II's specific prenomen had first been used by Rameses IV, and then by Amenemopet. However, its core *wsr-m3ʿt-rʿ* had been used by a number of kings since it had been first formulated for Rameses II. This would continue to be the case down to the end of the Third Intermediate Period. The renown of Rameses was clearly the reason for this frequent reuse, overturning the long-maintained custom of giving each new king an original prenomen, albeit sometimes composed on the pattern of that of an admired predecessor.[93]

The nomen of Osorkon II marks a change from those of his predecessors. Since the latter part of the Eighteenth Dynasty, it had been standard practice for nomina to comprise the birth name of the king, plus an epithet, usually *mry-ỉmn* ("beloved of Amun"). To this, Osorkon added *s3-bstt*, "son of Bastet," thus beginning a practice of incorporating a filiation from a goddess (either Bastet or Isis) into a king's nomen. This would continue until the radical revision of royal name formats during the latter part of the eighth century.

King and family

While the events of the years leading up to Osorkon II's accession remain obscure, clearly things were not entirely well with Egypt. This assessment is reinforced by an important inscription found at Tanis. This was placed on a stela that forms part of a kneeling statue of the king (fig. 43), and essentially sets out his policies for the administration of the state—what one might dub his "manifesto."[94] This includes the assignment of various key offices to his children. These include the High Priesthoods of Amun and Heryshef and the Great Chiefdoms of the Ma. That the latter are listed alongside the historic high priesthoods is an indication of the way that these Libyan chieftainships had now become key components of the Egyptian state.

The prominence given to these local chiefs implicitly reversed the centralization that had been a feature of the pharaonic kingdom since the late Twelfth Dynasty. At that time, the power of the various regional governors (nomarchs) seems to have been transferred to the royal center (to judge from the ending of the building of major provincial tombs for such individuals under Senwosret III and Amenemhat III). This centralization had been re-established under the New Kingdom, and maintained, at least in theory, even during the splits in the monarchy under the last kings of the Twentieth Dynasty and during the Twenty-first Dynasty. Now, however, the Great Chiefdoms had acquired territorial aspects, while some of them also held functions in the broader state and priesthoods. These points would contribute to the disintegrations that would begin before the end of Osorkon II's reign. The potential impacts of these developments must have been in the back of the mind of the king when he issued his Tanis text, and may already have been a factor in whatever situation had existed during the time(s) of Takelot I and the shadowy Shoshenq(s).

FIGURE 44 Relief of Osorkon II and Queen Karomama B; from Bubastis (BM EA1077). The queen's physique is unusual, and is reminiscent of later Nubian work.

In particular, an interesting reference requests that the god guard against any "brother being resentful of his brother." This indeed suggests royal concern at the inherently fissiparous nature of such a parceling out of fiefs to members of the royal lineage. References are also made to the royal children leading armies against the "*pywd*-Libyans," presumably a troublesome tribe on Egypt's west flank.[95] All this would seem to imply that Osorkon II was worried about the future of both his kingdom and pharaonic authority within it. In this he would prove to be justified.

The mother of the children who would take up these roles is given in the text as Karomama (B), the King's Great Wife (fig. 44). None of the children are actually named in the inscription, although Karomama is known from other sources to have been the mother of Princes Shoshenq D and Hornakhte C, together with Princesses Tashakheper, Karomama C,[96] and [Ta?]iirmer. Two other wives of Osorkon II are known, Isetemkheb G and Djedmutesankh iv, respectively the mothers of Princess Tjesbastperu A and Prince Nimlot C.

FIGURE 45 Block statue of the High Priest of Amun Nimlot C (Vienna ÄS5791).

Osorkon II and the temples of Egypt

In the event, no son of Karomama received the High Priesthoods of Heryshef and Amun. Rather, it was Djedmutesankh's son, Nimlot (fig. 45), who would come to hold them, in succession. Nimlot was certainly High Priest of Heryshef at Herakleopolis (fig. 46), in Year 16, also holding the title together with, inter alia, those of General and Great Chief of Per-Sekhemkheperre,[97] a military strongpoint established by Osorkon I in the vicinity of Herakleopolis. Many Herakleopolitan dignitaries were linked to the Twenty-second Dynasty royal family[98] and, indeed, it has been suggested that the city may have been its place of origin.[99]

One son of Osorkon and Karomama, Hornakhte, was given the High Priesthood of Amun at Tanis, perhaps in anticipation of translation to Thebes in the fullness of time, but died as a child (see page 149). Osorkon II's uncle, Nesibanebdjedet III, remained in office as High Priest at Karnak throughout at least the first decade of Osorkon's reign, before being followed by Nimlot in the position.

Although the pontificate of Ptah at Memphis is not mentioned in the Tanis text as a fief for a royal son, it passed to Osorkon and Karomama's son, Shoshenq D, perhaps their eldest.[100] He succeeded Merenptah Q, who had followed the last certain scion of the hereditary succession of Memphite High Priests that stretched back to the early years of the Twenty-first Dynasty. Shoshenq was in office by his father's Year 23, on the basis of a statue of him (fig. 47 right) that was apparently associated with the burial of an Apis bull in that year,[101] and was himself buried at Memphis under Shoshenq III (see pages 151–53).

FIGURE 46 The remains of the inner part of the temple of Heryshef at Ihnasiya el-Medina, ancient Herakleopolis.

FIGURE 47 The High Priest of Ptah, Shoshenq D. Left: image from the façade of his tomb from Memphis (Cairo JE88131; see figs. 119–120). Right: statue from the Serapeum at Saqqara (Budapest 51.2050).

Only a fragment of stela attests to work in the temples of Memphis under Osorkon II,[102] but further north considerable construction was undertaken at a number of Delta sites.[103] At Tanis itself, there was a significant expansion of the Amun temple, adding a new forecourt, with a pylon whose foundation deposits survived intact. Fragments of offering scenes, probably from the court, have been found in the Sacred Lake.[104] Osorkon II also erected the East Temple at the site, including the utilization of Old Kingdom columns that had already been reused at least once before, by Rameses II (fig. 6 bottom right).[105] At Bubastis (fig. 37), a large gateway was constructed to celebrate the king's *sed*-festival (fig. 48).[106] Also in the Delta, a usurped statue of Senwosret III at Leontopolis (Tell Muqdam) attests to work by Osorkon II at that city;[107] it is also possible that Queen Karomama was buried at the site (see pages 149–51).

FIGURE 48 Reconstruction of the gateway at Bubastis celebrating the jubilee of Osorkon II.

FIGURE 49 Fragment of the Karnak Priestly Annals, with entries of the reigns of Osorkon II and Shoshenq III (Fitzwilliam E.SS.67).

At Karnak, two blocks found to the northeast of Pylon VI preserve the remains of a decree of Osorkon II.[108] A number of entries in the Priestly Annals (fig. 49)[109] and private statues also belong to the king's reign.[110] Nile-level texts of Years 12, 21, 22, and 29 are preserved, with the height of the inundation very similar in all three cases (fig. 39[8, 9, 11, 12, 14]). Building work was, however, apparently restricted to some small chapels on the northeastern periphery of the complex (fig. 25).[111] These included two dedicated to forms of Osiris, a type of sanctuary that would become an important feature of building projects at Karnak through the Twenty-sixth Dynasty.[112] Of these, that of Osiris-Wepished seems to have been built under the auspices of the Letter Writer of Pharaoh Hor, an important figure who lived on into the time of Shoshenq VI (page 81).[113] Beyond Thebes, the remains of a stela of Osorkon II have been found at Aswan, on Elephantine Island.[114]

Foreign relations

While statuary of Shoshenq I and Osorkon I was found at Byblos (figs. 30b, 33), nothing is known from the time of Takelot I. However, the remains of a statue of Osorkon II were found at the Levantine port,[115] while a measuring jar bearing the king's names was discovered at Samaria in Palestine.[116] These items are the last substantive Egyptian royal remains known from Syria-Palestine until the Twenty-fifth Dynasty, likely reflecting the collapse of Egypt's internal fortunes around the end of the reign of Osorkon II.

FIGURE 50 Doorjamb of Horsieset I; Karnak.

Thebes (Semi)detached: King Horsieset I

As already noted, the earlier years of Osorkon II saw the pontificate at Karnak in the hands of his uncle, Nesibanebdjedet III, who was then followed in office by Osorkon's own son, Nimlot C.[117] However, toward the end of Osorkon II's reign, a separate king suddenly appears at Thebes, in the person of Hedjkheperre-setepenamun Horsieset (I)-meryamun (fig. 50):[118]

Horus		*kꜣ-nḫt ḫꜥ-m-wꜣst*
Prenomen		*ḥḏ-ḫpr-rꜥ stp-n-ỉmn*
Nomen		*ḥr-sꜣ-ꜣst mr-ỉmn*

His Nebti and Golden Falcon names are presently unknown.

As would increasingly be the case during the middle years of the Third Intermediate Period, this titulary is wholly unoriginal. The prenomen had been used already by Nesibanebdjedet I, Shoshenq I, and Takelot I, while the Horus name—of course wholly appropriate for a Theban king—was currently also in use by Osorkon II.

Horsieset's origins are obscure. For many years it was assumed that he had previously been High Priest at Karnak, and also a son of Shoshenq Q. However, while the latter did indeed have a son named Horsieset (A), there is no evidence that this Horsieset ever rose beyond the rank of Priest of Amun, his title on the Bes statue dedicated by his father (fig. 35) having been misread as a high-priestly one.[119] In addition, in the one inscription apparently naming a High Priest Horsieset alongside Osorkon II,[120] Horsieset's name and title are secondary (fig. 51), giving no certainty that

FIGURE 51 Block statue of the Royal Scribe of Documents, Nebnetjeru, dedicated by his son, with detail of the inscription on its right shoulder; from Karnak (National Museum of Alexandria CG42225).

they were truly contemporaries in office. Indeed, it is more likely that the High Priest Horsieset in question was the man now known as Horsieset B, who never became a king, and would fight a battle to maintain his High Priesthood that persisted for a quarter-century after Osorkon II's death (pages 68–77, 80–82).[121]

Alternatively, Horsieset could still have been Shoshenq Q's son, but had achieved his status without having passed through a documented stage of holding the Amun High Priesthood. Another option is that King Horsieset was a son of the former High Priest Nesibanebdjedet III, to judge by the fact that the latter's wife, [Isetem]kheb (S)-Ikhy, bore the title of "God's Mother,"[122] which can be used to designate the mother of a king.[123] Horsieset's own wife may have been Shebensopdet, a King's Wife who is of otherwise unknown affiliations, but was buried at Herakleopolis, whence came the evidence of the king's maternity.[124] Two daughters of Horsieset I are known: Isetweret i[125] and [Tadit]anebethen.[126]

Horsieset I had a son who was elevated to the High Priesthood at Thebes, but his only known monument is damaged, and only two signs of the pontiff's name are partly legible, giving a reading of [...]*dỉw*[...] or [...]*ʿw*[...] (fig. 52).[127] A name of the period of the appropriate form is Padubast, and this son of Horsieset I may be identifiable with an individual of that name who would be, alongside Horsieset B, another protagonist in the coming struggles for power at Thebes. Horsieset is also associated on a stela (fig. 53)[128] with the first God's Wife of Amun apparently of any prominence since the Twenty-first Dynasty, Sitamen Mutemhat Karomama (G)-meryetmut (fig. 54).[129] Although she nowhere bears the title of King's Daughter, all other known holders of the office were royal princesses, and thus it is likely that she was indeed the offspring of a king. Indeed, it is possible that Karomama G *was* the same person as Osorkon II's daughter Karomama C, but had decided not to use a title implicitly linking her with Osorkon. This might have been the case if Horsieset's assumption of kingship was based on a denial of Osorkon II's legitimacy.

FIGURE 52 The son of Harsiese I, as shown on a monument from Koptos. His name has suffered damage, but could be restored as [Pa]du[bast] (Cairo JE37516).

FIGURE 53 Fragment of stela, showing Horsieset I and the God's Wife Karomama G (Berlin ÄM14995).

FIGURE 54 Bronze figure of Karomama G (Louvre N500).

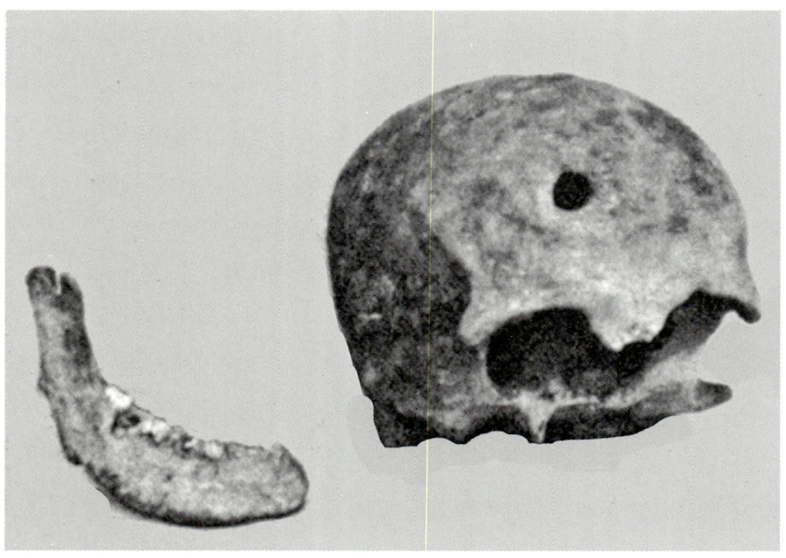

FIGURE 55 The skull of Horsieset I, showing the trepanned hole.

Unfortunately, no data are available to indicate the nature or chronology of Horsieset I's kingship. If he was indeed a son of Nesibanbdjedet III, it is possible that Horsieset's kingship, and his son's pontificate, directly followed the end of Nesibanebdjedet's period of office. On the other hand, it seems more likely that the demise of Nesibanebdjedet III was followed by the translation of Nimlot C to the High Priesthood of Amun, with the Horsieset/[Pa?]du[bast?] regime established somewhat later, after Nimlot's death or displacement from office. If this were the case, it may have been the first manifestation of the power struggles that would wrack the Thebaid over the next few decades. However, none of the monuments of the potential protagonists seem to bear any telltale signs of intentional mutilation,[130] while at least one statue has inscriptions that name both Osorkon II and Horsieset I (see just below).

FIGURE 56 Statue of the Fanbearer Nakhtefmut, dating to the time of Horsieset I (Cairo CG42208).

In any case, Horsieset I's effective rule may have been brought to an end through a collapse of his health. The skull found in his tomb (fig. 55; see pages 145–48) had "in the forehead a roughly quadrilateral hole which suggests a trepanation, [although he] lived for a long while after the infliction, whatever its nature may have been."[131]

It may have been in the wake of Horsieset's death that his son was supplanted by Nimlot C's son, Takelot F, as High Priest: the latter is mentioned in the Chapel of Osiris-Wepished at Karnak, built by Osorkon II.[132] However, around the end of Osorkon II's reign yet another High Priest had appeared on the stage, the aforementioned Horsieset B, who would remain on the scene—in and out of office—for some three decades. The fate of Takelot F will be discussed in the next chapter.

Of the lesser clergy at Karnak, the Fourth Priest Djedkhonsiufankh A had been followed by his son Nakhtefmut A-Djedthutiufankh B. He is shown to have been a contemporary of both Osorkon II and Horsieset I by the presence of both kings' names on one of his statues, explicitly given by favor of Horsieset I (fig. 56).[133] Horsieset's daughter, Isetweret i, was married to Nakhtefmut's son, Horsieset C, who went on to become Fourth, and ultimately Second, Priest, apparently before the end of Osorkon II's reign.[134]

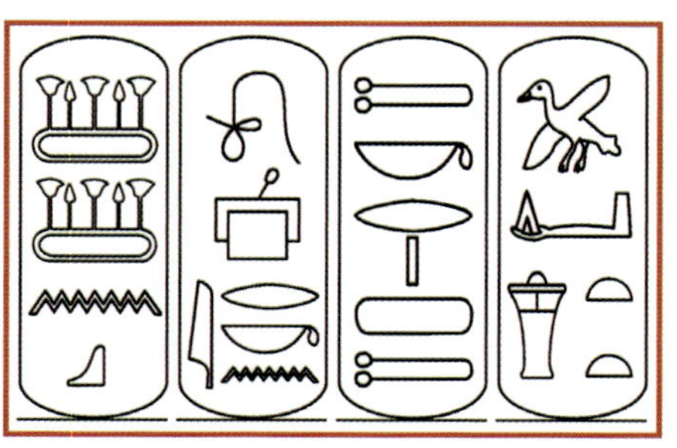

3 Disintegrations

Egypt may have been briefly reunited following the demise of Horsieset I, but before the end of Osorkon II's reign, another king had arisen in Thebes. The length of Osorkon's reign remains a matter for discussion. His highest certainly preserved regnal year is 23, from the stela of an Apis bull buried that year,[1] with a probable Year 29 among the Nile-level notations on the quay at Karnak (fig. 39[12]).[2] However, on the basis of broader chronological considerations, it seems probable that Osorkon lived on into at least the mid-30s of his reign.

The last years of the reign of Osorkon II mark a watershed in the history of the Third Intermediate Period. With it, the fissiparous tendencies that had been apparent since the last years of the New Kingdom finally became endemic, and would remain so for two centuries. First manifested in the dual kingships of the Twentieth/Twenty-first Dynasty transition, and then by the likely additional king(s) during the reign of Takelot I, and recently in the person of Horsieset I, they stood on the threshold of becoming institutionalized. Indeed, Osorkon's "manifesto" on his Tanis statue highlights the various nodes of power that he wished to secure in the persons of his sons, suggesting an unease at their being held by worthies without a direct connection with the pharaoh.

Those shown in that text as wielding levers of power within Egypt included not only the time-hallowed high pontiffs of the principal gods, but also various Chiefs of the Ma(shwesh), and also "Chiefs of Foreigners," presumably an umbrella term embracing such worthies as the Chiefs of the Libu and other tribes. This shows clearly how the political structure of Egypt had become transformed over the previous century, with holders of explicitly non-Egyptian titles now key players in the state.

There has been much debate over how far these title-holders and the lineages they represented contributed to the breakdown of centralized authority in Egypt during the ninth and eighth centuries. This has gone hand in hand with the question of the degree to which the situation stemmed from the underlying nature of Libyan society, which may have been antithetical to the very concept of a unitary monarchy.[3] Certainly, the glimpses of Libyan society revealed by Egyptian accounts of the various Rameside military entanglements indicate collective leadership exercised by multiple chiefs, rather than a single "king."

In the context of later Third Intermediate Period history, it seems likely that what is to be seen is a Libyan tribal-based "segmental" non-hierarchy running in parallel with, and in tension with, the historic Egyptian pharaonic hierarchy.[4] The importance of lineage can also be seen in the extensive genealogies set out on statues, on coffins, in graffiti, and in other contexts down into the eighth century—and, tellingly, disappear with the reimposition of a unitary state by Psamtik I (see pages 155–57). What is interesting is that these most overt displays of "Libyan-ness" come some time after the advent of Libyan kingship in the persons of Osorkon the Elder and Shoshenq I. They were presumably results of growing ethnic confidence and pride following on from the advents of these two kings, probably bolstered by further immigration into Egypt from the Libyan heartlands and settling in locations that were already the seats of Libyan Chiefs.

Thebes Detached: Takelot II

Down to the death of Osorkon II, the royal succession—in the main line at least—is guaranteed by the genealogy of Pasenhor B; after this, Pasenhor's ancestry diverges from the kingly sequence and is therefore of no further help. However, an autobiographical text of the High Priest Osorkon (see below, pages 71–73) states that he was a maternal great-grandson of Osorkon II, placing his own father, a King Takelot (II), one generation earlier and thus a successor to Osorkon II.[5]

For many years it was accepted that Takelot II was the direct successor of Osorkon II in the Twenty-second Dynasty line at Tanis (cf. chapter 7). However, it now seems clear that he was actually an independent ruler of Thebes, his reign running in parallel with the continuing line of Osorkon II at Tanis (see below). As for the origins of Takelot II, he seems most likely to have been none other than the High Priest Takelot F, son of the former pontiff Nimlot C and thus a grandson of Osorkon II. It is in any case clear that Takelot II became king prior to Osorkon II's death. This is because Takelot's Year 24 precedes Year 22 of Osorkon's successor at Tanis, Shoshenq III (for whom see pages 77–80), in the chronological list of endowments made by Takelot's son, Osorkon B, that are included in Osorkon's aforementioned autobiographical text.

FIGURE 57 Fragment of stela of Takelot II from Elephantine (Elephantine Museum).

Only three elements of Takelot II's titulary are currently known:

Horus		*kꜣ-nḫt ḫꜥ-m-wꜣst*
Prenomen		*ḥḏ-ḫpr-rꜥ stp-n-rꜥ*
		ḥḏ-ḫpr-rꜥ stp-n-rꜥ nṯr-ḥqꜣ-wꜣst
Nomen		*tklt sꜣ-ꜣst mr-ỉmn*

The king's names show little originality, the Horus name having only recently been (re)used by Osorkon II and Horsieset I, although "Strong Bull who appears in Thebes" was an obvious name for a king of the south. His prenomen was borrowed from Shoshenq I and Takelot I, although the epithet sometimes used, "divine ruler of Thebes,"

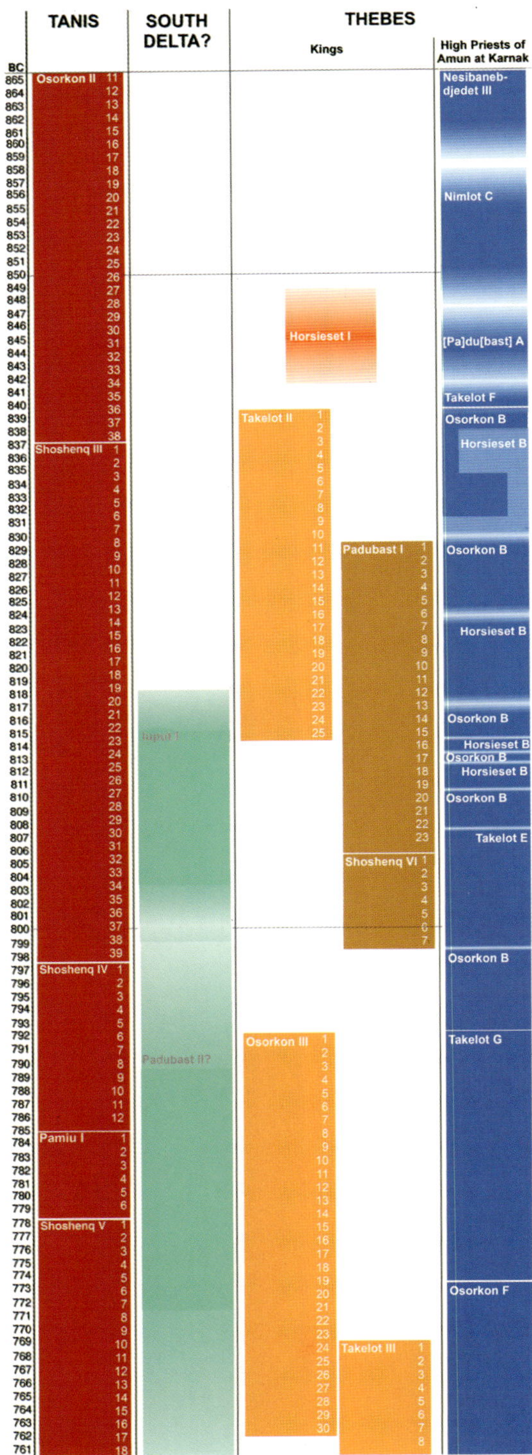

FIGURE 58 Chronology: ninth to eighth centuries BC.

had not been used since the Eighteenth Dynasty, and then always in the nomen. Its use was clearly another expression of the king's area of dominion and, interestingly, Takelot's Tanite contemporary, Shoshenq III, revived the "northern" equivalent, "netjerheqaiunu," "divine ruler of Heliopolis," for his own titulary (pages 77–78). This implies an understanding by both kings that their respective authorities were limited, rather than either one claiming untrammeled pharaonic authority. Takelot followed Osorkon II in incorporating a filiation from a goddess into his nomen, in this case Isis, rather than Bastet. This marked the beginning of the use of "sieset" as a marker for southern kings, contrasting with the use of "sibastet" by Osorkon II and later kings ruling from the north.

It would seem likely that Takelot F went directly from being Theban pontiff to Theban king, but it is unclear what happened to the High Priesthood at that point. Takelot II's aforementioned son, Osorkon B, held the office at various points over the following decades (see below), and a direct father–son succession is possible. However, a complicating factor is the aforementioned case of a statue (fig. 51) which has the name and title of Horsieset B inscribed alongside the cartouche of Osorkon II, potentially implying that they were contemporaries in office. However, as already noted, close inspection shows that the name of Horsieset was not carved at the same time as the cartouche, suggesting that it was added secondarily, in which case it might perhaps be seen as a gesture against the kingship of Takelot II. Horsieset B was clearly opposed to his rule, as the history of the next few decades is the story of the conflict between Horsieset and Takelot's son, Osorkon B, for possession of the High Priesthood of Amun at Thebes.

Little is in any case known of the earlier years of the new southern regime. Undated reliefs of Takelot II and the God's Wife Karomama G in Chapel e in the Montju complex[6] may date from this period. Similarly, a restoration text in the name of Takelot II in the Ptah temple at Karnak may also be dated to these times, as might a fragmentary stela from Elephantine. This piece demonstrates that when this monument was erected, the king's writ embraced—or was at least acknowledged at—Aswan (fig. 57).[7]

Takelot II had at least four sons. The eldest was Osorkon B, High Priest of Amun at Karnak and Generalissimo. His mother was Karomama D, a daughter of Nimlot C. She was thus a sister of her husband, if he had indeed previously been the High Priest Takelot F. Other known sons were Nimlot F,[8] [...]iuankh,[9] and the General Bakenptah.[10] There were also at least three daughters, Karomama E (fig. 62),[11] Isetweret ii, who married the Vizier Nakhtefmut C,[12] and Shepensopdet (v), who married the Fourth Priest of Amun, Djedkhonsiufankh C, son of his predecessor Horsieset C, and who was the mother of a further Fourth Priest, Nakhtefmut B.[13]

It is in Takelot's Year 11 that certainly-dated events begin, in particular with the first episode in a long text inscribed within the Bubastite Portal at Karnak. This is a key source for the next three decades of Theban history, together with the Karnak Nile-level texts and the Karnak Priestly Annals. Generally referred to as the Chronicle of Prince Osorkon,[14] it is made up of two distinct sections. The first section dates to Year 11 (figs. 59a, 60), while the second part covers Years 12 and 15 of Takelot II through Year 28 of Shoshenq III; a final coda is dated to the latter's Year 29. It was in this last year that the second section was apparently carved (fig. 59b, c).

The Year 11 section is dated to I *prt* 1, and recounts Osorkon's passage southward from El-Hiba, just south of the mouth of the Fayyum, with an army to put down a rebellion, which seems to have caused damage to towns as far north as Hermopolis (Ashmunein). Here, the pontiff instituted repairs before the army headed on to Thebes, where captured rebels were executed and their bodies burned, destroying their chance of an afterlife, according to Egyptian belief. This bloody episode was followed by the issuing of a series of decrees regarding the administration of the Theban temples. It was in the wake of these events that we find a priest named Hori petitioning Osorkon on I *šmw* 11 for the restoration of his hereditary rights within the Karnak temples (fig. 123).[15]

As to who Osorkon B's opponent(s) were, one Karnak Nile Level text (fig. 39[23]) seems to provide the key. This is dated to Year 6 of Shoshenq III, Osorkon II's successor at Tanis, and names the High Priest as being Horsieset B.[16] Since Shoshenq seems to have become king in Tanis two years after Takelot had done so in Thebes (page 68), this date corresponds to Takelot II's tenth regnal year. It thus reveals Horsieset as Osorkon's antagonist, pointedly using the reign of the contemporary Tanite king as his dating era.

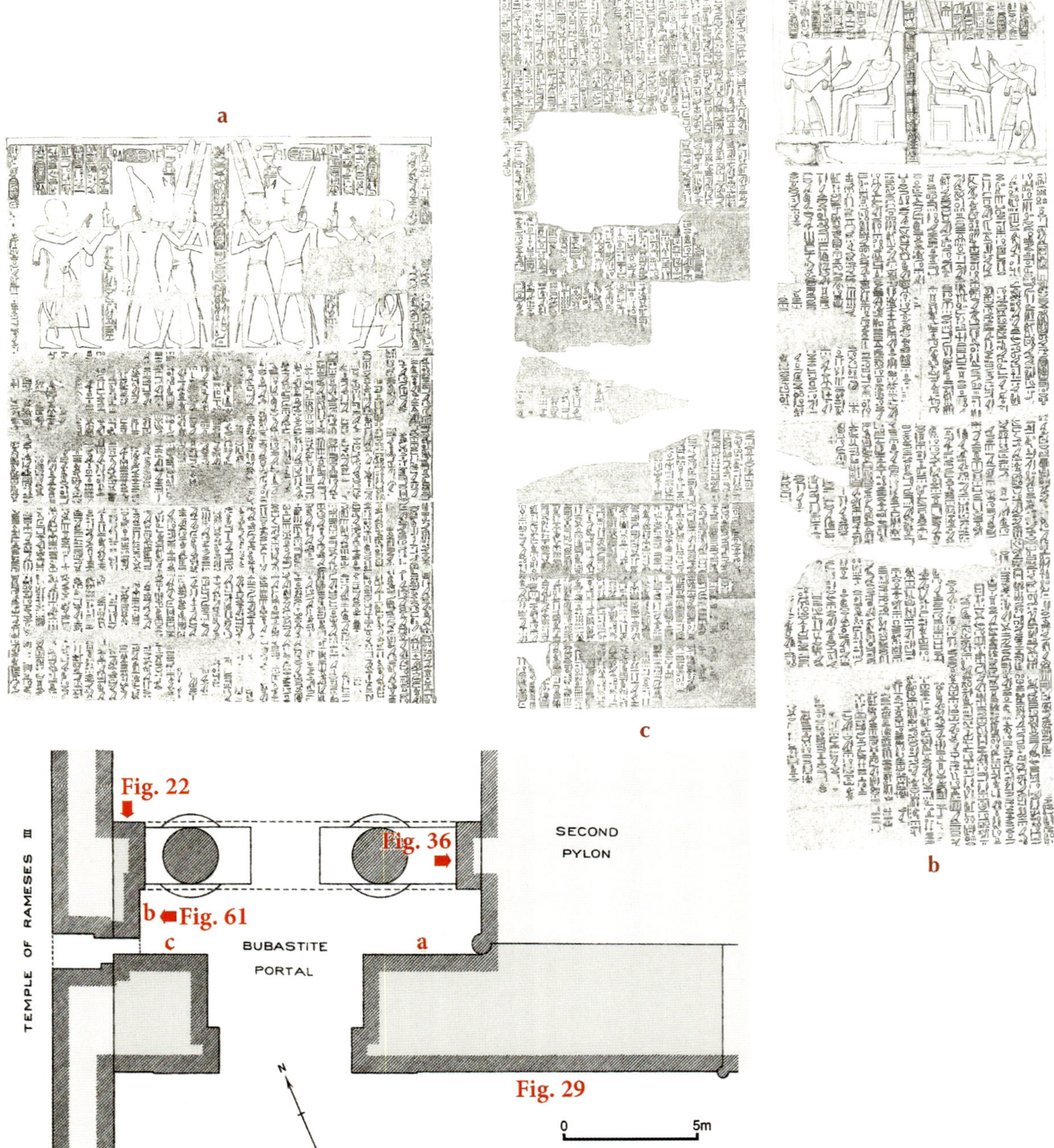

FIGURE 59 Plan of the Bubastite Portal at Karnak, with the texts comprising the Chronicle of Prince Osorkon. a. First section, dated to Year 11, headed by a double scene of Osorkon and his father (see also fig. 61). b, c. Second section, with a double scene of Osorkon and Amun at the top, and concluded on the inside of the western section of the Portal. This covered Years 12 and 15 of Takelot II through Year 28 of Shoshenq III, with a final coda in the latter's Year 29, in which year this second section was apparently carved.

FIGURE 60 The first section of the Chronicle of Prince Osorkon.

This may be linked with the already noted addition of Horsieset B's name alongside that of Osorkon II on an existing statue, and might suggest that Horsieset initially based his rebellion on at least nominal loyalty to the long-established line of kings in Tanis, rather than the "upstart" Takelot II. In any case, Horsieset survived the defeat of the rebellion and would continue in opposition to Osorkon B for the High Priesthood for another two decades.

Year 12 saw Osorkon in Thebes three times, bringing with him shiploads of offerings, his position apparently now secure. However, in Year 15, civil war broke out once again with renewed and unexpected intensity: indeed, Osorkon protests in the Chronicle that there had been no omen, such as an eclipse, which might have been expected to herald such a cataclysm.[17] Civil war would wrack southern Egypt for some twenty years.

Thebes Divided: Padubast I

It would appear that Horsieset had not been alone in his rebellion, as an anonymous Year 12 of another Nile-level text naming him as High Priest (fig. 39[24])—which can, nevertheless, be only that of Shoshenq III—is stated to correspond to Year 5 of a king with the following names:[18]

Prenomen	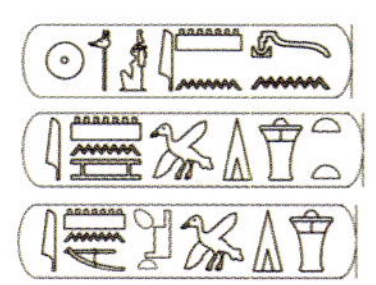	*wsr-mꜣꜥt-rꜥ stp-n-ỉmn*
Nomen		*pꜣ-dỉ-bꜣstt mr-ỉmn*
		pꜣ-dỉ-bꜣstt sꜣ-ꜣst mr-ỉmn

The associated Horus, Nebti, and Golden Falcon names remain unknown. The prenomen had been used by Rameses IV, Amenemopet, and Osorkon II, while the format of the nomen, with the epithet *s3-3st*, followed Takelot II's name. On the basis of the Nile-level text, this Padubast must have come to power in Shoshenq III's Year 8, that is, in or soon after Takelot's Year 10, and thus almost certainly coinciding with the Year 11 rebellion described in the Chronicle.

What then might have been the background of this further upstart king? A possibility is that he was none other than the High-Priestly son of Horsieset I, whose damaged name we have already noted (page 63, above) could potentially be restored as [Pa] du[bast]. Certainly, as the son of a former Theban king (and himself a former High Priest), this individual would be a credible candidate. Padubast I and Horsieset B would be closely associated over the next twenty years, with the Year 15 putsch putting them at the head of the Thebaid for the best part of a decade.

Of Padubast I's family, only a son, Padiamenet iii, is known, from a record in the Karnak Priestly Annals of his induction as a God's Father in the king's Year 7.[19] Friendly relations between the Padubast/Horsieset regime and the Tanite kings are suggested by the double-dating of the aforementioned Nile-level text, and a restoration of the doorway of Pylon X, at the southern entrance to the Karnak temple, by Pashedbast B, a son of Shoshenq III (fig. 61).[20]

FIGURE 61 The portal of Karnak's Pylon X, with the text of Pashedbast B, son of Shoshenq III, which was carved on the remains of the limestone gateway in the foreground; it is now destroyed.

FIGURE 62 Stela of Year 25 of Takelot II, and also naming the High Priest Osorkon B, donating land to his daughter, the Chantress of Amun, Karomama E, who is shown—most curiously—emerging from a chest or sarcophagus; from chapel of Osiris-Padedankh at Karnak (Cairo JE36159).

However, while control of Thebes was apparently maintained through Year 8 of Padubast I,[21] Osorkon B and Takelot II seem to have made a comeback during the latter's Years 24 and 25 (≈ Padubast I Years 14–15). During Year 24, the Chronicle records donations to Amun by Osorkon, while a stela at Karnak (fig. 62) is dated to Takelot II's Year 25—the last known for the king. It is possible that an oracle text potentially aimed against Horsieset B may date to this, or another, of Osorkon B's comebacks.[22] It seems likely that Takelot died shortly after the Year 25 stela was carved, as the Chronicle dates the next batch of donations by Osorkon to Shoshenq III's Year 22, corresponding to what would have been Takelot's Year 26—if not the latter part of Year 25 itself.

If the Takelotid revival had thus been followed shortly by the death of Takelot II himself, it is not surprising that soon afterward we find Padubast I once again appearing in a Nile-level text, dated to his Year 16.[23] Most interestingly, this is stated to correspond to Year 2 of a king ( ), Iuput-meryamun. This individual is an enigma. Although his Year 6 appears in graffiti on the roof of the Khonsu temple,[24] there is no unequivocal record of his prenomen. Furthermore, there is no evidence as to his background or affiliations. A statue base, from Tell el-Yahudiya in the southeast of the Delta,[25] bears the following prenomen and nomen:

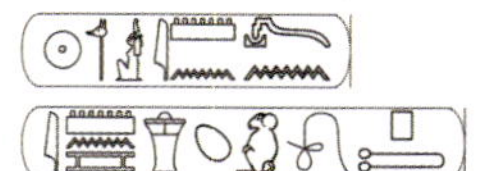

Prenomen — *wsr-mꜣʿt-rʿ stp-n-ỉmn*

Nomen — *ỉwpwt sꜣ-bꜣstt mr-ỉmn*

The format of the names fits well with a date in the late ninth century, but very similar names, albeit with Re, rather than Amun, referenced in the epithet within the prenomen, and a different spelling of the nomen, were also used by Iuput II a century later (see pages 114–15), so a question remains as to which of the Iuput kings commissioned the statue base.

The Karnak Iuput has generally been regarded as a Theban co-regent of Padubast, but does not necessarily follow: in his Year 5 Padubast had linked his reign with that of Shoshenq III, most definitely not a Theban. It has already been noted that, directly following Takelot II's death, Osorkon B began to date by Shoshenq III: Could it be that this act implies a break in the previous link between the Padubastid regime and that in Tanis, leading to another northern monarch (i.e., Iuput I) being thereafter recognized as the Padubastids' northern "partner"? The later Iuput II reigned at Leontopolis in the southeastern Delta, so this may have been true of his earlier namesake. We will return to the question of this south-Delta polity below.

Meanwhile in the North: Shoshenq III

As already noted, while Takelot II was establishing his separate regime in the south, Osorkon II was succeeded at Tanis by Shoshenq III. Nothing is known of Shoshenq III's origins: he cannot have been a son of Osorkon II, as the latter already had a son named Shoshenq (D, the High Priest at Memphis). This man was buried during Shoshenq III's reign, as shown by a bracelet placed on his mummy (page 151). It would therefore seem not unlikely that Shoshenq III was a grandson of Osorkon II, which would fit in with his rule lasting for four full decades. One possibility is that he was actually an eponymous son of Shoshenq D, with the latter dying (naturally or otherwise) around the same time as his father Osorkon II, accounting for his burial under Shoshenq III.[26]

As pharaoh, Shoshenq III adopted a titulary that included the following names (his Nebti and Golden Falcon names being thus far unknown):

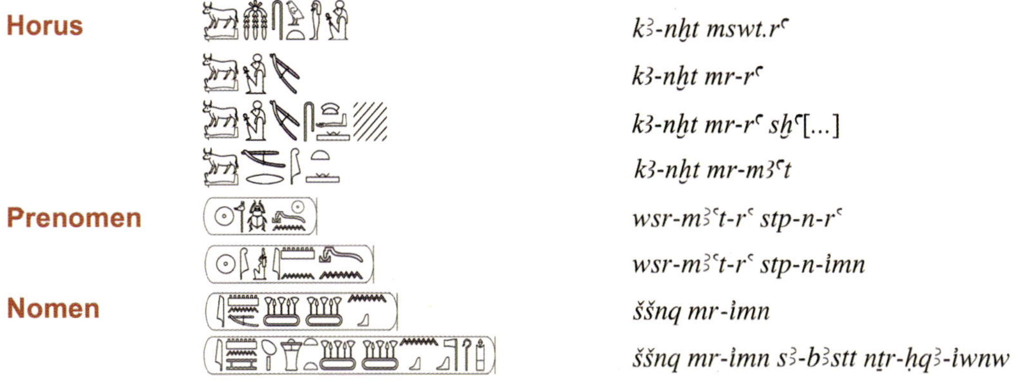

Of the three Horus names known for the king, the first one listed ("Strong Bull, offspring of Re") had not been used by any previous monarch. The second ("Strong Bull, beloved of Re") had already been used during the Twenty-second Dynasty by Osorkon I, while the incomplete extended version (". . . who has caused (him) to appear [...]") may have been identical with a similarly formulated Horus name of Shoshenq I. The final one had very recently been employed by Osorkon II and a range of earlier kings.

FIGURE 63 The granite gate of Shoshenq III at Tanis, largely built from the cut-up remains of a colossal statue of Rameses II (see also fig. 125 bottom).

The king's alternate prenomina had both been widely used since Rameside times, and as such could not be used on their own to identify the king, requiring the presence of a nomen as well for certainty. In the case of Shoshenq III, this could be of simple form, with just the epithet "beloved of Amun," or an extended version, continuing the approach inaugurated by Osorkon II. This incorporated not only the epithet "son of Bastet," alongside "beloved of Amun," but also added yet a further epithet, "divine ruler of Heliopolis." The latter epithet had originated back in the mid-Eighteenth Dynasty, and been revived during the Twentieth. It had then lain fallow until picked up again by Shoshenq III. As already discussed (page 70), this seems to have been a marker for Shoshenq's understanding that he was an effective ruler only in the north.

FIGURE 64 Stela from the burial of Apis XXIX in the Serapeum at Saqqara. Dated to Year 28 of Shoshenq III, it shows the Apis being adored by the Great Chief of the Ma, Padieset A (for whose coffin see fig. 119 bottom), and his sons, the High Priest of Ptah Peftjauawybast B, and the *sm*-Priest of the god, Takelot D. All are shown with the Libyan feather above their heads (Louvre IM3749=N413).

Shoshenq III's Great Wife was one Tentamenopet, with whom he had a daughter named Ankhesenshoshenq.[27] By another spouse, [Ta]dibast ii, daughter of Tadibast, he had Bakennefi A, who seems to have been heir to the throne in Year 14.[28] A third wife was Djedbastesankh, the mother of Takelot C, a Commander of All Troops.[29] Other offspring of the king included Pashedbast B (see page 75, below), the High Priest of Amun (at Tanis) Padebehenbast (active in Year 28),[30] and probably the Great Chief of the Ma, Pamiu, who is likely to be the future king of that name (see page 84).[31] Their mother(s) remains unknown.

At Tanis, Shoshenq III added a new monumental gateway to the brick enclosure wall of the Amun temple (figs. 63, 125 bottom).[32] The stone for this was obtained from earlier monuments, including granite blocks produced by cutting up a colossal statue of Rameses II. The king also built his tomb at Tanis (pages 142–43).

Aside from the mentions at Thebes, all known attestations of Shoshenq III come from the north of Egypt. Monuments exist in various parts of the Delta,[33] including a pylon at Tell Balamun and a gateway at Heliopolis.[34] From the same area come stelae recording the donation of land to local cults,[35] a similar stela from Herakleopolis being the king's most southerly substantive attestation.[36]

In the area of Memphis, stelae commemorated the burial of Apis bull XXIX at Saqqara in the king's Year 28[37]—although another bull must have been interred earlier in the reign, given that the previous known bull burial had been back in Year 23 of Osorkon II.[38] The stela that accompanied Apis XXIX to the grave reveals the Memphite hierarchy at that point in time, including their line of descent (fig. 64). The leading figure in paying homage to the deceased Apis is the Great Chief of the Ma, Padieset A, son of a like-titled Takelot B, who was in turn a son of the former High Priest Shoshenq D, the son of Osorkon II. The next figure is Padieset's son, the High Priest of Ptah Peftjauawybast (B), followed by another son, the *sm*-priest (i.e., second in the Ptah hierarchy) Takelot D. What is interesting here is that on the stela of Apis XXX, buried in Year 2 of Pamiu I (see below, pages 82–83), Pedieset A and Takelot B are retrospectively referred to with the additional titles of Memphite High Priest. It would thus seem that the family of Shoshenq D continued to hold the Memphite pontificate. However, Pedieset—and possibly Takelot—passed that office to a son while yet living, but retaining the Great Chieftainship. That the latter was regarded as senior to a pontificate—formerly second only to the king—is shown by the scale of his representation on the Apis XXIX stela. This seems to be an example of the way in which the tribal Libyan lineages subverted the ancient Egyptian hierarchies.[39]

The Struggle for Thebes

Surprisingly, Osorkon B did not claim Takelot II's throne on the latter's demise. Rather, he remained merely High Priest, and used the regnal years of Shoshenq III for dating purposes. This may suggest that the Tanite king was now supporting Osorkon in his struggle with Padubast I and Horsieset B, reversing the earlier situation that had led the latter to initially date his activities by the years of the Tanite pharaoh. As suggested above, it may be that Shoshenq was now threatened by a rival in the Delta in the form of Iuput I, and an alliance between the Tanite king and Osorkon was necessary to oppose the Padubast I–Iuput I axis.

The struggle between Osorkon B and his enemies can be traced partly through the records of the years in which the Chronicle states that offerings were made by the prince–pontiff, and partly through the dates, reigns, and individuals mentioned in the period's Nile-level texts. Thus, Osorkon seems to have been in control in Year 22 (of Shoshenq III), but lost power soon afterward. This is implied by the fact that we then find a Nile level labeled with the combination of Year 16 of Padubast I and Year 2 of Iuput I (≈ Year 24 of Shoshenq III: fig. 39[26]). Osorkon seemingly made a comeback immediately after this inundation, as he then records offerings in Years 24 and 25 (of Shoshenq III). But after this we find Padubast I back in control during his Years 18 and 19 (≈ Years 26/27 of Shoshenq III), as shown by Nile-level texts of those years (fig. 39[27, 28]). But Osorkon then records himself making offerings in Years 28 and 29 (of Shoshenq III), indicating that he had once again displaced Padubast from at least Thebes itself.

However, the entry of Year 29 would be the last one in the Chronicle, and the inundation of the following year was recorded as measured in Year 23 of Padubast I (fig. 39[29]). Interestingly, while Horsieset B had been mentioned in the Nile-level text of Padubast's Year 19, in Year 23 the contemporary High Priest is named as a Takelot (E). Presumably Horsieset had now died after contending with Osorkon B for the pontificate for over three decades. Nothing is known, however, of the origins of the new pontiff.

Not long afterward there was a further change of personalities, when Padubast I himself appears to have been succeeded by a Shoshenq (VI) of unknown origins. As with many kings of the era, his titulary is only partially known:

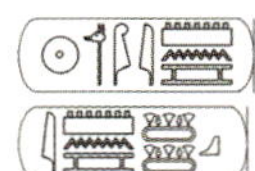

Prenomen *wsr-mꜣꜥt-rꜥ mr-ỉmn*

Nomen *šš(n)q-mr-ỉmn*

The king's prenomen, although with the now-banal "Usermaatre" core, differed from that of a number of recent kings in employing the epithet "meryamun," a combination previously used only by Rameses III, thus marking Shoshenq VI out from his Tanite contemporary, Shoshenq III. The new Theban king is known only from the Nile-level record of his Year 6 (fig. 39[25]), where he is accompanied by the High Priest Takelot E, and also from graffiti on the roof of the Khonsu temple in Years 4 and 6, and an entry in the Karnak Priestly Annals which has, unfortunately, lost its date.[40] He is also named on the funerary cones of the Letter Writer of Pharaoh, Hor, who had served since the days of Osorkon II.[41]

Shoshenq VI and Takelot E seem to have maintained their power in Thebes for some seven years, with no sign of any immediate renaissance by Osorkon B. Whether low-level conflict continued, or whether Osorkon retired for the time being, is uncertain, but a probable reference to him as "Osorkon-of-Teudjoy" may suggest that he was based at the latter city (modern El-Hiba). This had been a stronghold of the High Priests of Amun

FIGURE 65 Cartonnage mummy case of Sheamenimes, daughter of the Chief of the Ma Takelot Q (Cairo TR 21/11/16/5).

since the Twenty-first Dynasty.[42] If this identification is correct, the text in question indicates that Osorkon had married Sheamenimes, daughter of the Chief of the Ma Takelot Q (fig. 65). This will have been early in his career, as Meresamenet, daughter of Osorkon and Sheamenimes, is not called the offspring of a High Priest on her coffin, indicating that she must have died during these "wilderness years."[43]

The triumph of Osorkon

It is not long after Shoshenq VI's Year 6 that we find the following entry in the Karnak Priestly Annals:

> Year 39, I *šmw* 26 [of Shoshenq III]: Now [Osorkon B] was in Thebes carrying out the festival of Amun in concert with his brother, the General of Herakleopolis and Army Leader Bakenptah, while all the gods were satisfied with them in overthrowing everyone who had fought against them.[44]

It thus appears that, after nearly three decades of struggle, Osorkon had finally displaced his Theban opponents. Presumably this had involved the physical overthrow of Shoshenq VI and Takelot E, but nothing is known of their actual fates. However, Osorkon did not yet claim his father's throne, dating his triumph in terms of the reign of Shoshenq III. This presumably reflected long-term support that had been provided by the old Tanite, and it would not be until after his death that Osorkon finally assumed kingship in Thebes.

New Generations in the North

Tanis

Shoshenq III's last recorded regnal year is the Year 39 cited just above. From his last decades we have a number of documents that indicate, aside from the possible pharaonic challenge of Iuput I, his domains now included a patchwork of territories controlled by Great Chieftains of the Ma. Among the best-documented of these is that based at Mendes, with one Hornakhte A attested as Chief in Year 22 of Shoshenq III (fig. 66)[45] and further incumbents known down to the first part of the seventh century. In the western Delta there was a succession of Chiefs of the Libu, starting with Inamunnifnebu in Year 31 of Shoshenq III.[46] Other Chiefdoms of the Ma included one based at Pharbaithos (Hurbeit), twenty kilometers northeast of Bubastis, also first attested under Shoshenq III,[47] to whom they presumably owed some form of allegiance.

The chronology of the kings at Tanis directly following Shoshenq III can be calculated by reference to the stelae that commemorated the burial of Apis XXX in Year 2 of his second successor, Pamiu I (fig. 68).[48] This bull is stated to have been inducted in Year 28 of

FIGURE 66 Mendesian stela of the Chief of the Ma Hornakhte A, dated to Year 22 Shoshenq III. Hornakhte wears the Libyan feather (Brooklyn 67.118).

Shoshenq III and lived twenty-six years, showing that fourteen years separated Shoshenq III's last known regnal year (39) from Pamiu I's accession. Although for many years it was assumed that Pamiu was Shoshenq III's direct successor, it is now clear that a king now known as Shoshenq IV ruled for a decade between the two monarchs (see page 181).

Little is known about the king, including his family relationships, although as Pamiu I was probably a son of Shoshenq III, this is likely to be true of Shoshenq IV as well. Only his prenomen and nomen are currently attested:

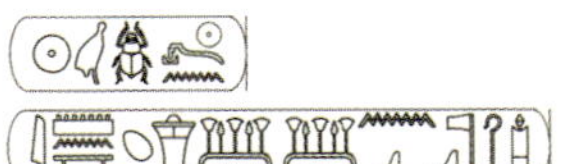

Prenomen	*ḥḏ-ḫpr-rʿ stp-n-rʿ*
Nomen	*ššnq sꜣ-bꜣstt mr-ỉmn nṯr-ḥqꜣ-ỉwnw*

Shoshenq IV's prenomen had previously been used by a range of kings, including Shoshenq I, but the addition of epithets to Shoshenq IV's nomen allow him to be distinguished from his illustrious ancestor.

Besides his burial at Tanis (page 143), Shoshenq IV is known from a bark-stand at that site (on which he bears the "Theban" epithet "-netjerheqawaset," rather than the usual "northern" "-netjerheqaiunu"), two donation stelae, dating to his Years 4 and 10, a statuette of Isis, and some smaller pieces.[49] The Year 10 donation stela[50] was in the name of a Chief of the Libu, Niumataped (A), who is also known from a donation stela of a Year 8 sometimes regarded as that of Shoshenq V, but may also actually date to the time of Shoshenq IV.[51]

The reign of his successor, Pamiu I (fig. 67), lasted at least seven years, as shown by a block originally from Heliopolis.[52] Like so many of the kings of his time, only the core elements of his titulary are known:

Prenomen		*wsr-mꜣʿt-rʿ stp-n-(ỉ)mn*
		wsr-mꜣʿt-rʿ stp-n-rʿ
Nomen		*pꜣ-mỉy mr-ỉmn*
		p(ꜣ)-mỉy

FIGURE 67 Bronze statuette of Pamiu I (BM EA32747).

The use of the core prenomen "Usermaatre" with versions existing citing both Amun (curiously, in all examples omitting the initial *ỉ*-sign) and Re in its epithets makes it completely useless as a means of identifying Pamiu I's monuments. On the other hand, Pamiu's nomen was hitherto unique for a pharaoh, meaning "The Cat," and marks Pamiu as the first Tanite pharaoh to have a non-Libyan name since the Twenty-first Dynasty. Most examples of his name write his name phonetically, but at least one example uses the cat hieroglyph instead, and also adds the epithets "sibast" and "netjerheqa[...]" to the usual "meryamun." However, some attestations of the king (including three inscribed blocks from Tanis)[53] omit all epithets, the first northern example of an archaizing simplification of royal names that was already developing at Thebes (see pages 88, 91).

A donation stela that may be assigned to the reign is known from Bubastis,[54] but the largest group of material from Pamiu I's reign derives from the Serapeum at Saqqara, where the aforementioned Apis XXX was buried in II *prt* of his Year 2. The principal stelae (fig. 68a–b)[55] once again show Padieset A as the leading man at Memphis, but with a younger son Horsieset H having replaced Peftjauawybast B as High Priest.[56] In addition, four further stelae

FIGURE 68 Stelae from the burial of Apis XXX in Year 2 of Pamiu. a., b. Padieset A and Horsieset H, both wearing Libyan feathers, adoring Apis and the Goddess of the West. The text gives the date of the bull's birth in Year 28 of Shoshenq III and its age at death, providing a key chronological datum. c. Dedicated by the priest Senebef. d. Dedicated by the priest Padja (Louvre: a. IM3697, b. IM3736, c. IM4205, d. IM3441).

were dedicated to the bull by other Memphite worthies (fig. 68c–d),[57] while a block statue and a stela datable to this reign also probably come from this city.[58]

The southern Delta

We have already noted the possibility that the Iuput I associated with Padubast I was a precursor of the Iuput II known to have ruled from Leontopolis during the second half of the eighth century. Another potential local king from, or near, the city is a Padubast (II), with the following known titulary:

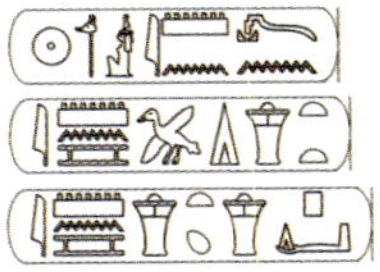

Prenomen	*wsr-mꜣꜥt-rꜥ stp-n-ỉmn*
Nomen	*pꜣ-dỉ-bꜣstt mr-ỉmn*
	pꜣ-dỉ-bꜣstt sꜣ-bꜣstt mr-ỉmn

These cartouches differ from those of Padubast I only in the epithet "sibast" replacing "sieset," and some have argued that they represent the same individual, using different epithets in the north and south. However, during the latter part of the Third Intermediate Period, it is clear that an epithet that would have been insignificant during earlier periods was indeed enough to distinguish between kings with otherwise identical names. Definite examples of this are Takelot I versus Takelot II, and Osorkon II versus Osorkon III.[59]

Exactly where and when Padubast II reigned remains a matter for debate.[60] A series of monuments from Memphis, plus another from Bubastis, bear his names, suggesting a dominion embracing the southern and southeastern parts of the Delta, while references in two of these documents suggest some degree of authority in Herakleopolis.[61] The form of his nomen, with its epithet, places him between the mid-ninth and mid-eighth century (cf. page 54).[62] As such, some have inserted him into the Tanite succession between Shoshenq V and Osorkon IV, on the basis that he is the "Petubastis" whom Manetho makes the founder of his Twenty-third Dynasty.[63] However, given that the king's Year 23 is attested,[64] overall chronological considerations make it impossible to fit him into this position. Others have suggested that Manetho's order is wrong, and that he was actually the successor of Osorkon IV.[65] However, the format of his names, both with epithets, is inconsistent with the slimmed-down names attested for Osorkon IV (pages 107–109). A possible alternative places Padubast II at Leontopolis, or elsewhere in the southern Delta, as a predecessor of Iuput II, and a potential successor of Iuput I.

The locations where Padubast II is attested include those previously containing monuments of Shoshenq III, suggesting—on our proposed timeline—that there may have been a significant realignment of allegiances following the death of the third Shoshenq.[66]

FIGURE 69 Padubast II. Left: bronze statuette (Gulbenkian 52). Right: fragment of shabti (Petrie UC38074).

That this did not involve hard borders is, however, indicated by the dating of the burial of Apis XXX in terms of the reign of Pamiu I. We may perhaps see the eighth century as a period of "blended authority," with a spectrum of local rulers, ranging from those holding pharaonic status, through the Chiefs of various Libyan tribes, to holders of traditional Mayoralties, without any attempting to arrogate overarching power.

The Last Years of Libyan Thebes

The importance of the death of Shoshenq III as a watershed is suggested by the fact that it was only after this that Osorkon B felt able to finally claim the pharaonic status that had been held by his father Takelot II until his death, nearly two decades earlier. Indeed, his assumption of pharaonic status may actually not have taken place until half a decade after Shoshenq III's death, since we have a Karnak Nile-level text dated to Year 5 of the reign of Shoshenq IV (fig. 39[3]).[67]

That the High Priest Osorkon B was indeed the same man as King Osorkon III who appears in the records from this point had been doubted, but the discovery of an inscription in which this monarch links his royal titles with that of High Priest of Amun—for so long Osorkon B's principal title—makes this a reasonable assumption.[68] It is also to be noted that Osorkon III states in Nile-level texts at Karnak (fig. 39[5–7]) that his mother was a Karomama[69]—doubtless the wife of Takelot II and mother of Osorkon B.

Unusually for the period, the king's titulary is known in its entirety:

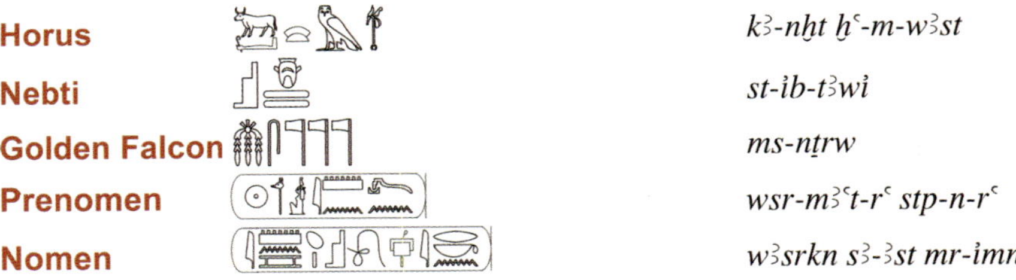

The Horus name was the one used by at least two of the preceding Theban kings, Horsieset I and Takelot II, and of course wholly appropriate to a king ruling from Thebes. Osorkon's Nebti and Golden Falcon names are interesting in being wholly unlike the expansive appellations used by kings since the Eighteenth Dynasty, being short pithy "mottoes," rather than the lengthy "manifestos" of previous centuries. The Nebti name, "The favorite of the Two Lands," had last been used (as a Horus name) by Niuserre of the Fifth Dynasty, a millennium and a half earlier, while the Golden Horus, "Born of the gods," was completely original, but in its brevity fully in keeping with Old and Middle Kingdom practice. This reference back to the past would soon be extended as part of a major overhaul of the presentation of the monarch. In contrast, Osorkon III's prenomen and nomen were wholly banal, copying those of Osorkon II, except for swapping the goddess proclaimed as the king's mother from the "northern" Bastet to the "southern" Isis.

When he finally assumed the Theban throne, Osorkon III must have been around sixty years old, if not older, depending on his age when he had first become High Priest.

It was probably in view of his advanced age at accession that he would later appoint his eldest son, Takelot G, co-regent around his Year 24, when he would have been around ninety. Contrary to what was long Egyptological lore, definite co-regencies are actually very rare in Egyptian history. Apart from during the Twelfth Dynasty, when they appear to have been used regularly by pharaohs to promote their heir to full kingly status while they yet lived,[70] all of the certainly attested later examples (Thutmose III and Hatshepsut; Akhenaten and Neferneferuaten) are "non-standard," with female kings ruling alongside males.[71] We have already noted Third Intermediate Period examples of double dates not representing co-regency of the Twelfth Dynasty type, but kings of separate lines proclaiming mutual recognition. But in the case of Osorkon III and (now) Takelot III we have a father–son combination that is unique for the period between the middle of the second millennium BC and the numerous episodes of joint rule found during the Ptolemaic Period. The extreme age of the elder king is, however, an ample explanation for this deviation from the norm.

Of Osorkon III's family, his Great Wife, Ka(ro)tjet(-meryetmut), is named on a stela of Year 15 at Hermopolis and in a filiation of her daughter Shepenwepet I in the temple of Osiris-Heqadjet at Karnak.[72] Another wife, Tentsai A, is named as the mother of Osorkon III's son and heir Takelot G (later King Takelot III) on a block, perhaps from Herakleopolis.[73] The other certain child of Osorkon III was Rudamun—later to be a king—who is called Osorkon's son on a memorial of his own daughter,[74] and may appear as such on the Hermopolis stela.[75] Less definite are Djedptahiufankh (F), son of a King Osorkon and known from the late Twenty-fifth Dynasty coffin of a great-grandson;[76] Irtiubast, a King's Daughter who was married to a King Takelot—and thus possibly sister-wife of Takelot III;[77] and potentially the later High Priest Osorkon F (see pages 92–93, below).

Perhaps as a result of his previous experiences, Osorkon III ensured his control over the Amun cult at Karnak by not only appointing Takelot G as High Priest (fig. 70),[78] but also making Shepenwepet I God's Wife, an office that she would hold for some six and a half decades.[79] As such she was granted the prenomen Khnemetibamen ("United with the heart of Amun"), beginning a sequence of prominent God's Wives that would continue until the end of the Twenty-sixth Dynasty. By their titulary and double cartouches they had quasi-pharaonic status, something first seen with Maatkare A at the height of her career back in the Twenty-first Dynasty.[80] Subsequently, only Karomama G is known to have been so endowed.[81] Indeed, Karomama's career could have lasted down to Osorkon III's accession[82]—although one or more (potentially rival) God's Wives may have come and gone in the interim.

An entry in the Priestly Annals and a number of private statues and other memorials are dated to Osorkon III's reign.[83] These include an indication that by its end the king's

FIGURE 70 Osorkon III and the High Priest Takelot G (later Takelot III) preparing to release birds during a ritual before Khonsu. Reused in the Taharqa colonnade, Karnak.

nephew Nakhtefmut B had succeeded Djedkhonsiufankh C as Fourth Priest.[84] Alongside two "average" floods of Osorkon's Years 5 and 6 (fig. 39[6, 7]), two extremely high Nile inundations are recorded during the reign (fig. 39[5, 13]).[85]

With the exception of one of Year 6 of Taharqa of the Twenty-fifth Dynasty, they are the highest of all the preserved Nile levels at Karnak. The higher of the two under Osorkon III, that of Year 3, is supplemented by a graffito of III *prt* 12 in the Luxor temple.[86] The latter records that the local citizens were "like swimmers in a wave" and the temples of Thebes "like swamps" (Luxor would have been flooded to over sixty centimeters above the level of its pavement). The text accordingly queries why Amun had sent such a disaster, given that temple ritual and offerings had been kept in order. Another exceptionally high flood is recorded in Osorkon III's Year 28; this is interesting in that it notes that this corresponded to Year 5 of "his son" Takelot III, attesting to the aforementioned co-regency between Osorkon III and Takelot III.

The revival of Theban fortunes during the peace of Osorkon III's reign is indicated by building work carried out during his time. This even extended as far north as the Fayyum region, where remains of Osorkon's reign have been found at Hermopolis.[87] However, most material from his time comes from Karnak (figs. 70, 71). Here, although modest by earlier standards, the chapel of Osiris-Heqadjet (fig. 72 top)[88] was a substantial monument, its decoration being completed during the period of co-rule between Osorkon III and Takelot III, with Shepenwepet I also featuring in the decoration (fig. 72 bottom).

A significant interesting feature of the scenes in the chapel is that the kings' prenomina are in some (but not all) cases written without the "setepenamun" epithets that had hitherto been integral parts of these names. Furthermore, while Osorkon III's nomen is always written in full, as is that of Takelot III in many cases, in others, the younger king's name is simply written as "Takelot." The following variations exist for the known elements of Takelot III's titulary:

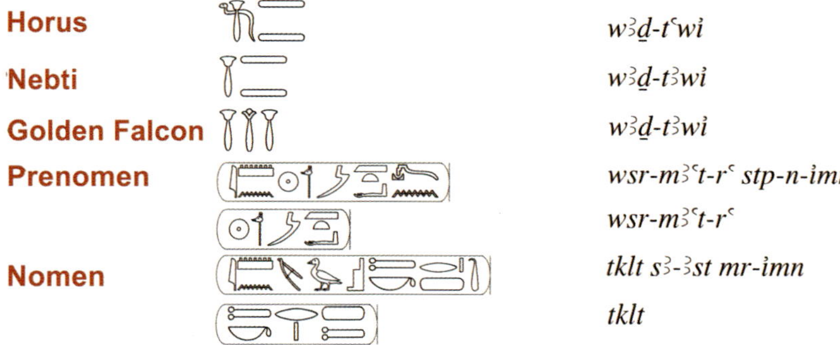

Horus	*wꜣḏ-tꜥwỉ*
Nebti	*wꜣḏ-tꜣwỉ*
Golden Falcon	*wꜣḏ-tꜣwỉ*
Prenomen	*wsr-mꜣꜥt-rꜥ stp-n-ỉmn*
	wsr-mꜣꜥt-rꜥ
Nomen	*tklt sꜣ-ꜣst mr-ỉmn*
	tklt

We have already seen how the Nebti and Golden Falcon names of Osorkon III had been composed on the Old/Middle Kingdom pattern. This was extended to the Horus name as well by Takelot III, who took matters yet further by repeating the same name ("Sturdy one of the Two Lands") for his Nebti and Golden Falcon names as well, albeit with slightly different orthographies. This name had previously been the Horus name of Unas at the end of the Fifth Dynasty.[89] While the king did make use of "complex" forms of his prenomen and nomen, with the embedded epithets typical of the period since Osorkon II, he was most frequently simply "Usermaatre" and "Takelot." Examples exist of Osorkon III with a plain "Osorkon" nomen (fig. 71), but it is possible that these may be posthumous writings of the name during the sole reign of Takelot III.

FIGURE 71 Osorkon III embracing a goddess; from Karnak (Cairo GEM 80855).

Osorkon III died soon after the great inundation of Year 28/Year 5, probably well into his tenth decade, as the next flood mark at Karnak is dated solely to Takelot III's Year 6, and records an exceptionally low Nile (fig. 39[4]).[90] Takelot III attained at least a thirteenth regnal year, as recorded on a stela from Amheda in the Dakhla Oasis.[91] It is possible that a Year 19 associated with the name of a God's Wife Shepenwepet in the Wadi Gasus belonged to him. However, it is quite possible that this is Year 19 of Taharqa, in association with the later God's Wife Shepenwepet II.[92] We have already noted a wife named Irtiubast, mother of a Priest of Amun Osorkon (see page 89, above); Takelot also fathered an Irbastwedjanefu (A) with the Favorite Kakat,[93] while a King's Wife Betjat may also have been married to this Takelot.[94] The mothers of Takelot III's other known children,[95] Diesetnesyt,[96] the Second Priest of Amun Djedptahiufankh (D),[97] Ankhkaroma,[98] Tentsai,[99] Ihsetamun,[100] and [...]ankh,[101] are unknown.

Irbastwedjanefu A married the vizier Pakharu, whose father, Pamiu i, bore a portfolio of offices. These ultimately included not only that of vizier, but also that of Third Priest of Amun and King's Son of Kush—the latter appearing for the first time since the Twenty-first Dynasty, and perhaps reflecting increasingly close links between the Theban polity and Nubia (cf. pages 101–102, below).[102] Ankhkaroma also married a future Third Priest of Amun—Pediamennebnesuttawy A/B.

Aside from his work in the Osiris-Heqadjet chapel, some blocks from another Karnak chapel,[103] and the aforementioned Dakhla stela, relatively little survives bearing Takelot III's name. Two block statues from Karnak date to the reign,[104] as does the graffito from the Khonsu temple there that included the genealogy naming Osorkon the Elder (see fig. 14), while, elsewhere, a statuette and a stela are known from the North Cemetery at Abydos.[105]

Takelot will have laid down his pontificate on becoming king, but nothing from his reign indicates the name of his successor as High Priest at Karnak. However, a High Priest Osorkon F can be placed in this general period by the stylistic dating of the stela

FIGURE 72 The temple of Osiris-Heqadjet at Karnak, built by Osorkon III and Takelot III, and later enlarged by Shabataka.

of his daughter Shepenwepet A to the latter part of the eighth century (fig. 73, left).[106] There has been debate over whether this Osorkon might be identical with the son of Takelot III of that name, and/or a High Priest and King's Son Oso[rkon] named on a block statuette from Karnak.[107] The issue here is that the mentions of Takelot III's

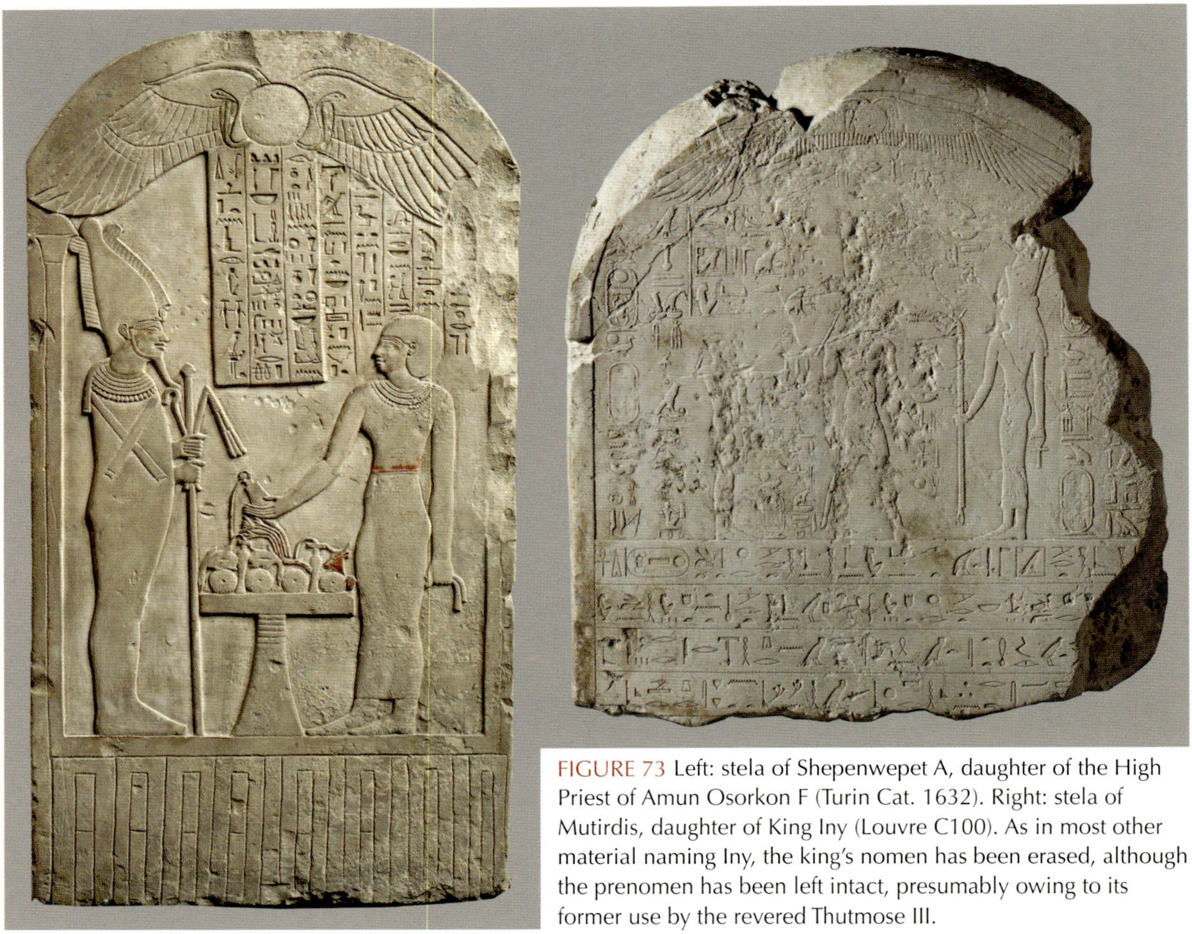

FIGURE 73 Left: stela of Shepenwepet A, daughter of the High Priest of Amun Osorkon F (Turin Cat. 1632). Right: stela of Mutirdis, daughter of King Iny (Louvre C100). As in most other material naming Iny, the king's nomen has been erased, although the prenomen has been left intact, presumably owing to its former use by the revered Thutmose III.

son—including on what seems to be his own coffin—only call him a simple Priest of Amun—not High Priest.[108] Unless these are all in error—which seems unlikely—the son of Takelot III must be distinguished (as Osorkon G) from the High Priest Osorkon F. It is not impossible that the latter was a younger brother of Takelot III, appointed to the High Priesthood by their father Osorkon III at the time Takelot III was elevated to the kingship. If he was a very much younger son, Osorkon F's period of office could have occupied a number of decades.

The length of Takelot III's reign is uncertain, but on broader chronological considerations seems to have lasted a little over a dozen years. Then he was apparently succeeded, not by one of his sons, but by a brother, named Rudamun, with the following cartouches:

Prenomen

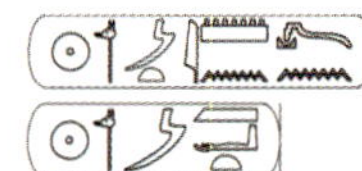

wsr-mꜣꜥt-rꜥ stp-n-ỉmn

wsr-mꜣꜥt-rꜥ

Nomen 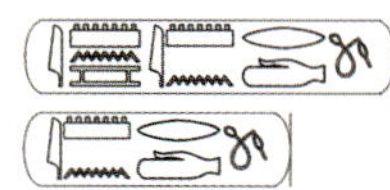 *rwḏ-ỉmn mr-ỉmn*

rwḏ-ỉmn

His assumed succession in Thebes is based on the presence of his painted cartouches in the chapel of Osiris-Heqadjet at Karnak,[109] and no certain year date is known, except for the potential Year 3 in a now anonymous Nile-level text at Karnak (fig. 39[43]).[110] But the days of the family of Takelot II as rulers of Thebes were numbered, and shortly the south of Egypt would fall under the control of rulers from an unexpected direction.

The mysterious King Iny

An individual who is difficult to fit into the history of eighth-century Egypt is a king for whom the following cartouche names are known from a number of sources:[111]

Prenomen *mn-ḫpr-rꜥ*

Nomen *iny*

This King Iny employed the former prenomen of the great Eighteenth Dynasty ruler Thutmose III—as did the Nubian king Pi(ankh)y of the mid-late eighth century (for whom see pages 101–107, below). That he reigned in the south of Egypt is indicated by the presence of bricks of his at Elephantine,[112] and the fact that his daughter Mutirdis held sacerdotal positions at Karnak (fig. 73, right).[113] A graffito of Iny's Year 5 also exists on the roof of the Khonsu temple at Karnak, as does a votive object in his name at Abydos. However, his exact date remains unclear, as does the way in which his tenure interfaced with that of the kings of the line of Takelot II at Thebes and the Kushite take-over of the south by Kashta.

Northern Egypt during the Eighth Century

Around five years before Takelot III joined his father on the Theban throne, Pamiu I of Tanis had been succeeded by his son,[114] Shoshenq V. His titulary was, like that of Osorkon III, an important waypoint in the move from the expansive "imperial" name forms embraced by his predecessors, and those following Old and Middle Kingdom tradition:

Horus *kꜣ-nḫt ḫꜥ-m-wꜣst*

wsr-pḥtỉ

Nebti *[...]sꜥꜣ-ḫpr(w)-(w)r[...]*

wsr-pḥtỉ

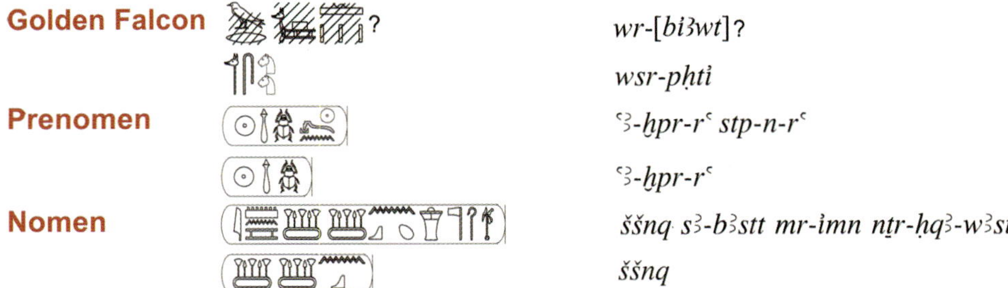

Shoshenq's "imperial" Horus, Nebti, and Golden Falcon names are only found on one set of blocks from Tanis,[115] with the latter two incompletely preserved. The Horus name was, of course, one used by many recent kings. However, the parallels for the surviving elements of the other two names are only to be found among those of Osorkon I (Nebti), and Horemheb and Amenmeses (Golden Falcon). The "long" prenomen had been that of Osorkon the Elder, the core name also having been used by Pasebkhanut I, with "Aakheper-X" names borne earlier by Thutmose I and II and Amenhotep II of the Eighteenth Dynasty. Shoshenq's nomen epithets included not only the "northern" one of "son of Bastet," but also "divine ruler of Thebes." This may have been a political statement of some kind, or may simply have served to distinguish Shoshenq V's nomen from that of Shoshenq III, who was "divine ruler of Heliopolis."

Interestingly, these "imperial" names come from the dismantled remains of a chapel decorated with scenes relating to the king's jubilee, found reused in the Sacred Lake at Tanis.[116] This would imply that they date from the latter part of Shoshenq V's reign, seemingly indicating a reversal of the situation apparently seen in Thebes, where "imperial" names gave way to those of Old/Middle Kingdom type. On the other hand, the nature of the chapel might indicate a special case in this instance. All other known monuments of Shoshenq V, including another dismantled building at Tanis,[117] employ epithet-free cartouches, and the same short motto, "Strong of might," for all three of his other names. Although of Old/Middle Kingdom form, this name had not actually been used by any pharaoh.

Shoshenq V's nomenclatural archaism was now combined with the appearance of an art style that also harked back to the past, specifically the early Old Kingdom (fig. 74),[118] a trend that would be deepened under Shoshenq's successor. The burgeoning power of the Chiefdoms under Shoshenq V is indicated by the Memphite High Priest Takelot H,[119] probably the latest scion of the line of Shoshenq D, who uniquely simultaneously combined his pontifical title with that of Great Chief [of the Ma]: Padieset A is found using the "Chief" title only after laying down the pontificate (page 80, fig. 64). Takelot H is also the last known High Priest at Memphis until the end of the Twenty-sixth Dynasty.[120] In the interim, it would appear that the *sm*-priest, hitherto the High Priest's deputy, was senior officiant.[121]

FIGURE 74 Shoshenq V. Left: fragment of statuette from Sacred Animal Necropolis, Saqqara (Fitzwilliam E.6.1969). Top right: lintel reused in Sacred Lake at Tanis. Bottom right: relief showing the king, followed by the High Priest of Ptah, Takelot H. It displays both the "simple" form of the king's nomen, and a style that recalls the art of the Old Kingdom. From Memphis (Cairo JE46915).

A range of material derives from Shoshenq V's reign of some four decades. A range of his regnal years, from 4 through 38, are attested by a donation stela and other documents.[122] These include material from two Apis burials at Saqqara, one in Year 11[123] and one in Year 37, from which came fifteen stelae.[124] These included the one dedicated by Pasenhor, which has already been noted as the genealogical key to the family ties of the earlier Libyan kings (fig. 75). Various minor items are known from Tell el-Yahudiya, Saqqara, and Bahariya Oasis, and of unknown provenance.[125]

By the time of Shoshenq V's death, it is clear that the progressive subdivision of Egypt into various independent or quasi-independent entities had been continuing apace. One in the western Delta was ruled by a line of Great Chiefs of the Libu who used the reigns of

FIGURE 75 The stela dedicated to Apis XXXIII by the Priest of Neith Pasenhor, whose genealogy is an important source for the family relationships of the Libyan royal family (Louvre IM2846).

the Tanite kings as their dating era. Beginning with Inamunnifnebu under Shoshenq III (see page 82, above), Niumataped then spanned the reigns of Shoshenq IV (see page 84, above), Pimay, and probably at least the first decade of the reign of Shoshenq V, the line continuing with Titaru in Year 15,[126] Ker in Year 19,[127] Rudamun B in Year 30,[128] and Ankhhor C, who appears at Memphis at the burial of Apis XXXIII in Year 37.[129]

Also in the western Delta, we find a number of Chiefs of the Ma, apparently based at Sais, of whom a certain Osorkon C seems to be the earliest known.[130] His probable successor was Tefnakhte, who is known from an undated statuette of Amun,[131] and from two of the donation stelae from the reign of Shoshenq V. One of these dates to Year 38,[132] but leaves the king's cartouches blank, although Shoshenq V is the only option, given the reign length involved. This suggests that Tefnakhte used the reign as no more than a dating era. The stela gives Tefnakhte (inter alia) the titles of Great Chief of the Whole Land, Army Leader, Great Chief of the Libu, and Ruler of the Nomes of the West. These seem to mark a progression from the titles affected by Tefnakhte two years earlier on a donation stela of Year 36—once again anonymous, but in this case with no space for a royal name—where he is just Great Chief of the Ma, Army Leader, and Great Chief of the Libu.[133]

It is unclear how Tefnakhte's last title related to that possessed simultaneously by Ankhhor C: Did each refer to a separate branch of the Libu tribe (cf. the multiple Great Chiefs of the Ma), or were they rivals, with Ankhhor driven out of the western Delta and in "exile" in Memphis when he played a part in the Apis burial of Year 37?[134] In any case, it is clear that by the close of the reign of Shoshenq V, Tefnakhte had grown to be a major figure in northern Egypt, with an eye to further expansion, and would come to play an important role in the events of the coming years.

There is no direct evidence as to who succeeded Shoshenq V. The data from the burials of the Apis bulls that is so useful for the transitions between the immediately preceding reigns is lacking after the burial in Year 37, the stelae associated with the next known burial (see page 117) lacking any information on the age or date of induction of the bull in question. While some have suggested that Padubast II should be placed next in the succession (page 86), it seems more likely that it was a king now known as Osorkon IV. This may be inferred from a remarkable document that is a fruit of an intervention in Egyptian affairs from an unanticipated direction, and will be discussed in the next chapter.

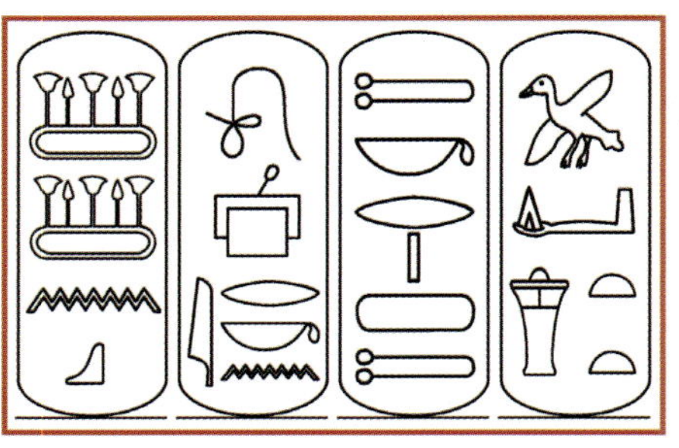

4 Eclipse

Nubia, the region straddling the border of the modern states of Egypt and Sudan, had a long history of interaction with Egypt, generally as a target for exploitation and colonization by the latter.[1] Then, at the end of the New Kingdom, the imperial control that Egypt had exercised for much of the previous half-millennium collapsed, and over the following three centuries a new Nubian (Kushite) state had come into being. This polity borrowed the institution of pharaonic kingship, its titles and forms, from its former overlord, along with the use of the Egyptian language for public monuments, the hieroglyphic script, and many gods, in particular Amun.

The evolution and expansion of the Kushite kingdom from its apparent heartlands around the Dongola Reach of the Nile cannot be traced until we find an entry in the Karnak Priestly Annals that seems to be dated to Year 1 of a Nubian King Kashta, who is also attested by a stela fragment from Elephantine.[2] Furthermore, a daughter of Kashta, Amenirdis I, is also to be found as the adopted daughter, and thus designated successor, of the God's Wife Shepenwepet I. All this makes it clear that, in the middle of the eighth century, the southern part of Egypt, at least as far north as Thebes, but probably further north as well, had fallen under Nubian control. But the mechanisms and timescales of this takeover remain wholly obscure.

Quite what this meant for the line of Takelot II is also unclear. It would appear that the rule of Rudamun at Thebes was terminated, but there is no evidence of any violent conquest, and it may be that Rudamun simply died soon after succeeding his father. In any case, his sister Shepenwepet I was left in place as God's Wife. While she was obliged to accept a Kushite princess as her heir, this would seem to imply that legal niceties were maintained, and two decades later we find a son-in-law of Rudamun as an ally of the Kushites (see just below). One might assume that the Kushite takeover in the south was thus ultimately a matter of negotiation, with the rump of the displaced royal line moving north.

It has already been noted how by the end of Shoshenq V's reign the Delta had become a patchwork of polities. This was also true of the northern portion of the Nile valley some two decades after Kashta's appearance as ruler of Thebes. Now, the Kushite/Theban throne was held by Pi(ankh)y,[3] and in his Year 21 a text of his (fig. 76) states that "one came to inform His Person that the Prince of the West ... Tefnakhte ... had seized the entire West from the coastal marshes to Lisht .... He was closing in on Herakleopolis, he had surrounded it without allowing anyone to leave or enter, fighting every day."[4]

Herakleopolis was the seat of King Peftjauawybast, of unknown antecedents, but a son-in-law of Rudamun, and bearing a name previously borne by a Memphite pontiff under Shoshenq III (pages 79–80).[5] His known names are:

Prenomen		*nfr-kꜣ-rꜥ*
Nomen		*pf-ṯꜣw-ꜥwy-bꜣstt*

In keeping with the spirit of the age, the king's nomen was devoid of epithets, while his prenomen was of ancient stamp, first used by Pepy II at the end of the Old Kingdom, and occasionally subsequently, most recently by Rameses IX and Amenemnesut. One of Peftjauawybast's wives was Irbastwedjanefu B, a daughter of Rudamun, and thus a clear link between him and the former Theban line of kings. Indeed, it has been suggested that Peftjauawybast was not only the son-in-law of Rudamun but also a successor of his as part of a Herakleopolitan–Theban dynasty.[6] With Irbastwedjanefu, Peftjauawybast had a daughter, Sopdet(em)haa(wt).[7] Another daughter was Irutj (or perhaps Ilot), whose mother was King's Wife and King's Daughter Tashereniset, named on two Herakleopolitan donation stelae, dated to the king's Year 10.[8] The identity of Tashereniset's royal father is unknown, especially with the number of individuals who were now coming to claim pharaonic titles. Two metal statuettes of Peftjauawybast's time survive, one of the ram god Heryshef, and one of the king himself (fig. 77).[9]

In addition to Tefnakhte, Peftjauawybast's antagonists included a king named Nimlot (, *nmlt*), who was ruling Hermopolis, to the south of Herakleopolis, with the title of king. However, only his nomen is preserved on the two small items naming him.[10] On the basis of his name, he is likely to have been a scion of the Twenty-second Dynasty royal line. Some links with Thebes are suggested by the naming of the God's Wife Shepenwepet I and her heir Amenirdis I on one object of his. It appears that Nimlot had been initially an ally of Pi(ankh)y, as the latter states that Nimlot had "gone off to

FIGURE 76 The victory stela of Pi(ankh)y; from Gebel Barkal (Cairo JE48862).

FIGURE 77 Bronze statuette, possibly representing King Peftjauawybast (MFA 1977.16). The cartouche on the piece is damaged, and its reading as Neferkare, Peftjauawybast's prenomen, is not certain.

be [Tefnakhte's] foot-man, [having] betrayed His Person" (i.e., Pi(ankh)y).

In response to the attack on Herakleopolis, Pi(ankh)y—at that time in Nubia—launched a relief expedition led by two of his Egypt-based generals, and comprising both forces already in Egypt and others sent from Nubia. This army defeated forces of Tefnakhte and Nimlot in open battle, and then laid siege to Hermopolis, while also moving to relieve the siege of Herakleopolis. By now an array of other local rulers had joined Tefnakhte and Nimlot, doubtless concerned that victory by Pi(ankh)y would, at best, constrain their power, and at worst remove it altogether. Thus, now gathered in Hermopolis were the Chiefs of the Ma Shoshenq E (of Busiris), Djedameniufankh (of Mendes), and Nesnayisu (of Hesebka)—and the Delta kings Osorkon IV and Iuput II.

However, the siege of Hermopolis proved protracted, and was only finally successfully concluded when Pi(ankh)y himself brought reinforcements from Nubia. First, envoys emerged from the city with gifts, including Nimlot's own crown, followed by members of his family, and finally Nimlot himself, bringing a horse as a present. In the meantime, Herakleopolis had been freed from its siege, the grateful Peftjauawybast bringing gifts, lamenting how he "did not find a friend in [his] day of distress, who would stand on the day of battle," now rejoicing that Pi(ankh)y had "driven darkness from" him.

The Nubian king then pushed north to mop up opposition, including seizing Memphis, and finally staging a set-piece event at Athribis, at which he took the submission of "those kings and mayors of the northland, all the chiefs who wear the (Libyan) feather, every vizier, every chief, every royal acquaintance from the west, from the east, and from inland islands, to behold the vitality of His Person." The only absentee was Tefnakhte, who had maintained resistance right up to this point, but subsequently sent a letter of submission. He then received a Kushite delegation in Sais, which administered an oath of allegiance on Tefnakhte and received gifts from him.

Following on from this, a second ceremony of submission was staged at Athribis, at which the four local Egyptian kings formally pledged their loyalty—not just the three who had sided with Tefnakhte, but also the loyal Peftjauawybast (fig. 76). But only Nimlot was

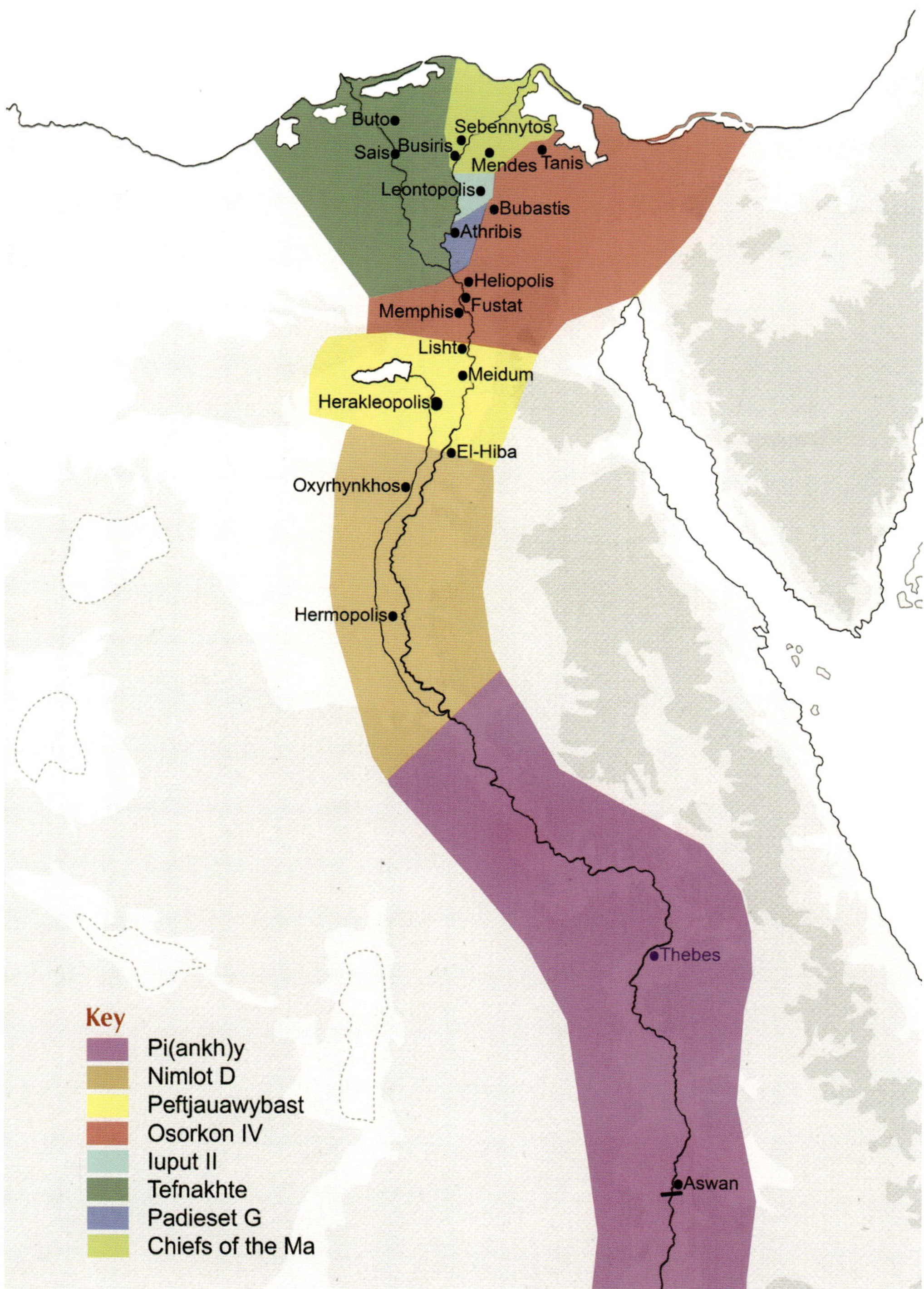

FIGURE 78 The political geography of Egypt at the time of Pi(ankh)y's campaign; the boundaries between the various polities are schematic only.

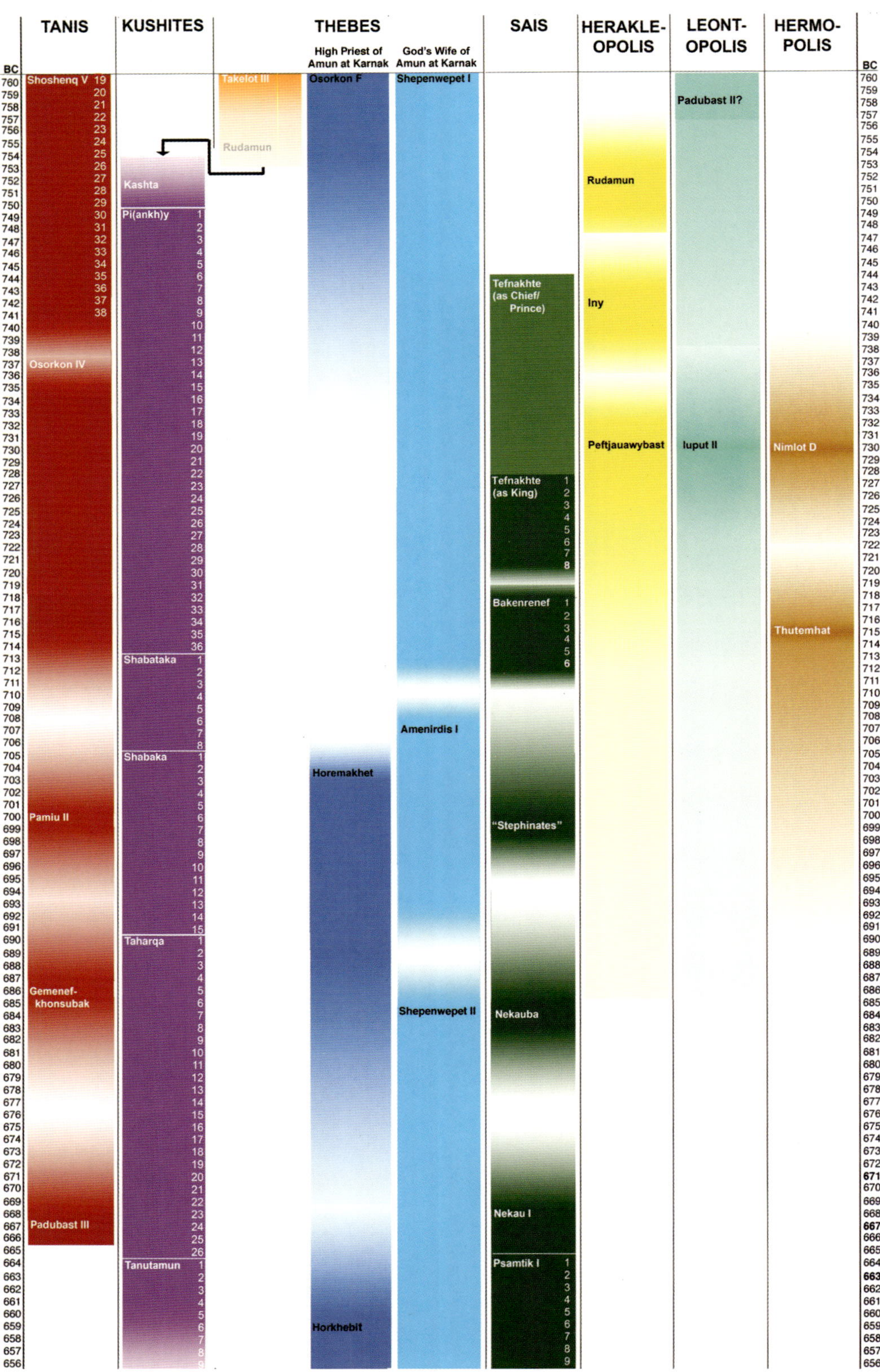

FIGURE 79 Chronology: eighth to seventh centuries BC.

received into Pi(ankh)y's residence. The other three had to remain outside "because they were uncircumcised and fish-eaters ..., an abomination to the king's house." Then, having become the suzerain of all local rulers in Middle and Lower Egypt, as well as being himself the king in Thebes, Pi(ankh)y returned home, apparently never to return to Egypt.

The Twilight of the Libyan Pharaohs of Egypt

Despite his all-embracing triumph, and in contrast to his successors on the throne of Kush (see pages 117–18), Pi(ankh)y was seemingly content with his direct control of Nubia and southern Egypt, leaving the north to its patchwork of kingdoms and lesser polities.[11] The four local kingdoms endured for some time, to be joined for a while by a fifth, some of them surviving until the first part of the seventh century.

Tanis and Bubastis

In Pi(ankh)y's account of his campaign, he characterizes King Osorkon IV as being from "Bubastis and *rʿ-nfr*." The latter was centered on what is now Tell Tebilla, some fifty kilometers to the north of Bubastis, but the term is generally regarded as embracing the area to the east, including Tanis.[12] That Osorkon was a member of the line at Tanis is in any case made clear by the presence of a number of blocks at that site that came from buildings decorated by him (fig. 80a–b).[13] It seems probable that he was therefore the successor of Shoshenq V, although no documents survive to confirm this. If Shoshenq V's successor, it is likely that Osorkon was that king's son, but the only data we have on his background is that his mother was named Tadibast (fig. 81).[14]

Only the king's cartouche names are known:[15]

Prenomen		*wsr-mꜣʿt-rʿ*
Nomen		*wꜣsrknw*
		wꜣsrk[n]

These are consistent with the epithet-free forms of names that were now being used, but are interesting in that the nomen is written at Tanis with a *nw*-sign at the end, rather than the usual *n*-sign. Its significance is unclear, and in the text of Pi(ankh)y "Osorkon" is written with its usual spelling. Given the ubiquity of the king's prenomen, and the abandonment of the use of epithets, it may be that the unusual orthography of the nomen was intended as a means of distinguishing the king from the earllier Kings Usermaatre Osorkon (II and III).

The Tanis blocks, found reused in the site's Sacred Lake, are also interesting in that their style is a direct imitation of that from the beginning of the Third Dynasty, two

a

b

c

d

FIGURE 80 Blocks in archaizing style, found reused at the Sacred Lake at Tanis, from monuments of Osorkon IV (a–b) and Gemenefkhonsubak (c–d).

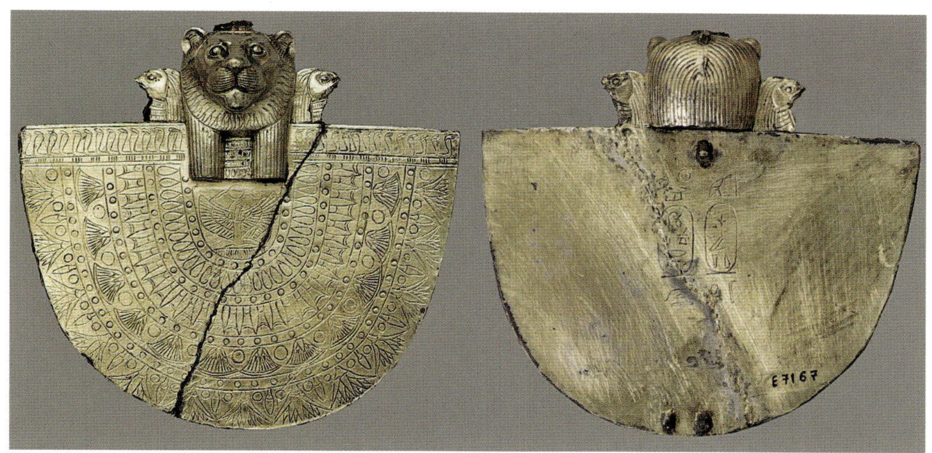

FIGURE 81 Aegis bearing the names of Osorkon IV and his mother, Tadibast (Louvre E7167).

millennia before Osorkon's time. We have already noted reliefs of Shoshenq V that recalled this remote era (fig. 74), but those of Osorkon IV are precise copies: indeed, previous finds of examples lacking identifying cartouches had been assessed as actual Third Dynasty works.[16] This would suggest that it was during the reign of Osorkon IV that the substructure of the Step Pyramid at Saqqara was cleared and elements of its decoration copied, as evidenced by grids drawn over two of the reliefs of the king in its substructure (fig. 82).[17] This would accordingly date a passageway cut under the southern part of the pyramid, and intended to allow the clearance of the interior, to the time of Osorkon IV, or perhaps Shoshenq V, rather than the Twenty-sixth Dynasty, as has long been assumed.[18]

That such efforts were made to probe the innermost recesses of this ancient monument indicates the importance of the project to reset the Egyptian monarchy with reference to earlier times. This worked in conjunction with the recasting of the formulation of royal names, again in the image of the remote past. The disintegration of the state, and its accompanying civil conflicts, must have given rise to these attempts to reconnect with what was doubtless perceived as a far-off golden age. Although such slavish copying of ancient representations would not continue, simplified royal names and art with an underlying inspiration from the Old and Middle Kingdoms would persist down to the fourth century BC.

Although now a vassal of the Kushite king, Osorkon IV appears to have played an important role in Egypt's relationship with the burgeoning Assyrian empire. Tiglath-Pileser III had become king of Assyria in 745 BC, a few years before the death of Shoshenq V. By the end of Tiglath-Pileser's reign, in 727, Assyria had taken control of all of Syria-Palestine, and was thus now a direct neighbor of Egypt, and specifically the eastern Delta realm of Osorkon IV.

As such, Osorkon IV is likely to have been the "So, king of Egypt" stated in the Old Testament as having been asked (unsuccessfully) by the Israelite king Hoshea for aid

FIGURE 82 Corridor probably cut during the eighth century BC to gain access to the interior of the Step Pyramid at Saqqara, and two stelae of Djoser under the pyramid with grid lines left by ancient copyists.

FIGURE 83 The Levant and Mesopotamia.

against Tiglath-Pileser's successor, Shalmaneser V (727–722 BC) during 726/5.[19] Osorkon was probably also the ruler who sent his army commander "Re'u" to aid a Palestinian rebellion against the next Assyrian king, Sargon II (722–705 BC), in 720—only to be defeated in battle at Rafah.[20] On the other hand, the Assyrian depiction of the battle[21] seems to show a Nubian as part of the defeated force.[22] This may suggest that it was a joint Egyptian–Kushite one, reflecting the fact that Osorkon IV's realm was now a dependency of Nubia (cf. page 118, below). A few years later, in 716, Osorkon IV was doubtless the "Shilkanni, king of Egypt" who sent a gift of horses to Sargon II, whose forces had at that time penetrated as far as El-Arish in northeastern Sinai.[23]

How much longer Osorkon's reign lasted is unknown, but he would appear to have been followed on the throne by a number of kings who are known from material at Tanis. The likely earliest of them bore the following names:[24]

Horus		*nṯr(i)-ḫꜥ*
Prenomen		*nfr-kꜣ-rꜥ*
		nfr-kꜣ-rꜥ [mry]-i[mn]
Nomen	,	*p(ꜣ)-miy(w)*

Unlike that of Pamiu I, the nomen of this second Pamiu is never written with the cat sign. His other two names were clearly inspired by those of Pepy II of the Old Kingdom, the prenomen Neferkare being taken from him directly, with the Horus name of Pamiu just missing the terminal *w* found in that of the ancient pharaoh. It is interesting to note that the same prenomen was affected by the Kushite king Shabaka and the Herakleopolitan Peftjauawybast (and possibly by a contemporary of Psamtik I as well [page 155]).

All that is known of Pamiu II are his names, although the style of his surviving reliefs at Tanis shows that he must have been of the same period as Osorkon IV, most probably as his successor. All known examples of Pamiu's nomen have been carefully erased, but whether this was through hostility toward him or simply the precursor to never-completed usurpation is unclear.

Another king commemorated by archaizing blocks at Tanis—and who also suffered from the later erasure of his nomen there—is Gemenefkhonsubak:

The king's nomen is of a form known from the New Kingdom through the Twenty-sixth Dynasty. His core prenomen, "Noble one of the *ka* of Re," had been used only once previously, back in the Fifth Dynasty, and is unusual for the period in adding an epithet, the novel "Who is begotten on Re." The Horus name of the king, "Who makes the Two Lands live," had previously been the Nebti name of Senwosret IV of the Thirteenth Dynasty. Like Osorkon IV, Gemenefkhonsubak is known at Tanis from blocks found reused at the Sacred Lake (fig. 80c–d), and also two minor items.[25]

A ruler named Padubast is attributed to Tanis by Assyrian texts referring to events of 671–667/6 BC (see pages 119–121 below), and would seem to be identical with a further king known from blocks at the Sacred Lake, and also from an unfinished statue (fig. 84) and doorjambs from Memphis:[26]

FIGURE 84 Padubast III. Top: reused block at the Sacred Lake at Tanis. Bottom: lower part of statue found at Memphis.

Padubast's prenomen ("He who makes the heart of Re content") had been originated by Amenemhat I, founder of the Twelfth Dynasty, and in the interim used by a king of the Thirteenth Dynasty, while his Golden Falcon name ("He who contents the gods") was new, albeit of ancient form.

Leontopolis

King Iuput II of Leontopolis is known, outside Pi(ankh)y's narrative, from three definite sources, and another possible one which may, however, actually belong to Iuput I (page 76). One of the former is a hieratic donation stela dated to his Year 21, another a bronze door hinge, which also names his wife, Tintka, and the third a faience plaque depicting the king (fig. 85a).[27]

FIGURE 85 a. plaque of Iuput II (Brooklyn 59.17). b. fragment of model palette depicting Thutemhat (Swansea EC2018). c. stela of Tefnakhte (Athens 32).

The style of the latter is very much that employed for depictions of the Kushite kings after they assumed the direct rule of Egypt around 710 BC (see pages 117–18, below). The model employed an Old/Middle Kingdom–inspired body, but facial features and a cap crown that are typical of Nubian royal representations. This clearly dates the piece to a decade or more after Iuput's submission. Curiously, unlike the door hinge, which gives the king abbreviated names typical of the time, the plaque carries cartouches with epithets more characteristic of earlier times (cf. page 76 for the problem as to which King Iuput was the owner of a statue base carrying "long" cartouches). Iuput II therefore seems to have used the following cartouches:

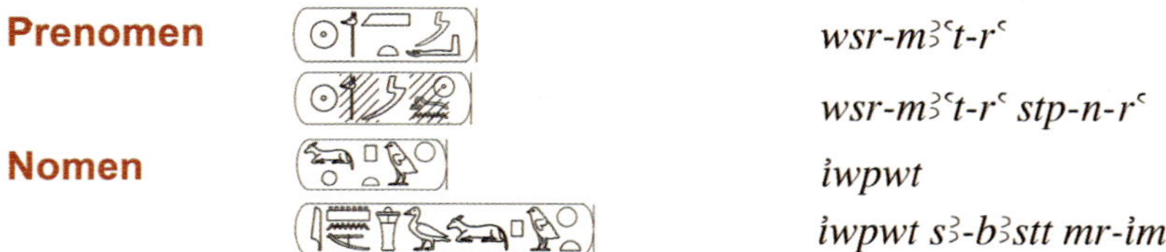

It may be noted that Shabataka, the founder of Kushite kingship in Egypt, did employ an "imperial" titulary at the beginning of his reign, and this may have influenced some of the subordinate kings to follow suit, before the Kushite monarch (and his successors) standardized on Old/Middle Kingdom–style titularies.

No further king can be attributed to Leontopolis, and no specific ruler of the city is mentioned by the Assyrians in 671–667/6 BC. It had presumably been absorbed into one of the neighboring polities in the interim.

Herakleopolis

That Peftjauawybast continued to rule into the period of Kushite dominion over Egypt is suggested by the fact that, like Iuput II, he was depicted in Kushite royal manner on his statuette (fig. 77). The local kingship does not appear to have survived him, as no later Herakleopolitan monarch is known, and by the beginning of the seventh century the key figure in the city seems to have been the Shipmaster and High Priest of Heryshef, in the person of one Padieset.

Hermopolis

Nothing is known of Nimlot after his submission to Pi(ankh)y, but another king is known from the city, Thutemhat (fig. 85b):[28]

That he was only king in Hermopolis and its environs is made clear by his Horus name, "Appearing in the Hermopolite nome"; his nomen also cites the local god, "Thoth is in front." His core prenomen ("Vital form of Re") is intriguing, in that it differs only in writing *ḫpr* in the singular from Akhenaten's core prenomen, Neferkheperure. Both names are unique, and of course Akhenaten's capital, Tell el-Amarna, lay directly opposite Hermopolis, where many blocks from the site were reused in Rameside times. Could it be that Thutemhat adopted a prenomen that had a clear local reference, to go with his "local" nomen and Horus name? If so, it would shed an interesting light on the survival of Akhenaten's memory, in spite of attempts at his cancellation following his death.

From Assyrian records, a Nimlot was ruler of Hermopolis at the beginning of the 660s, but there is no Egyptian material to indicate whether he presented himself as a king or a holder of lesser titles.

Sais

To the four kingdoms that had submitted to Pi(ankh)y was soon added a fifth: Sais. Tefnakhte had declined to submit in person, and given this and his previous activities, it seems almost certain that he was the person of the name whom we find with the following cartouches:[29]

Horus		*siꜣ-ḫt*
Nebti		*siꜣ-ḫt*
Prenomen		*špss-rꜥ*
Nomen		*tꜣ.f-nḫt*

As with many kings of the era, the Horus and Nebti names are repetitions of each other, albeit with slightly different orthographies. The name in question ("One who understands self") was a new one, but of ancient stamp, names of the form *X-ḫt* having been adopted by two kings of the Third Dynasty. The prenomen ("Noble of Re") is interesting in containing only two elements, in contrast to almost all other prenomina, which contain three. Two donation stelae survive from Tefnakhte's reign,[30] one being dated to his Year 8 (fig. 85c).

Although there is no contemporary data to confirm the information, it seems clear that Tefnakhte was followed on the Saite throne by Bakenrenef:

Prenomen		*wꜣḥ-kꜣ-rꜥ*
Nomen	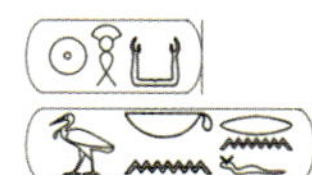	*bꜣ-kn-rn.f*

The king's prenomen ("Enduring of the *ka* of Re") had previously been used by Iaib of the Thirteenth Dynasty.

Apart from a stone fragment at Tanis and a donation stela, the principal material dating to the reign of Bakenrenef comes from the burial of an Apis bull in his Year 6 (fig. 86).[31] Unfortunately, the stelae in question are all private votive examples, and thus do not include the details concerning the bull's birth date and lifespan that would have anchored Bakenrenef's reign in relation to those of earlier kings.[32] However, later tradition calls Bakenrenef ("Bokkhoris" in Greek) the son of "Tnephtichthus," transparently Tefnakhte.[33] This tradition also praises the king for his wisdom and as a lawgiver, and finds its way into a range of Classical sources, including Diodorus Siculus[34] and Tacitus,[35] while Manetho alleges that during his time a lamb spoke, prophesying the future. Remarkably, a jar bearing the king's name was found in an Etruscan tomb in central Italy (fig. 122) and a scarab from Pithecusa in the south of that peninsula.[36] We will return to Bakenrenef's reputation below (page 157).

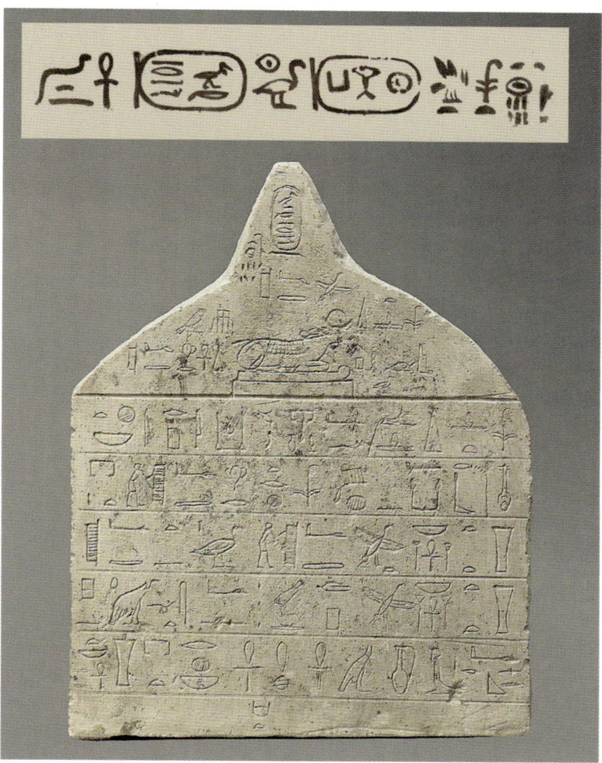

FIGURE 86 Stela from the interment of Apis XXXIV under Bakenrenef (Louvre IM 1258), and the graffito dating this to the king's Year 6.

Another statement by Manetho regarding Bakenrenef is that the first king of his Twenty-fifth Dynasty, "Sabacôn, … t[ook] Bocchoris captive [and] burned him alive"—although the version of Eusebius' epitome of Manetho preserved by St. Jerome states that he was only sent into exile. While the truth of the way in which Bakenrenef's reign ended remains unknown, that his career was cut short by Shabataka seems not open to doubt, and marked a new phase in the history of the Libyan kingdoms in Egypt.

Kushites, Assyrians, and Saites

With the exception of the self-elevation of the former Princedom of the West to a kingdom, Pi(ankh)y's settlement apparently remained in place until his death, around a decade and a half after his great campaign into northern Egypt. However, his successor, Shabataka,[37] seems to have taken a very different approach, by sending an army into Egypt. He was also probably crowned at Karnak in his Year 3 (c. 711 BC),[38] as may be implied in a Nile-level text of that year (fig. 39[33]). That he was now more than "just" a king of Kush and southern Egypt, as Pi(ankh)y had been, is shown by the way in which he and his successors placed a double uraeus on their brows, one for Kush and one for Egypt (fig. 87).

Nevertheless, apart from Sais, the remaining extant local kingdoms—and other lesser independent/quasi-independent polities—were left in place. Indeed, after a period when Sais was seemingly put in the hands of a Kushite nominee (one version of Manetho follows Bakenrenef by "Ammeris the Ethiopian"), we find a succession of kings listed by Manetho as the first members of his Twenty-sixth Dynasty. They begin with "Stephinatês," probably a second Tefnakhte, who is followed by "Nechepsos." The prototype of the latter was probably the bearer of the following two names, although there is no source that places them together:[39]

Like Bakenrenef, this king features in much later tradition, in this case as co-author of an astrological manual, and it has even been suggested that the prophetic lamb of Bakenrenef was actually Nekauba, perhaps through some misunderstanding of the ram hieroglyph in the latter's name.[40]

The cartouche names of the next Saite king, Nekau I, are attested by only a handful of items (fig. 88):[41]

The prenomen had been that of the great Thutmose III, and by adopting it Nekau was clearly making a statement of intent: he would indeed play an important role in the events of 671–667/6 BC.

A major change that followed Shabataka's taking overall control of Egypt was that the Tanites were no longer the pharaohs interacting with the Levant, in particular the Assyrians. Now it was the Kushite kings. They and their homeland were something new to the Assyrians, Sargon II calling Nubia "an inapproachable region" which had "never—from remote days until now—sent messengers to enquire after the health of my forefathers."[42] But now they became involved in the affairs of Syria-Palestine, Shabataka's successor, Shabaka, sending troops to aid those in Palestine who were opposing Assyrian hegemony in the region.[43]

FIGURE 87 The Nubian king Shabataka, as depicted on the façade of his extension of the temple of Osiris-Heqadjet.

FIGURE 88 Statuette of Horus, with names of Nekau I on the rear (Petrie UC14689).

Ultimately, Assyria resolved to bring Egypt under its control as well. After an abortive attack in 674 BC, Esarhaddon (680–669 BC), second successor of Sargon II, invaded again in 671 BC, forcing the current Kushite king, Taharqa, to retreat, wounded, into the far south. The Assyrian king then "deported all Nubians from Egypt, leaving not even one to do homage." Everywhere in Egypt, he "appointed new kings, governors, officers, harbor overseers, officials and administrative personnel." Sargon then "initiated regular sacrificial dues for Ashur and the great gods" and "imposed upon them tribute due to … an overlord, annually without ceasing."[44]

Many (if not all) of the "new" rulers and officials were actually those who had been fulfilling the roles under the Kushites, whom many may have seen no more desirable

FIGURE 89 Relief of the Assyrian king Ashurbanipal in his chariot; from North Palace, Nineveh (BM WA124946).

as overlords than the newly arrived Assyrians. Doubtless some were influenced by the millennia-old Egyptian propaganda that had raged against "vile Kush." This Assyrian hegemony was, however, short-lived, as by 669 Taharqa had returned to Memphis, prompting Esarhaddon to once more march west—only to fall ill and die that November, while still in Palestine.

Although this provided Taharqa with a brief respite, the new Assyrian king, Ashurbanipal (fig. 89), initiated a fresh invasion in 667/666,[45] which again resulted in the Kushites retreating southward, beyond Thebes, which was then sacked by the Assyrians. The local kings and other rulers, who had "left their offices in the face of the advance of Taharqa and had scattered into the countryside," once again swore allegiance to Ashurbanipal, who then returned home to his capital at Nineveh. The rulers involved included King Nekau I at Sais and Padubast III at Tanis, the Chiefs of the Ma Shoshenq F at Busiris and "Buiama" at Mendes, Nimlot E at Hermopolis, Nespamedu A at Thinis, Bakennefi C at Athribis, and Montjuemhat, Mayor and Fourth Priest of Amun, at Thebes.[46]

However, most of these worthies seemingly came soon to the view that they had been better off under Kushite rule after all, since they plotted together to restore Taharqa, sending messengers south to him. Unfortunately, Assyrian officers left behind in Egypt got wind of the plot, intercepted the messenger, and rounded up the local rulers, who then were dispatched to Nineveh to face Ashurbanipal's wrath. In parallel, the inhabitants of their cities were massacred, with corpses flayed and hung from city walls. The only Egyptian ruler to be spared was Nekau I: Ashurbanipal relates that he had him "dressed in a garment with multicolored ornamentation, placed a golden chain on him as the insignia of my kingship, and put gold rings on his hands .... I returned Sais to him ... and gave Athribis to his son."

Although it appears that new local rulers were appointed to replace the executed individuals, Nekau I was clearly Assyria's principal vassal in Egypt, and apparently the only one with pharaonic status. Yet his days were finally numbered, as 664 saw Tanutamun, nephew and successor of Taharqa, who had died soon after his final retreat into Nubia, undertake a further reconquest of Egypt.

Tanutamun advanced northward, and at Memphis "out came the children of rebellion to fight His Person; His Person made a great bloodbath among them, their number being unknown."[47] Among the dead seems to have been Nekau I; his son Psamtik, the ruler of Athribis, fled to Assyrian-controlled Syria.[48] However, Ashurbanipal was soon back in Egypt, Tanutamun abandoning Memphis for Thebes, and the various local rulers submitting to the Assyrian king. It is likely that Psamtik returned to Egypt with Ashurbanipal—as a king, as he counted his regnal years from the death of Taharqa. By ancestry and background, it is quite clear that Psamtik I was a "Libyan" but, as will be discussed in chapter six, his reign marked the extinction of "Libyan" rule in Egypt.

5 Houses of Eternity

Although the kings of the latter part of the New Kingdom appear to have primarily been resident in the north, the construction of royal tombs in the Valley of the Kings at Thebes continued down to the end of the Twentieth Dynasty, although it appears that neither Rameses X nor Rameses XI were actually buried in their sepulchers there. However, with the advent of the Twenty-first Dynasty, the royal cemetery shifted to Tanis, where many kings down to the eighth century are known to have been buried.

In the Delta (and also the alluvial areas of the Nile valley), tombs were historically of a very different kind from those on the desert margins of the valley and beyond. In the latter, burial places generally had at least their substructures tunneled into the rock. However, in alluvial areas tombs had to be built on, or sunk into, such places where gravel beds were high enough to remain out of reach of the annual inundation. These areas were of course also required for the habitation of the living, so that cemeteries generally existed cheek-by-jowl with settlements. High-status sepulchers were often incorporated into local cult complexes, which was certainly the case at Tanis. Here, the royal cemetery developed directly south of the axis of the Amun temple. When the last major addition was made to this structure under Osorkon II (fig. 7), the position of its outer pylon was constrained by the presence of the cemetery.

Alluvial-land tombs comprised structures of stone or mud brick, placed as high as possible above the maximum level of the annual Nile flood, as damp is a key enemy of organic materials, including embalmed remains. The royal tombs at Tanis were primarily built of stone, some of it recycled (like much of the masonry at the site) from earlier monuments, especially those of the dismantled city of Per-Rameses. It is likely that they

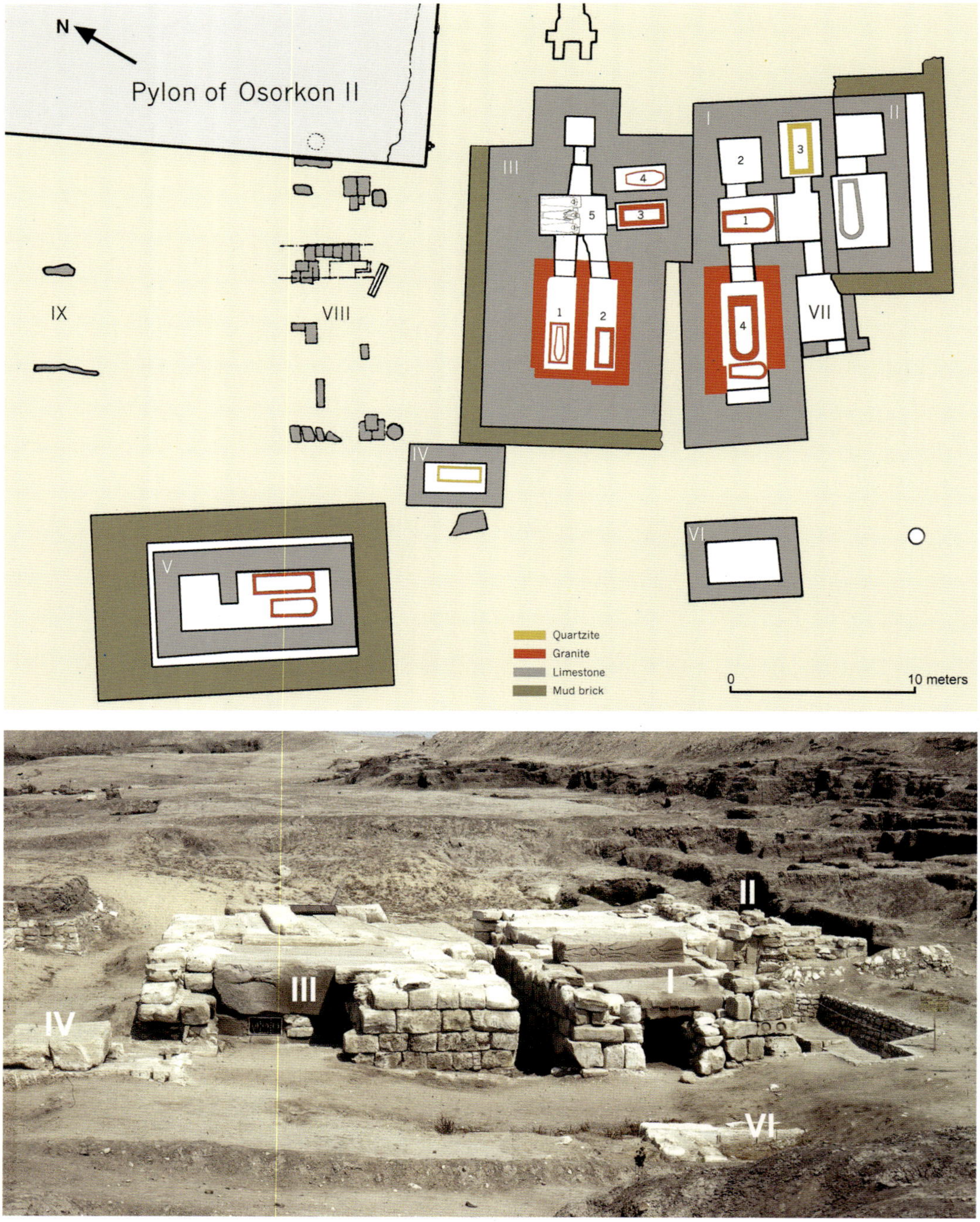

N
Pylon of Osorkon II
IX
VIII
III
I
II
VII
IV
V
VI
Quartzite
Granite
Limestone
Mud brick
0
10 meters

FIGURE 90 The royal necropolis at Tanis.

were surmounted by funerary chapels, probably of brick,[1] but no traces were reported during excavations.

The earliest surviving tomb decoration at Tanis is that in tomb NRT-III, built for Pasebkhanut I and his wife, each of them possessing their own granite burial chamber, embedded in a limestone structure that included an access shaft, an antechamber, and two secondary burial chambers (fig. 90).[2] However, it is clear that the adjacent NRT-I had been built before NRT-III, as the northeastern part of this tomb had been cut back to accommodate the construction of the southeastern part of NRT-III.

Accordingly, NRT-I must have been constructed for a predecessor of Pasebkhanut I, with Nesibanebdjedet I the only real option, although nothing bearing his name has been identified in the tomb. That Nesibanebdjedet was buried at Tanis is likely not only as the founder of the Tanite dynasty, but also because one of his canopic jars was allegedly purchased nearby.[3] However, its earliest surviving decoration dates to the reign of Osorkon II, when the layout of the tomb also underwent alterations (see pages 129–40).

As well as the interment of Pasebkhanut I, NRT-III had also been used for the burials of a number of that king's successors. First, Amenemopet's coffin and mummy had been placed in the chamber and the sarcophagus originally provided for Pasebkhanut's Queen Mutnedjmet.[4] Nothing is known of the burial of Osorkon the Elder, but both Siamun and Pasebkhanut II were buried (or reburied) in the antechamber of NRT-III, where were found their shabtis and the two totally decayed coffins and mummies that must have been theirs.[5]

Shoshenq I and Osorkon I

The burial places of Shoshenq I and Osorkon I are unknown, although the canopic chest of the former was acquired on the antiquities market some time before 1891. This piece (fig. 91)[6] is of square naos form, decorated with winged goddesses at its corners, with the interior carved into four cylindrical compartments. These have diameters of approximately fifteen centimeters; there can be no question of conventional canopic jars ever having been placed within. Accordingly, the visceral bundles would have been placed either directly in these cavities, or in metal coffinettes of the kind found in the tomb of Tutankhamun, and employed in the burial of Shoshenq IIa a few decades later (fig. 92c). This kind of chest is otherwise unknown during the Third Intermediate Period,[7] but was the standard type used by kings from Amenhotep II through the Nineteenth Dynasty.[8]

While Shoshenq's chest differs in detail and execution from New Kingdom examples, it is identical in concept, suggesting that its designer had seen, or heard described, a New Kingdom chest. Since the final reinterment of the New Kingdom royal mummies

FIGURE 91 The canopic chest of Shoshenq I (Berlin ÄM11000).

seems to have taken place during Shoshenq's reign (page 28), this would not be particularly surprising. How long this revival of the old form lasted is unclear, given that the burial of Osorkon I is unknown, but as the reburial of Shoshenq IIa included silver coffinettes, it is possible that the original burial might have had such a chest. However, the coffinettes were actually found in reused canopic jars (see page 129).

As to the potential locations of the missing tombs of Shoshenq I and Osorkon I, there is certainly no space for them in the known royal cemetery at Tanis. One possibility is that their sepulchers lay at Bubastis, which Manetho calls the place of origin of the Twenty-second Dynasty,[9] although nothing of them has been reported in the extensive necropolis at that site. Herakleopolis and the precinct of Ptah at Memphis, both of which later received high-status burials of the period, are also possibilities, with Memphis certainly hosting a "Mansion of Millions of Years of Shoshenq-meryamun"—that is, a mortuary establishment—that is known from texts of the latter part of the Twenty-second Dynasty.[10] However, textual mentions of such structures at Memphis go back to the New Kingdom, during which time pharaohs were of course buried at Thebes, with their associated Mansions of Millions of Years (memorial temples) nearby.

That the cemetery of the early Twenty-second Dynasty was in some low-lying location is suggested by the state of the reburied remains of Shoshenq IIa. The trough of the coffin had been broken prior to being placed in its final location, while grass roots and soil were found among the royal bones, all suggesting that the coffin had spent some time in standing water—which was never present in the Tanite royal cemetery, in which his encoffined mummy was found.[11] This might suggest that Shoshenq IIa's burial had been moved to the Tanite necropolis after the evacuation of another cemetery in the wake of serious flooding. It is also perhaps instructive that Takelot I had his ultimate burial place provided in the tomb of his son Osorkon II, at Tanis (pages 135–38).

Shoshenq IIa

Shoshenq IIa's mummy, cartonnage mummy case, coffin, canopic coffinettes, and shabtis were found in the antechamber of Pasebkhanut I's NRT-III, having been placed between the coffins of Siamun and Pasebkhanut II (fig. 128). The coffin (figs. 42, 92b), and the cartonnage mummy case placed within (fig. 92a; cf. pages 175–77), each had the head of a raptor, rather than a human being. This feature is also present with the coffins of Osorkon II and Horsieset (pages 139, 146, fig. 114). Its meaning remains unclear, but it perhaps invoked the mortuary falcon deity Sokar. Another, or perhaps linked, possibility is that this was a new manifestation of the avian aspect seen in royal coffins dating between the Seventeenth and mid-Twenty-first Dynasty. These had a feathered *(rishi)* decorative pattern, which may have originated in a desire to represent the deceased

FIGURE 92 Funerary equipment of Shoshenq IIa from NRT-III. a. The reconstructed cartonnage mummy case (Cairo JE72196). b. Upper part of the silver coffin (JE72154, fig. 42). c. Canopic coffinettes (JE72159-62).

as a human-headed bird *(ba)*.[12] In contrast, the bodies of Shoshenq's coffin and cartonnage were decorated in a manner that recalls contemporary private cartonnages (cf. figs. 21 right, 32, 65).[13] Although the king's employment of a cartonnage follows contemporary private practice, the contained mummy of Shoshenq IIa deviates in employing a mask as well. This was human-faced, with the flesh composed of beaten gold (fig. 93); the remainder had utterly decayed when found (fig. 129 left), but was probably made of cartonnage.

FIGURE 93 Gold face from the mask of Shoshenq IIa; the rest was probably made from cartonnage (Cairo JE72163A).

As already noted, the coffin was accompanied by a set of silver canopic coffinettes (fig. 92c), which were found in reused canopic jars lying near the coffin.[14] It is unclear whether these jars had been appropriated for the reburial, or had been used for the king's original interment. They certainly did not comprise a matched set. Remarkably, the bundles found within the coffinettes proved to not to be real mummified viscera, but imitations in stiffened linen.[15] From late in the Twentieth Dynasty it become the custom to return the viscera to the body after mummification, but canopic equipment had become such a fundamental part of the burial outfit that high-status individuals continued to include visceral containers.

Takelot I and Osorkon II

As previously discussed, it is possible that Takelot I may also have been the subject of evacuation and reburial, as his ultimate interment was in the tomb of his son, Osorkon II. On the other hand, the circumstances of his obscure reign may have prevented his construction of a suitable tomb, leaving it to his son to make appropriate arrangements for his father.

As already noted, Osorkon II's sepulcher, Tanis NRT-I (figs. 94, 95),[16] seems originally to have been constructed for Nesibanebdjedet I, but was then reconstructed for the later king. The full extent of Osorkon's rebuilding of this sepulcher is not wholly clear, but certainly involved the tomb's complete (re)decoration,[17] and the provision of a new entrance from the west, with a granite lintel (figs. 94[1a], 95[1a], 96), superseding the original shaft on the east of the tomb (figs. 94[2], 95[2]).

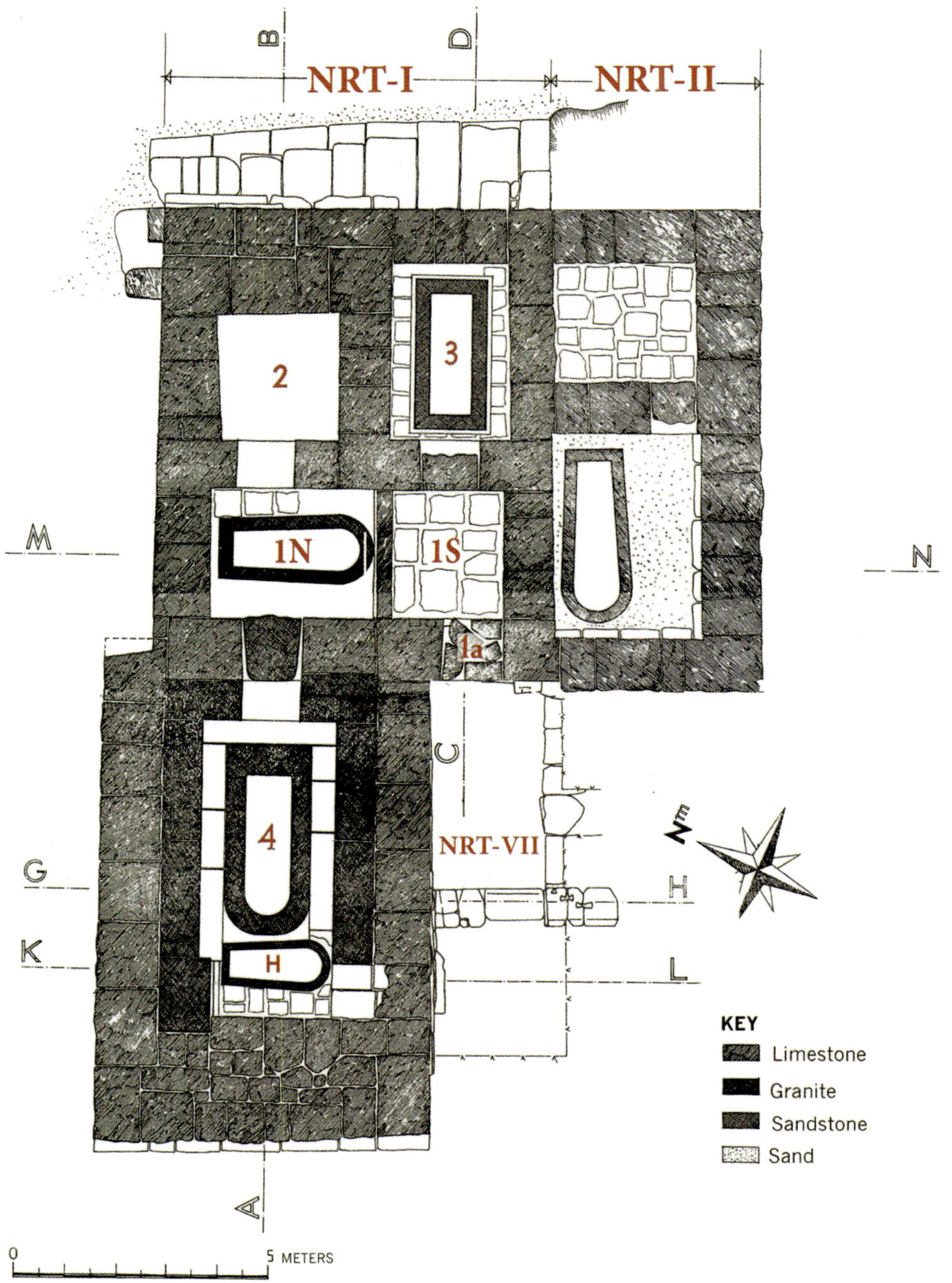

FIGURE 94 Plan of NRT-I and II.

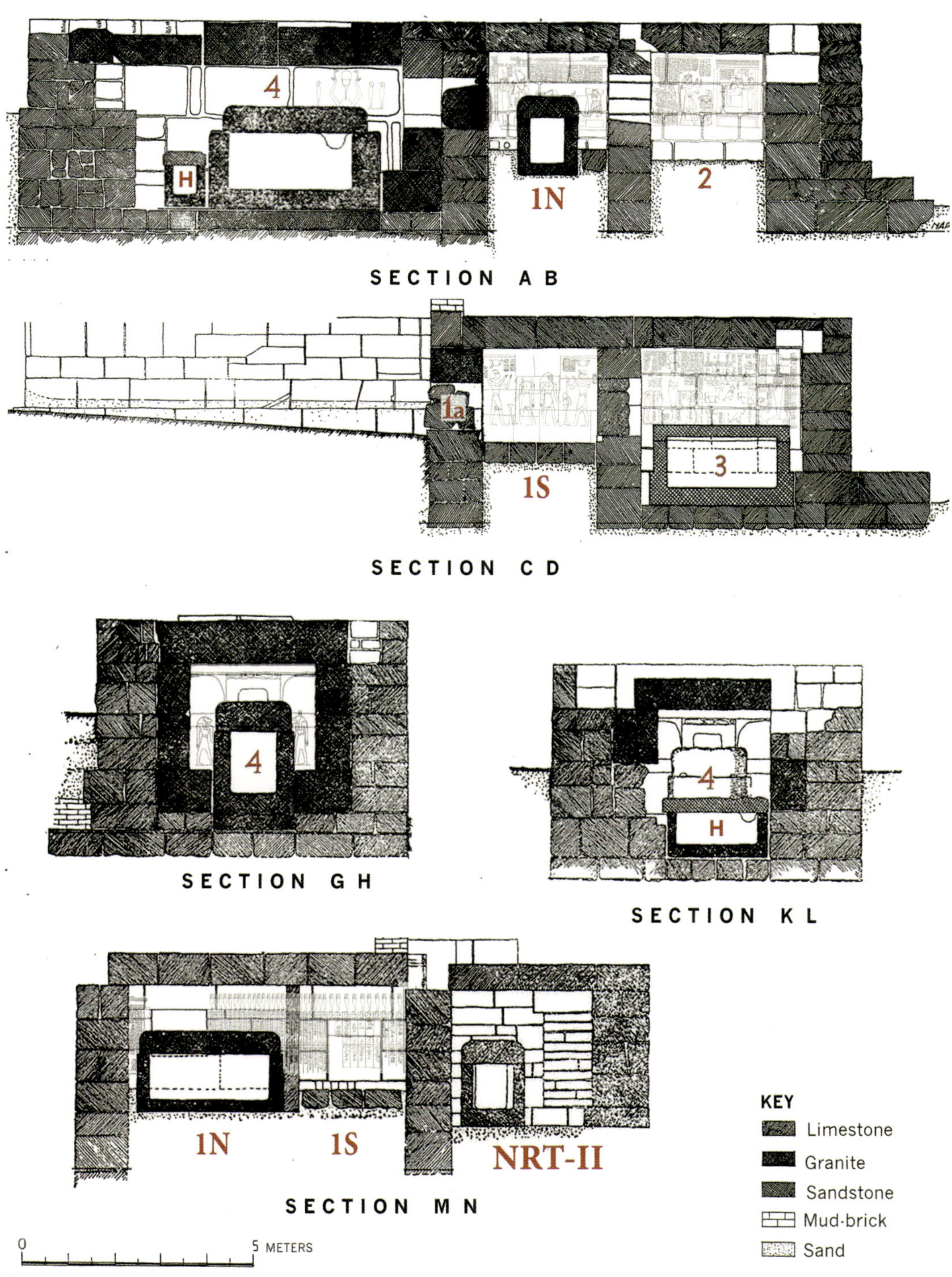

FIGURE 95 Sections of NRT-I.

The new doorway contained an unusual tableau (visible on the left of fig. 96 bottom) in which the General Pashereneset is shown mourning and reciting an elegy for the late King Osorkon.[18] That a king should be mourned like a mortal is a new departure. The text ends with the laconic note "Kapus made it for him." This has often been interpreted as an indication that Osorkon II's mother Kapes (the names are different, but within the potential boundaries of orthographic variation) outlived him and acted as intermediary

FIGURE 96 NRT-I. Top: entrance. Bottom: view from entrance (with text of Pashereneset), through chamber 1S, into chamber 3 (Takelot I).

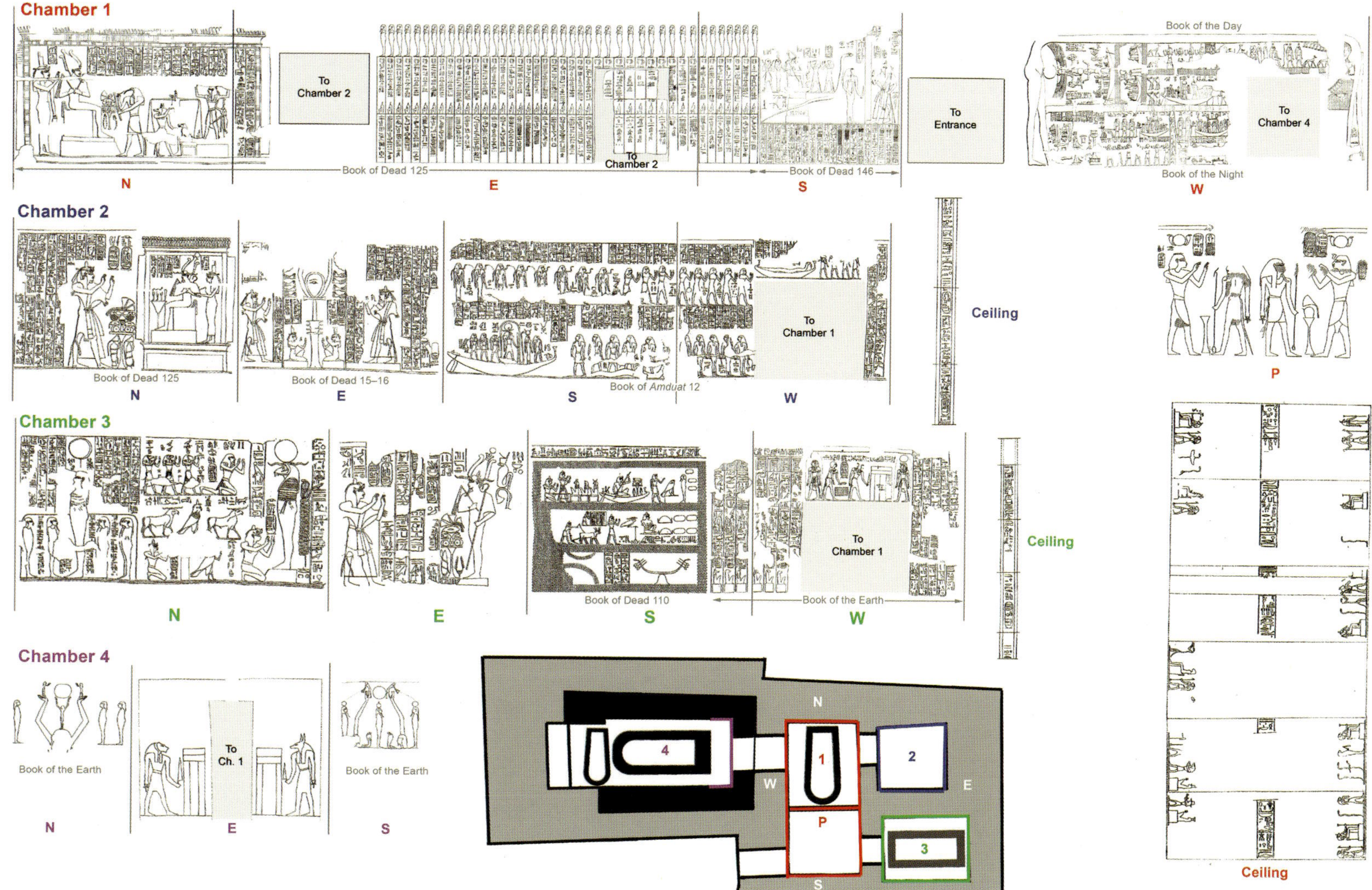

FIGURE 97 The decoration of NRT-I.

in allowing Pashereneset to add his elegy—or even provided the king with his tomb. However, the lady in question is given no title, while Osorkon II's mother is unlikely to have still been alive at the end of her son's four-decade reign. Accordingly, "Kapus" may have been a daughter of the king, if a member of the royal family at all.

Beyond this new entrance lay what was initially a single antechamber (figs. 95[1N+1S], 96[1N+1S], 106), but which was later subdivided into two spaces (see below). Three walls of the chamber were devoted to extracts from the Book of the Dead, the fourth to the Books of the Day and the Night (see fig. 97);[19] the ceiling also bore astronomical tableaux. These latter elements were typical of the decoration of royal tombs of the Nineteenth and Twentieth Dynasties. The Book of the Dead elements in the room included the weighing of the heart and the Negative Confession from BD125. These were standard elements of suites of funerary texts provided for a commoner or royal family member. However, although the Negative Confession is found in the tomb of Merenptah of the Nineteenth Dynasty (KV8), the accompanying scene showing the judgment of the king himself (fig. 98)—and not just simply an image of the judgment hall—is unheard-of in any kingly tomb of the New Kingdom. Now, it appears that the king is no longer a god on earth gone to join his brothers in heaven, but one who must now submit to judgment like a mere mortal.

More of the Book of the Dead, including the final vignette from BD125 (fig. 99 top), adorned the north and east walls of the former Twenty-first Dynasty entrance shaft (figs.

FIGURE 98 The judgment scene on the north wall and north end of the east wall of chamber 1, from Chapter 125 of the Book of the Dead.

94[2], 95[2]). This room had its other two walls decorated with the twelfth hour of the Book of *Amduat* (fig. 99 bottom), part of the original suite of ritual texts introduced into royal tombs of the early Eighteenth Dynasty. The Book of the Dead vignettes in NRT-I (and in the Memphite tomb of Osorkon II's son, Shoshenq D [pages 151–53]) are very similar to those found in the papyrus of Nesitanebetashru, daughter of Panedjem II.[20]

Another space opening into the antechamber, and directly opposite the Twenty-second Dynasty entrance to the tomb (figs. 94[3], 95[3], 96 bottom), was employed for the interment of Takelot I. On the east wall, Takelot is shown in the form of Osiris, being adored by his son, Osorkon II. Takelot is also seen as a small figure kneeling before Amun-Horakhty on the north wall of the chamber, which also includes kneeling figures of Osorkon II. The south and west walls are adorned with the depiction of the next world from Book of the Dead chapter 110 (fig. 100 top), and material from the Twentieth Dynasty Book of the Earth (fig. 100 bottom).

Takelot I was interred in a quartzite sarcophagus originally made for a late Twelfth Dynasty Chancellor named Ameny (fig. 101), and probably derived from a tomb in the Fayyum.[21] No attempt was made to change the original texts, the king's name being simply added in ink on the lid and the ends of the coffer, which was sunk in the floor of the chamber. Surviving items of Takelot I's funerary equipment included four canopic jars (fig. 102a–c), a large calcite jar with the name of Osorkon I, shabtis, and, inside the sarcophagus, a fragment of a gilded coffin and a gold mask, together with elements from items of jewelry (fig. 103 top).

FIGURE 99 Top: Osorkon II adoring Osiris on the north wall of chamber 2, from the final vignette of BD125. Bottom: figures from the upper part of the twelfth Hour of the Book of *Amduat* on the south wall of chamber 2.

FIGURE 100 Chamber 3. Top: detail of the scene of Book of Dead Chapter 110 from the south wall. Bottom: west wall, with parts of the Book of the Earth.

FIGURE 101 The sarcophagus of Ameny, usurped for Takelot I. The piece is of a design typical of the reigns of Senwosret III and Amenemhat III, with paneling around the base modeled on the enclosure wall of Djoser, whose pyramid complex was an inspiration for those of these kings.

FIGURE 102 Canopic jars from NRT-I and NRT-V. a–c. Takelot I; d–e. Osorkon II; f. Shoshenq III; g–h. Shoshenq IV; i–j. Pamiu I.

FIGURE 103 Top: shabtis and fragments of funerary equipment of Takelot I. Bottom: shabtis of Osorkon II (upper row) and Hornakhte (lower row).

The main burial chamber, of Osorkon II himself (figs. 94[4], 95[4], 104 top), was built from granite, as had been those constructed for Pasebkhanut I and his wife in NRT-III, suggesting that this was an original part of the tomb's structure. It had minimal decoration, concentrated around its entrance, comprising two vignettes from the Book of the Earth and two demons on the doorjambs. However, unlike the usurped examples in the Tanite tombs of the Twenty-first Dynasty,[22] and in the burial of Takelot I, the sarcophagus of Osorkon II seems not to have been taken over from a previous burial. It is likely, however, that it had been manufactured from a previously quarried piece of granite, something certainly true of the lid, cut from what had once been a dyad of Rameside times. This had a slightly raised representation of the king on its upper surface (as also seen on the sarcophagus lid of Shoshenq III: fig. 109) and his prenomen. This full-face depiction of the king was clearly an echo of the three-dimensional images of kings that had appeared atop royal sarcophagi of the mid-Nineteenth to mid-Twentieth Dynasties.[23]

Surviving fragments indicate that Osorkon II had a silver coffin and a gilded cartonnage, both with raptor heads. Four inscribed canopic jars were found (fig. 102d–e), and a few fragments from jewelry, as well as a heart scarab of Osorkon II, and also one of Takelot I. Over three hundred shabtis of Osorkon II were present in the chamber (fig. 103). As well as debris from the king's burial, the sarcophagus contained three badly decayed mummies, one of a child and two of individuals about 1.5 meters tall (fig. 104 bottom), presumably later intrusive interments.

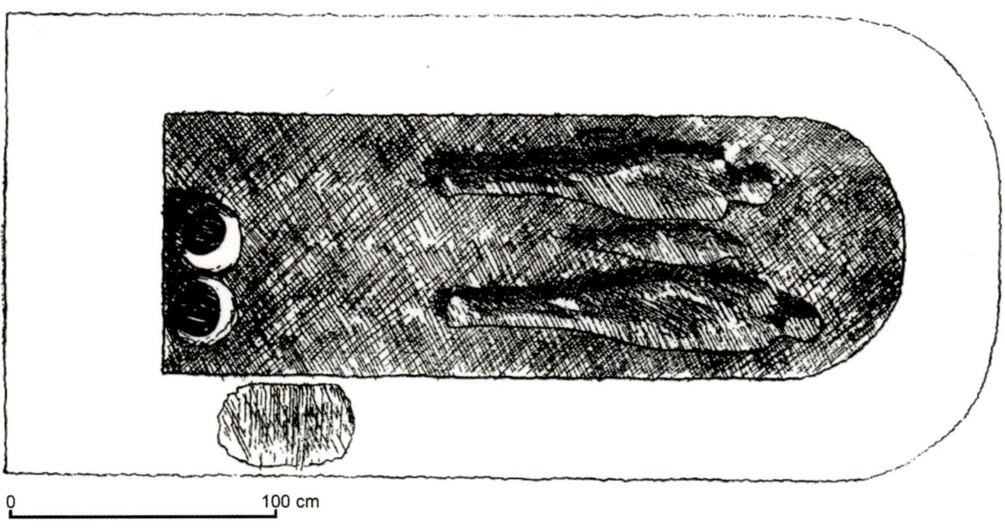

FIGURE 104 Top: the burial chamber of Osorkon II, seen from the west. Bottom: the contents of the sarcophagus as found.

FIGURE 105 The wall erected under Shoshenq III to divide chamber 1 into two parts.

At some point during Osorkon II's reign, the western end of the royal burial chamber was partly dismantled, and reconfigured for the burial of the king's young son, Hornakhte. The tomb was also modified during the reign of Shoshenq III, when a dividing wall was inserted into the antechamber, the wall adorned with scenes of Shoshenq and Osorkon II adoring unlabeled divine figures (fig. 105).[24] Into the northern half of the chamber (figs. 94[1N], 95[1N], 106) was inserted a large sarcophagus with a rounded head-end, sides that tapered inward from the shoulders, and a lid made from a statue of Rameses II. The tapered plan of this sarcophagus is all but unknown during previous epochs,[25] but then becomes a standard type through the Ptolemaic Period.

The owner of this sarcophagus is unclear. While fragments of shabtis of a king Shoshenq-sibast-meryamen were found, and Shoshenq III was represented on the exterior of the dividing wall,[26] Shoshenq III had his own tomb some way away (see below). One option is that the sarcophagus was intended for the burial of a member of the royal family (perhaps a widow of Osorkon II), with the shabti fragment a "stray" from the burial of Shoshenq V (see further, page 144).

FIGURE 106 The northwest corner of chamber 1.

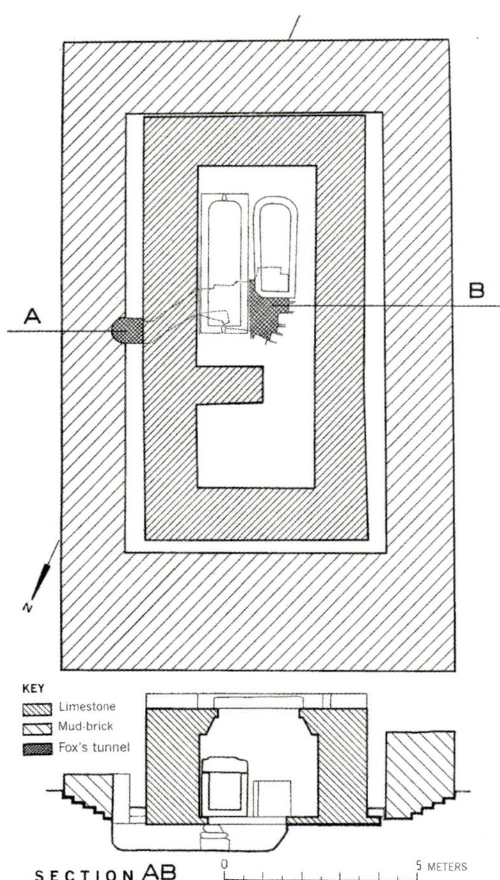

FIGURE 107 Plan and section of NRT-V, the tomb of Shoshenq III.

Shoshenq III and IV

For his tomb, NRT-V,[27] Shoshenq III selected a location to the northwest of the earlier sepulchers, at a significantly higher level—perhaps a reaction to the flooding of the necropolis in which Shoshenq IIa had originally been buried. NRT-V was of a simple design, comprising a single compartment, divided into an antechamber and a burial chamber (fig. 107, 109), and entirely constructed from reused blocks. Its decoration (fig. 108)[28] is largely taken from the Book of the Night, with the exception of the south wall and the cornices of the chamber. The latter are adorned with extracts from the Book of the Dead, while the upper part of the south wall bears a tableau previously found in the tombs of Rameses VI and IX (KV9, KV6) in the Valley of the Kings. Its lower part has a tableau employed previously in the tomb of Rameses VI, and also in the Osireion cenotaph of Sethy I at Abydos. This composition would later be employed in the Twenty-fifth Dynasty pyramids of Tanutamun and Queen Qalhata at El-Kurru.

Shoshenq III's sarcophagus was very similar to that of Osorkon II, in having a recumbent figure of the king on the lid in very shallow relief (fig. 109). Although the

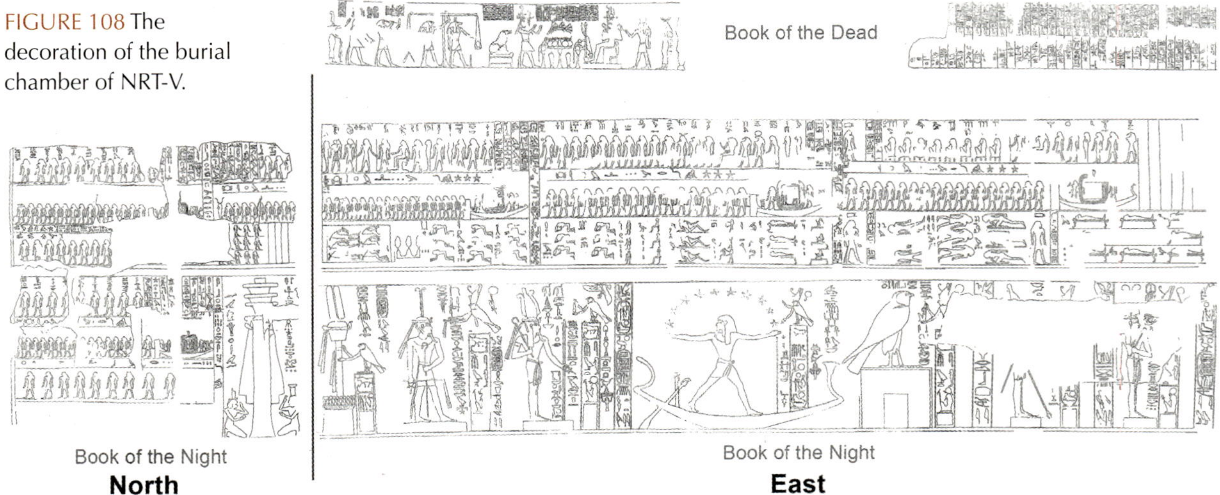

FIGURE 108 The decoration of the burial chamber of NRT-V.

FIGURE 109 The burial chamber of NRT-V, with the sarcophagus of Shoshenq III on the left, and Shoshenq IV on the right.

lid had a rounded head-end, this was only true of the interior of the coffer, which was externally of rectangular form. The coffer had been cut from a reused lintel of Thirteenth Dynasty date, the underside still preserving the Horus names of Kings Auibre Hor and Sekhemre-khutawy (nomen unknown) of the Thirteenth Dynasty.[29]

Next to the king's sarcophagus was found a second, smaller, example, lacking a lid. Its owner is revealed by fragments from two canopic jars, one of which preserved the names of Shoshenq IV (fig. 102g–h). Heart scarabs for both kings may have been found in the tomb (fig. 110).[30] An uninscribed canopic jar of Middle or early New Kingdom date was also found in the tomb (fig. 102f), which probably belonged to the burial of Shoshenq III.

FIGURE 110 The heart scarab of Shoshenq III (Brooklyn 61.10).

FIGURE 111 Tomb NRT-II at Tanis, the sepulcher of Pamiu.

Pamiu I

The latest firmly datable royal tomb at Tanis is NRT-II, built against the south wall of NRT-I, and of the same basic plan as NRT-V (figs. 94, 95, 111).[31] It was undecorated, but a fragment of canopic jar was found inscribed with the name "Usermaatre-setepenamun" in ink (two of the three complete, but uninscribed, examples are shown in figs. 102i–j). This indicates that NRT-II was the tomb of Pamiu, since the only other Tanite users of that prenomen, Osorkon II and Shoshenq III, have known sepulchers. Apart from a limestone sarcophagus and its lid, the remains of two gilded wooden coffins, possibly also a silver coffin, a gilded silver finger stall, scarabs, and fragments of amuletic jewelry survived.

Shoshenq V

It was noted above that a fragment of a shabti of a King Shoshenq was found in the antechamber of NRT-I. It is possible that he was Shoshenq V and, if so, the latter might have been buried in NRT-VII, a chamber constructed outside Osorkon II's entrance to NRT-I (fig. 94), but subsequently dismantled.[32]

Horsieset I

Of the Libyan kings ruling at Thebes, the tomb of only one, Horsieset I, has been located. This lay within the Medinet Habu complex at Western Thebes, directly south of the Eighteenth Dynasty temple there, and on the north side of the processional way leading from the gate of the Rameses III complex toward his memorial temple (fig. 112).[33] It thus followed the Tanis tombs in lying within a temple precinct, but the design was rather different. This

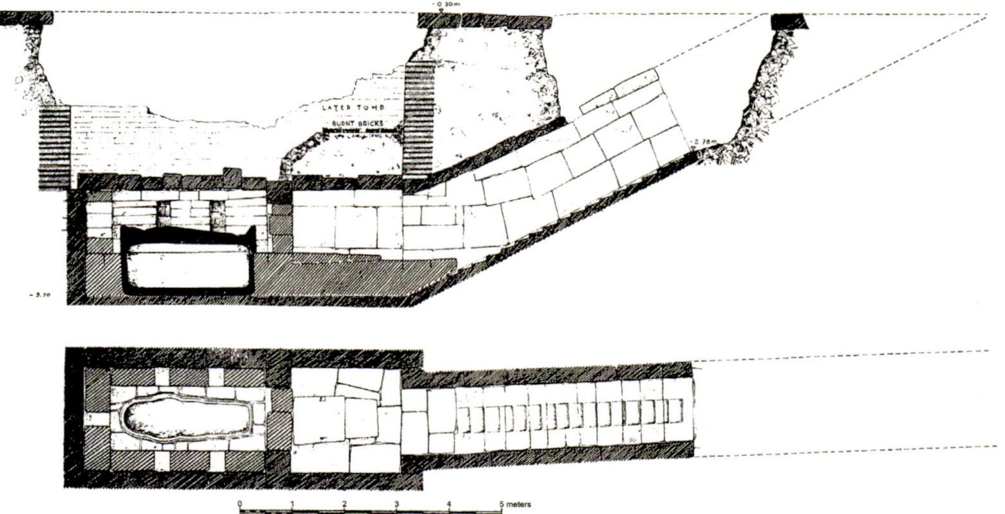

FIGURE 112 Top: view from the pylon of the memorial temple of Rameses III toward the Small Temple and migdol gate at Medinet Habu, with the location of the tomb of Horsieset I marked. Bottom: plan and section of Horsieset's tomb.

FIGURE 113 View from Horsieset's burial chamber toward the entrance to the tomb, and the king's set of canopic jars (Cairo JE59900), probably originally placed in niches in the side walls of the chamber.

comprised a burial chamber and antechamber approached from the east by a sloping passage, with a staircase down the middle (fig. 113 top). The structure was built largely from reused sandstone blocks, most coming from the buildings of Rameses III at the site.

The king's body, of which only the skull, jaw (fig. 55), and an arm bone are now extant, had been placed in an anthropoid granite coffin trough sunk in the floor of the burial chamber, closed with a raptor-headed lid (fig. 114). While the lid had been made for Horsieset, the trough had been taken from the tomb of the sister-wife of Rameses II, Henutmire (QV75), in the Valley of the Queens. Four canopic jars (fig. 113 bottom) had been placed in niches in the side walls of the burial chamber, a new arrangement for such items that would continue into the Late Period, while at least 250 shabti figures were recovered.

FIGURE 114 The granite coffin of Horsieset I, the lid with a raptor's head, as in the case of other kings of the period. The trough was usurped from Rameses II's sister, Henutmire (Cairo JE59896 + JE60137).

FIGURE 115 The three surviving miniature canopic jars of Takelot III (RMO CI.280, 283, 284).

No superstructure survived, but there may have been a chapel above, perhaps along the lines of those later provided for the sepulchers of the God's Wives of Amun of the Twenty-fifth and Twenty-sixth Dynasties, just to the south. To such a structure may have belonged a sandstone block with Horsieset's cartouche, found reused in the Ptolemaic gate directly to the east of the tomb.

Osorkon III and Takelot III

While no other kingly tomb has been identified for a Third Intermediate Period king at Thebes, there is evidence for the existence of two such structures. First, Theban documents of the Twenty-sixth and Twenty-seventh Dynasties mention a *ḥwt* (temple/tomb) of a king *wsrtn*, who seems likely to have been Osorkon III.[34] Given that Horsieset I had his tomb at Medinet Habu, and that Osorkon III's daughter Shepenwepet I and her successors as God's Wives were also buried there, it seems likely that this lost tomb was also located there.[35] Second, three miniature dummy canopic jars of Takelot III (fig. 115)[36] came to light before 1824; unfortunately, their place of discovery remains unknown. Also of unknown provenance is a now destroyed falcon-headed cartonnage[37] that might potentially have come from the burial of a king of Libyan times.[38] However, the discovery of the remains of a non-royal hawk-headed coffin at Tell el-Balamun extends the usage of the type beyond the king himself.[39]

Royal Family Tombs

The tomb of Pasebkhanut I had incorporated a dedicated chamber for the king's wife (and also a son), but no such arrangements were made in the Twenty-second Dynasty royal sepulchers at Tanis. However, a son of Osorkon II, Hornakhte, had his burial inserted into the southern end of his father's burial chamber.[40] This comprised a granite sarcophagus coffer, manufactured from a lintel of Rameses II, with a cut-down Twenty-second Dynasty quartzite lid (fig. 116),[41] a Middle Kingdom quartzite canopic chest, a set of calcite canopic jars inscribed for the prince, finger- and toe-stalls from the mummy, and over three hundred shabtis (fig. 103 bottom, lower row). Although robbed, it was possible to identify the remains of a silver coffin and a gilded mummy cartonnage, accompanied by a huge number of amulets, many of gold.

Of the queens of the period, we have already noted the possibility that the sarcophagus introduced into the antechamber of NRT-I might have been intended for a king's wife, but the only definitely known burial of a queen is at Leontopolis. Here, Kaꜣ(roma)ma, presumably the spouse of Osorkon II of that name, occupied one of a pair of vaulted chambers.[42] The room appears to have been decorated along the same lines as the tombs of Osorkon II and Shoshenq III, and contained a granite sarcophagus, cut from

FIGURE 116 The sarcophagus of Prince Hornakhte, from Tanis NRT-I.

FIGURE 117 The Ramesseum, whose subsidiary buildings were a popular place of burial during the middle of the Third Intermediate Period.

a block of Rameses II. The latter was intact, but with its contents water-ruined. Nevertheless, the queen's heart scarab, items of jewelry, canopic jars, and some shabtis survived. The second chamber, with a limestone sarcophagus, had been robbed out, but presumably had once held the body of another member of the royal family.[43]

Other senior members of the royal family for whom tombs are known possessed them by virtue of their sacerdotal offices. The God's Wives Karomama G and Kedmerut (turn of the ninth/eighth centuries BC) had tombs in the area of the Ramesseum (fig. 117), which was a key high-status cemetery from the end of the tenth century, on the basis of the discovery of canopic jars (Karomama) and shabtis (both) in that location.[44]

FIGURE 118 Plan of the tomb of Iuput A at Abydos, and a block from its burial chamber reused in the White Monastery at Sohag.

In contrast to these God's Wives' burial at Thebes, the High Priest of Amun Iuput A was interred at Abydos,[45] as had also been the case for the Twenty-first Dynasty pontiff, Menkheperre,[46] and one of the latter's sons.[47] Iuput's lay just south of the processional way from the Osiris temple to the god's "tomb" at Umm el-Qaab, and comprised a 120-meter-long brick-lined and roofed cutting in the bedrock, terminating in a burial chamber, its walls lined with granite slabs, decorated with the Book of *Amduat* (fig. 118); an incomplete room lay to its south. Much of the granite was taken away for reuse during the reign of Ahmose II in the sixth century BC.

Another royal High Priest, of Ptah, with a known tomb is Shoshenq D. The sepulcher lay just outside the southwest corner of the enclosure of the Ptah temple at Memphis (fig. 47, 119, 120),[48] as the first of a series of high-priestly tombs in this location. The principal part of the tomb comprised a room decorated principally with material from the Book of the Dead, with not-unexpected parallels with the decoration of the tomb of Osorkon II. Its blocks were all reused from earlier structures. The mummy, found intact, but water-damaged, was placed in a nest of two coffins, in a cutting in the floor, closed by a reused sandstone stela of Amenhotep II, adorned with a bead net and numerous amulets, and accompanied by canopic jars and 312 shabti figures. The cemetery was subsequently used by, among others, Shoshenq's son and successor as High Priest, Takelot B, and his grandsons, Padieset A and Horsieset Q.[49]

FIGURE 119 Top: the cemetery of the ninth/eighth century BC High Priests of Ptah at Memphis, with the gable roof of that of Padieset A visible. Middle: burial chamber of Shoshenq D (Cairo JE88131). Among other reused stones was the lintel over the entrance, on which Tutankhamun is still visible. Bottom: the silver coffin of Padieset A (Cairo JE86109).

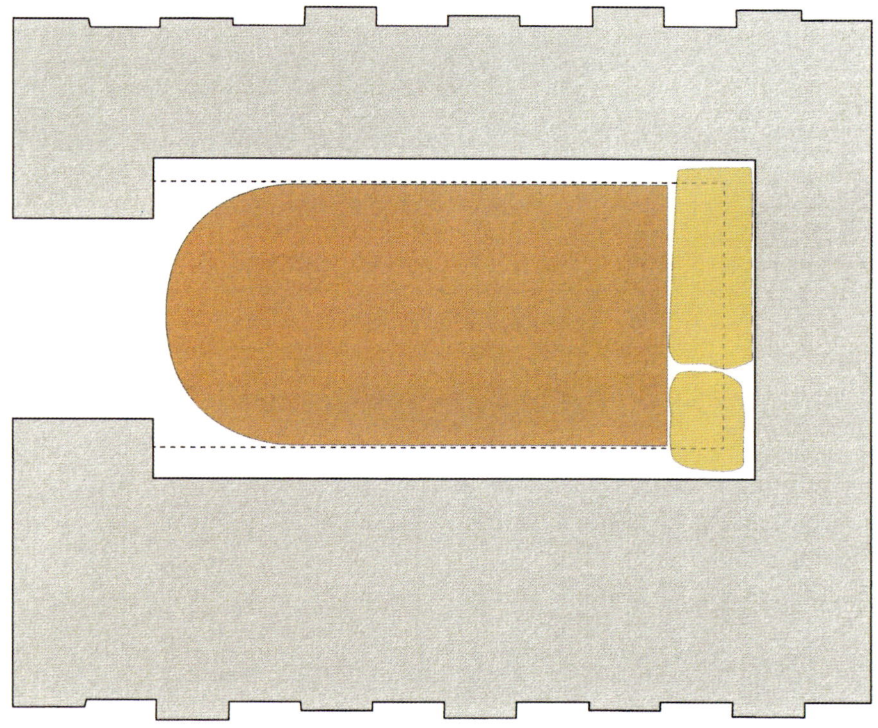

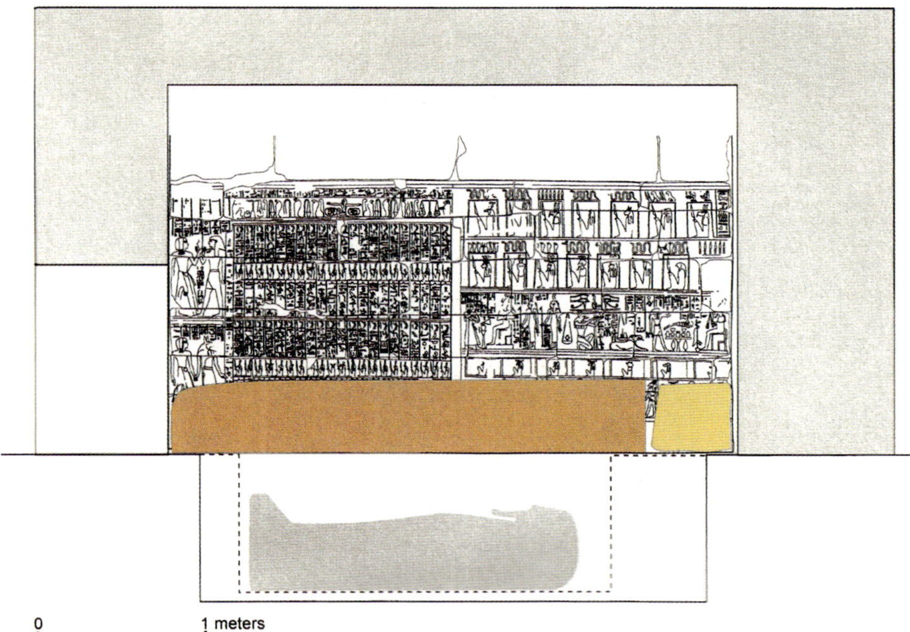

FIGURE 120 Plan and section of the burial chamber of Shoshenq D. The lid of the burial cist was a reused stela of Amenhotep II (Cairo JE86763).

6 Aftermath and Limbo

The End of Libyan Egypt

The reign of Psamtik I would last over five decades, his titulary running as follows:

Horus		*ꜥꜣ-ỉb*
Nebti		*nb-ꜥ*
Golden Falcon		*ḳnw*
Prenomen		*wꜣḥ-ỉb-rꜥ*
Nomen		*psmtk*

The king's prenomen copied that of Bakenrenef. The Horus name ("Great of heart"), the Nebti name ("Strong armed"), and the Golden Falcon name ("Brave") were all new, however, and seem very much intended to present the king as a strong warrior.

Psamtik was certainly of Libyan ancestry, but his accession can be seen as ending the era of "Libyan" kings—both great and small. In contrast to the approach taken by the Kushites—acting as overlords of the patchwork of local kings, chiefs, and other potentates—it seems that Psamtik's fundamental policy was to once again have but one single pharaoh, who was the sole font of legitimate royal power. Doubtless the ease with which the Assyrians had conquered the country, and the way that they had made use of the political situation to their own ends, helped Psamtik—who had been deeply involved in the events—to strengthen his resolve in this. Nevertheless, the existence of a sistrum handle with the prenomina Wahibre and Neferkare,[1] and a fragment of a screen wall from Athribis alternating the two names,[2] may attest to a final cohabitation between Psamtik and a rival.

FIGURE 121 Psamtik I. Left: relief at Edfu. Right: fragmentary colossal statue from Heliopolis (Cairo).

Although only Psamtik's final act of reunion, with the Thebaid in Year 9, is recorded in extant Egyptian material (see below), echoes of what seems to have happened over the preceding years are to be found in a story recounted by the fifth-century BC Greek traveler Herodotus.[3] This tells that at first Psamtik was but one of twelve coequal kings, subsequently deposing the other eleven with the help of Greek mercenaries to become sole king of Egypt. This would fit well with a scenario of Psamtik gradually removing from power the local rulers and absorbing their territories into his own. There would certainly be significant settlement by Carians in Egypt during and after Psamtik's reign, with mercenaries from the Aegean forming a significant part of the Egyptian army throughout the Twenty-sixth Dynasty.

As the end of the first decade of Psamtik's reign approached, it seems that the whole of Egypt north of the Thebaid was under the control of the Saite kings. It is possible that it was after Psamtik's mercenaries had helped him beat off a final attempt by Tanutamun to regain his Egyptian throne[4] that the final reunification was achieved in Year 9. Then Psamtik's daughter, Neitiqerti, arrived in Thebes to be adopted by Amenirdis II, daughter of Taharqa and the adopted heir of Pi(ankh)y's daughter, the current God's Wife, Shepenwepet II.[5] This accordingly reversed the process by which the Kushites had confirmed their absorption of Thebes a century earlier.

Psamtik's task of recentralizing authority under a single pharaoh was doubtless aided by the execution of most of his potential rivals by the Assyrians in 666 BC, and the possible killing of yet more by Tanutamun, at the same time as his own father had been killed. What is clear is that not only is there no sign of any local pharaohs during Psamtik I's reign, but the Libyan titles that had been so common over the past three centuries had vanished from the Egyptian scene. We even now find a campaign against Tehenu-Libyans recorded in Year 11.[6] Likely symptomatic of the evaporation of Libyan conceptions is the almost total disappearance of significant genealogies from the record, suggesting that distant lineage was no longer important in most contexts.

Instead, we find a further extension of the appeals to Egypt's remote past that had first appeared during the eighth century in art and royal titularies. During the Twenty-sixth Dynasty we find revivals of the cults of kings from the very earliest dynasties, including priesthoods of Menes, founder of the unified Egyptian state, and Djoser, builder of the Step Pyramid, the oldest standing monument then remaining in Egypt—and the burgeoning cult of Imhotep, reputed to be the architect of the latter structure.[7]

We have had cause to remark on the curious reputation in later tradition of Psamtik's ancestor, Bakenrenef, as a great lawgiver.[8] One wonders if this derived from Psamtik presenting Bakenrenef as the true font of Psamtik's own reforms. If so, perhaps it was seen as a way of stifling or diverting opposition to the dismantling of the "Libyan" traditional and legal accretions that would seem to have been fundamental to Psamtik's settlement. A further way in which Bakenrenef's memory may have been manipulated by Psamtik could lie in his death at the hands of the Kushites. As such, Bakenenef could be seen as a "hero ancestor," whose fate paralleled that of Psamtik's father, Nekau I. This might have served to further legitimate Psamtik's kingship—not just at Sais, but as ruler and protector of the whole of Egypt.

The Greeks who came to Egypt during the time of Psamtik and his immediate successors would have accepted this propaganda, and when legal ideas were transmitted back to the Aegean as "the wisdom of Egypt" they were associated with their ascription to Bakenrenef. By allegedly influencing the reforms of Solon in Athens at the beginning of the sixth century, Bakenrenef's status as a lawgiver will have been cemented across the wider Mediterranean world, helping to explain why an Etruscan would have wished to take to their grave a jar decorated in honor of Bakenrenef (fig. 122).

FIGURE 122 Vase of Bakenrenef, found in an Etruscan tomb (Museo archeologico nazionale, Tarquinia).

Fading Memories

Bakenrenef had a long afterlife in literature of the Classical world. Another Egyptian "law-giver" mentioned in such sources is Sasuchis, potentially based on Shoshenq I. The latter may also have been one of the prototypes, along with one or more Senwosrets of the Twelfth Dynasty, and New Kingdom monarchs such as Thutmose III and Rameses II, for the hero-king "Sesostris," whose stories were told by Herodotus during the fifth century BC. Indeed, it has been suggested that Shoshenq might also appear separately in Herodotus' work under the alias "Asuchis."[9] It was probably around the same time that the parts of the Old Testament mentioning "Shishak" (Shoshenq I) and "So" (probably Osorkon IV) took their established form, fixing at least two Libyan monarchs in broader historiography.

It was in the third century BC that an official history of Egypt was commissioned from the Egyptian priest Manetho, traditions differing over whether this was by Ptolemy I or Ptolemy II. The original work is lost, and survives only in excerpts and epitomes quoted by later writers, in some cases clearly a number of iterations beyond the original.[10] Some parts are clearly corrupt, but it is difficult to tell whether this derives from problems with Manetho's original work, or mistakes in transmission and redaction.

Three sources of Manetho survive for the Twenty-first through Twenty-sixth Dynasties, and run as follows (excluding the Nubian Twenty-fifth Dynasty):

Sextus Julius Africanus (d. c. AD 240)		**Eusebius of Caesarea** (d. AD 339)		**Eusebius of Caesarea** Armenian version	
Twenty-first Dynasty (seven kings of Tanis)					
Smendês	26yrs	Smendis	26yrs	Smendis	26yrs
Psusen(n)ês	46yrs	Psusennês	41yrs	Psusennês	41yrs
Nephercherês	4yrs	Nephercherês	4yrs	Nephercherês	4yrs
Amenôphthis	9yrs	Amenôphthis	9yrs	Amenôphthis	9yrs
Osochôr	6yrs	Osochôr	6yrs	Osochôr	6yrs
Psinachês	9yrs	Psinachês	9yrs	Psinachês	9yrs
Psusennês	14yrs	Psusennês	35yrs	Psusennês	35yrs
TOTAL	130yrs	TOTAL	130yrs	TOTAL	130yrs
Twenty-second Dynasty					
(nine kings of Bubastis)		(three kings of Bubastis)		(three kings of Bubastis)	
Sesônchis	21yrs	Sesônchôsis	21yrs	Sesônchôsis	21yrs
Osorthôn	15yrs	Osorthôn	15yrs	Osorthôn	15yrs
Three other kings	25yrs	—	—	—	—
Takelôthis	13yrs	Takelôthis	13yrs	Takelôthis	13yrs
Three other kings	42yrs	—	—	—	—
TOTAL	**120yrs**	**TOTAL**	**49yrs**	**TOTAL**	**49yrs**

Africanus		Eusebius		Eusebius (Armenian)	
Twenty-third Dynasty (four kings of Tanis)		(three kings of Tanis)		(three kings of Tanis)	
Petubatês (in his reign the Olympic Festival was first celebrated)	40yrs	Petubastis	25yrs	Petubastis	25yrs
Osorchô (the Egyptians call him Hêraclês)	8yrs	Osorthôn (the Egyptians called him Hêraclês)	9yrs	Osorthon (whom the Egyptians named Hercules)	9yrs
Psammûs	10yrs	Psammûs	10yrs	Psammus	10yrs
Zêt	31yrs	—		—	
TOTAL	89yrs	TOTAL	44yrs	TOTAL	44yrs
Twenty-fourth Dynasty (Sais)					
Bochchôris (in his reign a lamb spoke)	6yrs	Bochchôris (in his reign a lamb spoke)	44yrs	Bocchoris (in his reign a lamb spoke)	44yrs
Twenty-sixth Dynasty (Sais)					
—		Ammeris the Ethiopian	12yrs	Ameres the Ethiopian	18yrs
Stephinatês	7yrs	Stephinathis	7yrs	Stephinathes	7yrs
Nechepsôs	6yrs	Nechepsôs	6yrs	Nechepsos	6yrs
Nechaô	8yrs	Nechaô	8yrs	Nechao	8yrs
Psammêtichus	54yrs	Psammêtichus	45yrs	Psametichus	44yrs
Nechaô II	6yrs	Nechaô II	6yrs	Nechaô II	6yrs
Psammuthis II	6yrs	Psammuthis II	17yrs	Psamuthes II	17yrs
Uaphris	19yrs	Uaphris	25yrs	Uaphres	25yrs
Amôsis	44yrs	Amôsis	42yrs	Amosis	42yrs
Peammecheritês	6mths	—			
TOTAL	150yrs 6mths	TOTAL	167yrs	TOTAL	167yrs

All names are presented in Greek forms, with most of them fairly transparent as to their Egyptian originals (cf. pages 163–64), although some are more obscure,[11] and a few without any obvious Egyptian equivalent (e.g., "Zêt"). The Twenty-first Dynasty succession is consistent across all three sources, with differences restricted to a few reign lengths. It is also coherent with modern reconstructions of the dynasty, including "predicting" the discovery of Amenemnesut ("Nephercherês"—a rendering of his prenomen, Neferkare) and Osorkon the Elder ("Osochôr"—cf. page 179). It should be noted, however, that most studies have assumed, explicitly or implicitly, the basic correctness of the Manethonic successions, with a consequent risk of circular reasoning.

At the other end of the sequence, the Twenty-sixth Dynasty succession from "Nechaô" (Nekau I) onward is wholly consistent with independent data, but this is not the case with reign lengths, which are demonstrably incorrect in a number of cases. The most glaring example is that all versions are a decade short in the case of the reign of Nekau II. Eusebius' listings of Psamtik I are both a decade short, and his reckoning of Ahmose II's reign is short by two years; furthermore, he omits Psamtik III.

The Manethonic Twenty-sixth Dynasty spans the Twenty-fifth Dynasty to link up with the Twenty-fourth Dynasty, to provide a continuous Saite succession running in parallel with the Nubians. The was doubtless a result of Psamtik I's previously discussed propaganda implying that the Saite rulers represented Egypt's "true" kings from Bakenrenef onward. As far as the latter's entries are concerned, Africanus' six-year reign is consistent with contemporary data; Eusebius' forty-four years may simply be a dittography of the same writer's total for the preceding Twenty-third Dynasty.

The extant versions of the Twenty-second and Twenty-third Dynasties are all problematic. For example, Eusebius ignores in his totals the unnamed kings who appear in Africanus' version of the Twenty-second Dynasty; he also omits the Twenty-third Dynasty "Zêt." Such issues make it difficult to invoke Manetho credibly in support of any particular historical hypothesis, and doubtless reflect the difficulties experienced by earlier compilers when trying to make sense of the data available, from a period with multiple competing lines.

A common feature of king-list traditions, whether in Egypt or elsewhere—for example, in Assyria—was that they were intended to reinforce the concept of a single royal succession, going back to the time of the gods. Where this was not the case, problems arose, although Manetho does include dynasties that we know ran in parallel (although they are not acknowledged as such in the surviving extracts, which treat them as consecutive), for example during the First and Second Intermediate Periods. However, the disintegrations of the ninth and eighth centuries went well beyond binary north/south divisions, and what survives of Manetho's coverage of this period may simply represent such names as the compiler could most easily isolate.

These are likely to have been in particular those known in the northeast Delta, where Tanis and Bubastis continued to be major centers through the Ptolemaic Period. Interestingly, in doing so, no hint was given as to the kings' Libyan background—unlike in the case of the explicitly "Phoenician" (in Africanus' version) Fifteenth and "Ethiopian" Twenty-fifth Dynasties. Rather, the Twenty-second and Twenty-third dynasties were simply attributed to Bubastis and Tanis, with the division possibly reflecting the sources of data, rather than any deep understanding of the politics of the era.

Against this background, we therefore find the sequence beginning with the unproblematic Shoshenq I and Osorkon I, and beyond them probably Takelot I and Padubast II. Precise identifications become problematic as to which Osorkon (II or IV) is represented by "Osorchô/Osorthôn," and there are no obvious candidates for "Psammûs" and "Zêt."[12] One curious feature of the Twenty-third Dynasty listing is the glosses added to the entries for "Petubatês" and "Osorchô." The correlation of the former with the first Olympic Games would place his reign around 776/775 BC, the traditional placement of that event, which would actually fit with the present work's estimate of Padubast II as having reigned during the first part of the eighth century. The equation of "Osorchô" with the classical hero Heracles is interesting, as it revives a number of such equations in Manetho's treatment of the Eighteenth and Nineteenth Dynasties.[13]

As well as these "historical" references to Libyan kings, there are also preserved in first/second century AD Demotic papyri fabulous stories from a cycle that are clearly grounded in events and personalities from the time of Assyrian invasions of Egypt.[14] There is a King Padubast of Tanis (probably based on Padubast III), and characters named Padieset, Bakennefi, and Padikhonsu, all known from that period, alongside one of the key heroes, Inaros, son of Bakennefi of Athribis (presumably modeled on Bakennefi C). Even Taharqa is mentioned in one tale. The geography of the events is also in keeping with that present in Egypt during the late eighth/early seventh centuries. As such, the stories represent an interesting survival of all-but-forgotten persons in a literary context.

7 Resurrection

Rediscovering the House of Shoshenq

The end of paganism in Egypt, and the concomitant demise of the hieroglyphic script, at the end of the fourth century AD removed any possibility of engagement with ancient monuments on their own terms. All attempts to access and interpret the ancient Egyptians over the next millennium and a half would perforce be through the lenses of Classical and biblical data.

In 1822, the first workable scheme for the decipherment of hieroglyphs was published by Jean-François Champollion* (1790–1832), allowing historians access once again to original ancient Egyptian documents. However, this work initially only allowed the transliteration of names and the accurate translation of a limited number of words and phrases. It would not be until the 1850s that complete texts of significant length could be read with confidence. As a result, the initial outputs from the first generation of Egyptologists had to lean heavily on the "pre-decipherment" sources, in particular Manetho and the Old Testament in the case of the Libyan kings. These were regarded at that time as authoritative sources, and much of early history-writing for ancient Egypt comprised attempts to slot the newly available hieroglyphic material into the picture created by the time-hallowed Classical and biblical sources.

Champollion immediately recognized that Manetho's "Sesônchis/Sesônchôsis" and "Osorthôn" were equivalents of the hieroglyphic names Shoshenq and Osorkon, and that the biblical "Shishak" was also a Shoshenq.[1] Soon afterward, in 1826, he spotted that "Takelôthis" had to be a rendering of the hieroglyphic Takelot.[2] However, when linking the Manethonic names with specific titularies, while he was correct in making "Sesônchis/ Sesônchôsis" our Shoshenq I,[3] he equated "Osorthôn" with Osorkon II, and "Takelôthis" with Takelot II.[4] When at Karnak in November 1828, Champollion believed he was able to confirm his equation of "Shishak" with Shoshenq I by identifying a name ring on the latter's triumphal relief as reading "King of Judah."[5] It would not be until 1887 that Max Müller* (1862–1919) would point out that Champollion had erred in this,[6] and not until the 1980s that anyone would doubt that "Shishak" was indeed Shoshenq I—or even a Shoshenq at all (see pages 179–80). Champollion and his team also made the first copies of the nearby Chronicle of Prince Osorkon texts and accompanying tableaux, as well as the first element of the Karnak Priestly Annals to be recorded (fig. 123).

In the meantime, Gardner Wilkinson* (1797–1875), resident in Luxor since 1821, had been gathering evidence and making his own assessments. Among the fruits of his fieldwork was the copying of an inscription "at the doorway" of a now lost tomb (TTA18—fig. 17).[7] This linked a nomen cartouche now known to be that of Pasebkhanut II with a damaged prenomen, which Wilkinson interpreted as "Hedj⌈heqa⌉[. . .]re," but may more likely have been originally "Hedjkheperre," the prenomen of Shoshenq I (page 23).

Wilkinson agreed with Champollion in the identification of Manetho's "Sesônchis/Sesônchôsis" with Shoshenq I, but correctly saw "Osorthôn" as Osorkon I. He thus shifted Osorkon II to after "Takelôthis" (still seeing the latter as Takelot II), and then adding Shoshenq III at the end of his sequence.[8] He was, however, agnostic over whether "Shishak" should be seen as Shoshenq I or Shoshenq III. Ippolito Rosellini* (1800–43) also recognized the existence of Shoshenq III, but his succession ran Shoshenq I—Osorkon II—Shoshenq III—Takelot II—Osorkon I.[9] It would turn out to be Wilkinson's basic succession that would stand the test of time although, like everyone else, he assumed that Mathetho's "Takelôthis" was Takelot II. The existence of the shadowy Takelot I would not be revealed until the 1850s (see below).

By 1837, Wilkinson was in agreement with his colleagues that "Shishak" was indeed Shoshenq I, and had placed his accession in 981 BC.[10] Regarding the name ring identified by Champollion as "Judah," Wilkinson noted that while it was "a name whose component letters agree with the hieroglyphics, . . . the place it holds is not sufficiently marked to satisfy the scruples of a rigid sceptic."[11] He classified Shoshenq I, Osorkon I, and Takelot II as comprising the Twenty-second Dynasty, followed by Osorkon II and Shoshenq III as the first rulers of the Twenty-third. They were succeeded by "probably, one or more kings, occupying a space of about 50 years."[12] Wilkinson's succession accordingly corresponded with the core ordering of kings as understood today.

On the other hand, in 1838, Conrad Leemans* (1809–93), delving further into the material, added the High Priest Shoshenq Q into the pharaonic succession, creating a complication that would endure down to the end of the twentieth century.[13] While Shoshenq Q was recognized as being the son of an Osorkon, the name of his

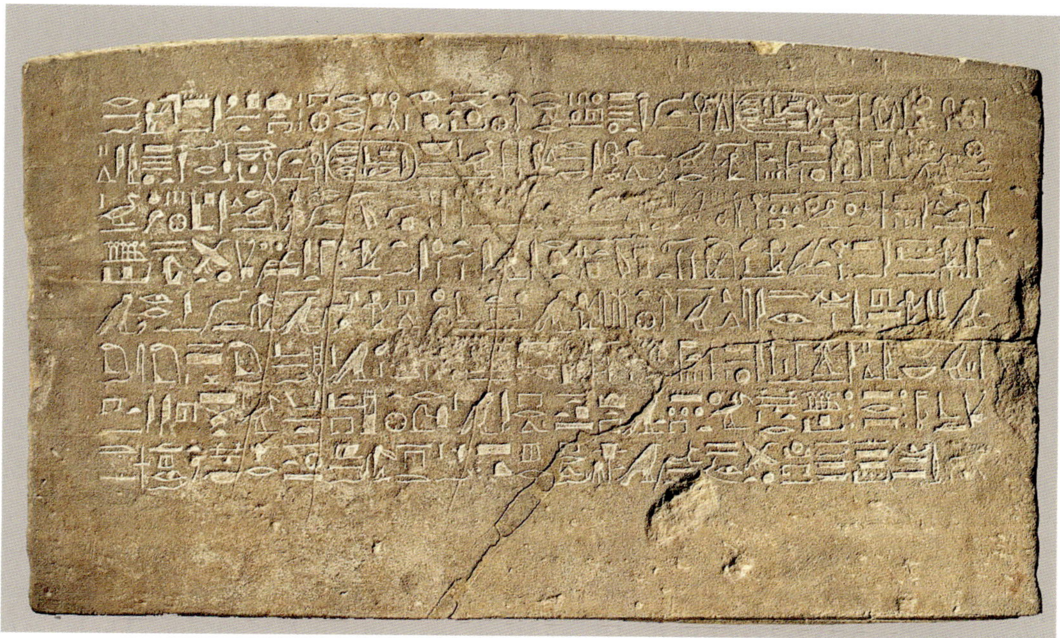

FIGURE 123 Slab with section of the Karnak Priestly Annals; from Festival Hall at Karnak (Louvre E3336=C258).

grandfather, Pasebkhanut II, was misread as being that of his mother. Leemans' succession ran Shoshenq I—an Osorkon—Shoshenq III—Osorkon II—Shoshenq Q—Takelot II—Osorkon I—Takelot III—Osorkon the Elder.

The next attempt at understanding the royal succession was made by Richard Lepsius* (1810–84) during the early 1840s, while leading the Prussian expedition to Egypt. His first study produced the succession Shoshenq I—Osorkon II[14]—Pasebkhanut II—Osorkon II[15]—Shoshenq Q[16]—Takelot II—Osorkon I—Shoshenq III—Takelot II for the Twenty-second Dynasty, and Padubast IV—Osorkon the Elder—Pashermut for the Twenty-third.[17] His latter dynasty thus mixed kings actually belonging to the sixth, tenth, and fourth (Padubast IV) centuries—an early illustration of the difficulty of doing anything meaningful with that element of the Manethonic chronicle.

However, as far as the Twenty-second Dynasty was concerned, things were clarified following the discovery by Auguste Mariette* (1821–81) of the Lesser Vaults of the Serapeum at Saqqara in February 1852. These contained a series of stelae dating from the second half of the dynasty, a number of which provided data on the royal succession of that time. Perhaps most importantly, the stela of Pasenhor (fig. 75) not only revealed the existence of Takelot I, but traced Pasenhor's ancestry back through the earlier kings of the dynasty to the Chiefs of the Ma.

Unfortunately, owing to the corruption of the text at a crucial point, the first publication, by Mariette himself,[18] read the stela as showing the Chieftains as the direct ancestors of just Pamiu I, rather than the whole Twenty-second Dynasty line. This therefore left the then-current chronology and genealogy of the dynasty untouched, with Pasebkhanut II as the third king of the dynasty. However, Lepsius soon argued for an emendation that did indeed make them the ancestors of Shoshenq I, and in 1856 produced a new sequence based on the Serapeum data.[19] Running Shoshenq I—Osorkon I—Takelot II—Osorkon II—Shoshenq Q—Takelot III—Shoshenq III—Pamiu I—Shoshenq V, this represented a real step forward in making sense of the period down to Shoshenq V. Nevertheless, it still had problems, particularly with the identification of the Takelots, and the inclusion of Shoshenq Q as a king "Shoshenq II." The latter issue was perhaps most pernicious, as the prenomen attributed to the alleged king, (Seshesh/Sekhemkheperre-meryamun), seems to have been a variant/misreading of that of Osorkon I, and never found with any Shoshenq nomen.

This "Shoshenq II" was enshrined in Lepsius' *Königsbuch*,[20] for many years the standard reference book for the names of the kings of Egypt and, as a result, this "zombie pharaoh" continued to stalk histories of Egypt into the twentieth century. Despite being dismissed with comments such as "[t]here is a universal silence of the monuments about his time,"[21] it was not until 1914 that his nonexistence was finally pointed out by Henri Gauthier* (1877–1950).[22] Yet a "Shoshenq II," now of unknown prenomen, continued to feature in histories, generally as an alias of Shoshenq Q. Then, in 1939, the discovery of the previously unknown Heqakheperre Shoshenq (pages 175–77) provided a new candidate for being "Shoshenq II"; the further history of this royal designation is picked up below.

Lepsius also attempted to make progress with the Twenty-first Dynasty, recognizing the correct position of Pasebkhanut II as a scion of that line and a key genealogical link between the two dynasties. Numerous issues were, nevertheless, outstanding, and would not come close to resolution until the discovery of TT320 (page 28) in 1881 brought much additional material to light.

In 1850, Samuel Birch* (1813–85) had apparently been the first to comment on the non-Egyptian nature of the royal names of the Twenty-second Dynasty, and also some of the names of the sons of Herihor.[23] He argued that they should be analyzed as of Aramaic and Assyrian origin, pointing in particular to the possible equivalence of the name Nimlot with the biblical "Nimrod," and Osorkon with "Sargon." He explained the appearance of such names by intermarriage between the Egyptian and Assyrian royal houses. The idea was embraced by Mariette,[24] but played down by Lepsius, although acknowledging that the names were of foreign origin. Her further agreed that they were probably Asiatic, but saw them as simply indicating that the dynasty sprung from a family that had immigrated into Egypt and was now settled there, but persisted in using ancestral names for their children.[25]

The idea that the Twenty-second Dynasty were Assyrians became a popular one, and Heinrich Brugsch* (1827–94) built on it, in his second work on the history of Egypt, published in German in 1877 and English in 1879, to propose a full-scale invasion at the time of Panedjem I.[26] He translated the title "Great Chief of the Ma," as borne by Nimlot A, Shoshenq A and B in the latter's Abydos stela, as "Great King of Assyria," with Nimlot leading the alleged invasion. Brugsch suggested that this invasion might nominally have been in support of the deposed house of Rameses, since he saw Mehytenweskhet A as a likely daughter of Rameses XI. He wove into his scenario the disorders recounted in both the Abydos stela and the Banishment Stela of Menkheperre (page 18). The former stela was used to argue that, Nimlot having died in Egypt, his tomb had become neglected, and that the measures mentioned in the stela were carried out by Shoshenq A, King of Assyria, on a visit to Egypt (not by Shoshenq B, the future Shoshenq I). With Nimlot dead, Shoshenq B became king in Egypt, ruling from Bubastis, with Pasebkhanut I as "under-king" in Tanis and Menkheperre continuing as High Priest in Thebes.

Gaston Maspero* (1846–1916) was highly critical of Brugsch's interpretation of the data in an 1880 review of his book.[27] He pointed out that "Ma" (not "Mat," as read by Brugsch), was actually an abbreviation of "Mashwesh," as had already been noted by Emmanuel de Rougé* (1811–72) from a study of stelae from the Serapeum,[28] and this was already being viewed as being the name of a Libyan tribe. In addition, there was no place in the Assyrian king lists for the alleged "Assyrian" monarchs, Shoshenq A and Nimlot A.

In 1883, Ludwig Stern* (1846–1911) demonstrated to the satisfaction of most that the Twenty-second Dynasty line was indeed of Libyan ancestry, but it was not until 1921 that a final study by Max Müller* (1862–1919)[29] finally demonstrated Berber linguistic affiliations to the satisfaction of the broad Egyptological community. In the interim, a number of scholars had continued to prefer Asiatic origins, Brugsch now making the "Mā" a "new race of ruler" located on "the east of Mesopotamia" (rather than Assyrians), but with his basic narrative unchanged.[30] In 1891, Peter Le Page Renouf* (1822–97) rejected Stern's argument that *tḥn*, used to designate Buyawawa on the Pasenhor stela, denoted that he was a Libyan. Rather, Renouf asserted that it was simply the Egyptian word "shining" or "splendid," and preferred an origin for the Twenty-second Dynasty in the area of Susa, in western Persia.[31] Eugène Revillout* (1843–1913) called Shoshenq I a "Chaldean satrap" in a work published in 1903,[32] while Flinders Petrie* (1853–1942), writing in 1905, not only supported Renouf's position, but also preferred Mariette's "split" reading of the Pasenhor genealogy, making the descent from Buyawawa irrelevant to the origins of the kings down to Osorkon II. For him, "we must look to some Babylonian or Persian adventurer in the service of the Tanite kings for the source of the [Twenty-second] dynasty."[33]

Scholars who unequivocally embraced the Libyan identity of the Twenty-second Dynasty kings included Édouard Naville* (1844–1926), in his 1891 publication of his fieldwork at the temple at Bubastis, which contained much material of Osorkon I and II (see further, page 171).[34] James H. Breasted* (1865–1935) also accepted the view in his highly influential *History of Egypt*, published in 1905.[35] In doing so, Breasted declared them, however, completely Egyptianized, a view that would not be widely challenged until the 1980s. In exploring the second part of the period, Breasted used Manetho's characterization of the Twenty-third Dynasty as "Tanite" to place Padubast I and the other actors of the period in the Delta, which would remain orthodoxy until the 1990s.

It seems likely that the tomb of Shoshenq I was found by plunderers around the beginning of the 1890s, as his canopic chest was purchased by Julius Isaac and presented to the Ägyptisches Museum in Berlin in 1891. The available historical data for the period was expanded during the latter part of the decade by the excavations of Georges Legrain* (1865–1917) at Karnak.

First, in March 1896, the area of the podium on the former riverfront of the Karnak complex was cleared, uncovering the Nile-level texts there (fig. 39). Legrain published them the same year, with some initial historical conclusions.[36] English translations and further conclusions were published by Breasted in his *Ancient Records of Egypt* in 1906.[37] Legrain's work during the 1898/99 season in the area of the former Middle Kingdom temple had brought to light forty-five fragments of the Priestly Annals.[38] Two more fragments from this corpus were acquired at an unknown date by the Fitzwilliam Museum, Cambridge (fig. 49), but may have been "strays" from Legrain's work.

The year 1905 saw the publication not only of Breasted's aforementioned *History of Egypt*, but also the third volume of the similarly titled work by Petrie. Both scholars agreed in seeing the known kings of the tenth through eighth centuries as essentially running in a single succession although, as noted above, they differed over their background (Breasted: Libyan; Petrie: Asiatic). As for the kings involved, both presented a succession that ran initially Shoshenq I—Osorkon I—Takelot I—Osorkon II. Two co-regents were then attributed to the latter, beginning with Shoshenq Q ("Shoshenq II"), and followed by seven years with Takelot II ruling alongside Osorkon.

Breasted and Petrie followed Osorkon II by a succession that ran Takelot II—Shoshenq III—Pamiu I—Shoshenq V—a Padubast (I [Breasted]/III [Petrie])—an Osorkon (III [Breasted]/the Elder [Petrie]). Their principal areas of difference here were based on the (even now still problematic!) question of the identities of the various Padubasts, and ongoing failures in distinguishing among Osorkon the Elder, I, II, and III, and Takelot II and III. These latter issues led to a long-standing belief in a co-regency between Osorkon II/Takelot II (actually Osorkon III/Takelot III). Breasted also placed the High Priest

Iuwlot (pages 42, 50) in the eighth century, as a son of his third-placed Osorkon, rather than a century earlier, under Osorkon I. Nevertheless, the basic succession set out by Breasted and Petrie down to Shoshenq V would remain the basis for most histories produced until the end of the 1980s.

Breasted and Petrie both saw the Twenty-second and Twenty-third Dynasties as essentially a continuum, but in 1913 Georges Daressy* (1864–1938) published a paper that took a very different view of the structure of the period.[39] This posited a split in royal authority fifteen years into the reign of Osorkon I, with Takelot I now heading a Theban line, which he continued as running Horsieset I—Padubast II—Shoshenq VI—Takelot II—Osorkon III—Takelot III—Rudamun. Daressy then placed Osorkon II as Osorkon I's direct successor, followed by a king whom he created from the version of the titulary of Shoshenq III that employed the epithet "setepenamun" in the prenomen (hereafter "Shoshenq IIIA"). Daressy's subsequent succession ran Iuput I—Shoshenq III (setepenre: "Shoshenq IIIR")—Pamiu I—Shoshenq V. While not willing to endorse the whole of Daressy's package, Petrie felt in 1914 able to accept a split in the kingship on the accession of Shoshenq III. He saw the second line as headed by Horsieset I, followed by a Padubast, a Takelot, and an Osorkon, and then Manetho's Psammus and Zêt.[40]

This basic structure, involving a split between Tanite and Theban kings somewhere during the ninth century, was employed in the presentation by Henry Hall* (1873–1930) in the first edition of the *Cambridge Ancient History* in 1925.[41] Content to call Shoshenq I and his descendants Libyans, Hall recognized the confusion over the identification of the Osorkons and Takelots, and successfully distinguished between the ninth- and eighth-century holders of the names, thus demonstrating that the Osorkon/Takelot co-regency attested by the Karnak Nile-level text was between Osorkon III and Takelot III, not Osorkon II and Takelot II. Hall also expressed doubts about the kingly status of Shoshenq Q. He preferred to bestow the ordinal of "II" on Shoshenq IIIA, under whom he placed the division of the kingship between the north and south, following him on the northern throne with Shoshenq IIIR, Pamiu I, and Shoshenq V.

Under this scheme, Shoshenq IIIA was the direct successor of Osorkon II, Takelot II being regarded as a Theban king, and placed third in a Theban succession that began with Horsieset I, followed by Padubast I, with Iuput I as a co-regent. Takelot II, Osorkon III ("probably" equated with Osorkon B), and Takelot III then followed. With the exception of his splitting of Shoshenq III into two people, and failing to recognize Takelot II and Padubast I as antagonists—Hall sees Osorkon B's enemy as "the Chief of Heracleopolis, or the king Sheshonk [IIIR], or both, perhaps in alliance with a rebellious noble family, or combination of noble families, in Thebes itself"—this comes close to most reconstructions published since 1989.

FIGURE 124 The Egypt Exploration Fund's excavations at Bubastis. Édouard Naville is the figure in the center of the upper image, wearing a pith helmet; to his right reclines William MacGregor* (1848–1937).

However, it soon became clear that Shoshenq IIIA and IIIR were the same person, something that had already been favored by Gauthier within a year of Daressy's paper,[42] and was finally confirmed in 1940, with the discovery of the tomb of Shoshenq III (see just below). As a result, Takelot II was returned to the Tanite main line, in part through a need to maintain overall chronologies. This idea was seemingly confirmed by the discovery in 1939 of a tomb-chamber at Tanis that seemed to be that of Takelot II (see also below), although it was actually of the first king of the name.

Excavating the Cities of the Libyan Pharaohs

The tomb of Horsieset I was found at Medinet Habu by a team from the Oriental Institute, University of Chicago, toward the end of 1927, further enhancing the material known from the area relating to the Libyan kings. However, elsewhere in Egypt, standing monuments of the tenth through seventh centuries are rare. The principal sites with significant temple remains from the period, Tanis, Bubastis, and El-Hiba, were all noted by early investigators. The first two were seen by the expedition of Napoleon Bonaparte in 1798, and El-Hiba by Joseph Bonomi* (1796–1878) in June 1831, the site being mapped by Wilkinson, who also made notes at Bubastis. The latter site was subject to large-scale clearance and recording by Naville, working for the Egypt Exploration Fund (EEF), during 1887–89 (fig. 124).

Auguste Mariette worked at Tanis during 1859–61, before Flinders Petrie carried out excavations for the EEF during the first part of 1884 (fig. 125). Shoshenq I's temple at El-Hiba was first investigated by Ahmed Kamal* (1851–1923) and Georges Daressy in 1902, and then fully cleared by Hermann Ranke* (1878–1953) in 1913.[43] It was in 1929 that a long-term excavation project was launched at Tanis by Pierre Montet* (1885–1966). A successor project continues to work at the site today, with important outcomes (cf. fig. 108), but it was during 1939–40 that Montet made the most spectacular finds relating to the kings of the Third Intermediate Period.

The discovery of the royal tombs at Tanis

Since 1934, Montet's team (fig. 126) had been working among mud-brick structures, including sculptors' workshops, along the inside of the southern enclosure wall of the Amun temple at Tanis (cf. fig. 7). In February 1939, while many more sculptural pieces were being recovered, a robbers' hole was found cutting through the brick down to a limestone surface. A wider clearance was initiated to reveal this surface, also bringing to light three canopic jars and a number of shabtis, one in the name of Shoshenq-meryamun-sibast.

On the morning of 27 February 1939, a missing slab was noted at the point where the robbers' hole met the pavement. At 14:00 that afternoon, Montet dropped through the gap into what proved to be Room 2 (see fig. 94) of tomb NRT-I, where he was able to

FIGURE 125 Top: Tanis after a storm that took place during Flinders Petrie's work there in February 1884. Bottom: blocks from the gate of Shoshenq III (fig. 64). The fact that the inscribed block came from a cut-up statue is clearly apparent..

FIGURE 126 The team that excavated the royal necropolis at Tanis. Left to right: Georges Goyon* (1905–96); Jean-Louis Fougerousse (1879–1953); Paul Bucher* (1887–1966); Pierre Montet.

read the names of Osorkon II. From here, Montet passed into Room 1N, noting the large granite sarcophagus and the thin wall that separated it from Room 1S, and a doorway in the east wall, obstructed by rubble and blocks of limestone (fig. 127).

The room beyond this blocking (3) was accessed two days later by removing its roofing slabs, and found to be largely full of mud, from which were extracted canopic jars and a calcite vase, before revealing the sarcophagus and shabti figures, of a King Takelot. Going back to Room 1N, Montet observed an opening in the west wall, sealed by a large block of granite. Gaps around the block allowed glimpses of a granite room, filled by a giant granite sarcophagus, on the cover of which could be seen the lids of canopic jars. Since there was no space to draw the granite block into Room 1, excavations were made around the exterior of the granite room, revealing a robbers' hole toward the western end of its south wall. Removing the mud that filled much of the chamber revealed a further sarcophagus, which turned out to be that of Prince Hornakhte.

FIGURE 127 The blocked doorway of chamber 3 of NRT-I, seen from inside that room.

FIGURE 128 The antechamber of NRT-III as revealed in 1939, with the coffin of Shoshenq IIa on the right, and the west wall of the antechamber in the background, which concealed the burial chambers of Pasebkhanut I and Mutnedjmet/Amenemopet. The silver coffinettes of Shoshenq were found in four of the jars to the left.

Montet's team then worked northward from the place where they had entered NRT-I until they came across what proved to be the entrance shaft of NRT-III. Covered with three slabs, it was filled with debris and concealed an intact blocking at the bottom. Removing this revealed a rectangular chamber, decorated in the name of Pasebkhanut I (fig. 128).

> The floor of the main chamber was raised in the northern part to accommodate a large electrum sarcophagus and two mummies. The sarcophagus had the shape of a mummy's sheath but with a remarkably executed falcon's head at the neck .... This beautiful work was executed for a Pharaoh whose names did not appear so far in the Book of Kings: Heqa-Kheper-rê sotep-en-rê, the beloved of Amon Chechanq. The coronation name differs only by a single sign, , instead of , from that of Chechanq I, but this difference prevents us from identifying these two kings and we must admit the existence of a new Chechanq, whose rank in the XXII dynasty remains to be fixed.
>
> The lid was simply placed on the trough. This contained the royal skeleton, entirely enclosed in a cartonnage envelope with gold appliqués which reproduced in every detail the decoration of the lid.[44]

This spectacular find resulted in the Egyptian Antiquities Service sending a team to Tanis as soon as possible, consisting of Guy Brunton* (1878–1948) and Mahmud Hamza* (1890–1976), of the Egyptian Museum in Cairo, and the conservator Alfred Lucas* (1867–1945). As reported by Brunton,

> [o]wing to the extremely decayed state of the mummy, its coffins and wrappings, which required the greatest possible care in their examination and removal, M. Montet felt that his expedition was not adequately equipped to deal with such an unexpected and difficult task. We accordingly reported to this effect to the Director General, with the result that I was ordered to superintend the necessary operations. Mr. Lucas, with his great experience in the treatment of delicate antiquities from the tomb of Tut-ankh-amen, most generously lent his invaluable help. We started work on April 3rd; Lucas stayed till the 6th; and on the 9th I returned to Cairo with the silver coffin, and other antiquities. M. Montet had taken the greater part of the jewellery to Cairo when he left on the 6th.
>
> Work in the tomb was difficult; the space was confined, the light was poor, the air very damp. The humidity in which the burial had been for so long lying had entirely rotted the organic remains, so that there were no tissues left on the

FIGURE 129 The interior of the coffin of Shoshenq IIa, showing the utter decay of organic materials, leaving the bones of the king layered with gold foil from the cartonnage (fig. 92a) and jewelry that had been placed within the wrappings.

mummy, scarcely a vestige of linen, and the wood had been mostly reduced to brown powder; the greater part of it was under the bones and round the head. The thick paint on the cartonnage had turned black or nearly so; the blue frit inlay of the jewellery had retained its colour but had disintegrated and much of it had fallen out; and the blue faïence amulets and beads had become a dirty grey.

Before we arrived M. Montet had lifted off the lid of the silver coffin, taken some photographs, and removed the gold foil of the hawk's head which formed part of the cartonnage. Our first view of the remains gave us little hope of removing intact any of the cartonnage or bead network, which underlay it. All had fallen to pieces and dropped to lower levels except where the bones of the skeleton had served as a support. Round the waist had been placed a belt of electrum; this retained its form and stood high in the centre of the coffin with the gold foil of the cartonnage lying far beneath it on either side. As the cartonnage consisted almost entirely of the gold foil, with very little left of its underlying stucco and linen body, and was so broken up and displaced, there was nothing to be done but to remove it piecemeal in the largest fragments possible. But every effort was made to save the vertical band of bead tapestry which ran down the centre of the network, and which could be seen here and there in the *débris*. At first a strong solution of celluloid was tried. But this could not penetrate under the gold foil, and eventually the usual hot paraffin wax was employed. This had the unwelcome result of consolidating under-layers which were not yet visible, so that

> all had to be lifted out together. However it was found that the head band had mostly fallen between the bones, and no method whatever could have recovered more than a few sections of it.
>
> After the removal of the cartonnage, the bead network, and the few remaining traces of the wooden coffin-lid, the jewellery on the chest, neck, and arms, was laid bare and removed without difficulty. Next came the bones. There then remained a thick layer of wood dust, under which was more bead network, and the underside of the cartonnage in contact with the body of the silver coffin. As this latter was badly broken, and as the cartonnage was obviously undisturbed, it was decided to strengthen the whole and transport it as it was to Cairo, where the various layers could be dissected at leisure and in a good light. M. Goyon covered the surfaces with newspaper and flooded the whole with a thick layer of plaster. This treatment was most effectual; nothing was disturbed in the transit by motor-lorry; and the lower layer of cartonnage was eventually successfully removed by Zakki Eff. Iskander[* (1916–79)], chemist at the Museum. The whole of the cartonnage has now been skilfully reconstructed and mounted on a plaster model coffin by Iskander Eff. after over three months work and is very nearly complete. Mr. Alan Rowe[* (1890–1968)] has greatly helped by his study of the inscriptions, and Ahmed Eff. Yusef has drawn in the missing hieroglyphs and decorations.[45]

The outbreak of the Second World War in September 1939 meant that the next season did not begin until January 1940. The most important work was the opening of the burial chambers of NRT-III, with the intact burials of the Twenty-first Dynasty kings Pasebkhanut I and Amenemopet. However, the burial chamber of NRT-I was properly investigated, and Shoshenq III's NRT-V found and cleared. The team left in May 1940, having transferred some material to the Egyptian Museum and secured the tombs. However, in 1943, the Tanis excavation house and its storerooms were looted, and NRT-I broken into, with some damage to the decoration. As a result, all canopic jars from NRT-I (except those of Hornakhte, which had gone to Cairo), many shabtis, and other material were stolen, and most remain lost. Around the same time, a safe in the basement of the Egyptian Museum was forced open, and a number of small items stolen.

Work was resumed in April 1945, when the copying of the decoration of NRT-I was begun. The sarcophagus of Pasebkhanut I was also extracted from NRT-III for transport to Cairo. Copying continued the following season, when Hornakhte's sarcophagus was taken out of NRT-I, and the intact burial of the Twenty-first Dynasty General Wendjebaendjed found in a hidden chamber of NRT-III. The full documentation of NRT-V was completed during 1951, 1955, and 1956.

FIGURE 130 Excavations at Tanis in March 1940, showing the exposed roofs of the royal tombs.

Another intact royal burial had been found in March 1942, when Ahmad Badawi* (1905–80) found the tomb of High Priest Prince Shoshenq D at Memphis, along with the sepulchers of some of his descendants (pages 151–53). Only summary reports were published at the time, and it was not until 2023 that the tomb of Shoshenq and its contents were fully published.[46]

In parallel with finishing off work in the royal necropolis, Montet's team began the excavation of the northeast corner of Tanis's Sacred Lake (see map, fig. 6) in 1948. The lake's construction had involved the large-scale reuse of earlier blocks,[47] which ranged in date from the time of Rameses II to that of Psamtik I, and material found at this time included the remains of buildings of Tanite kings of the eighth/early seventh centuries (figs. 74 top right, 80c–d, 84 top). More blocks continued to be found into the twenty-first century, including examples that revealed the long-sought prenomen of Osorkon IV (fig. 80a–b).[48]

Histories

The 1950s saw the full publication of the Bubastite Portal at Karnak by the University of Chicago's Epigraphic Survey.[49] Its Chronicle of Prince Osorkon was then studied and published by Ricardo Caminos* (1915–92),[50] who also published Shoshenq I's Silsila stela.[51] However, in spite of this, a number of other detail studies, and the excitement around the discoveries at Tanis, Sir Alan Gardiner* (1879–1963) felt in 1961 that the problems of the Third Intermediate Period remained "most baffling, nor can they be tackled with much profit until the scattered and fragmentary inscriptions have been collected anew, accurately copied, and properly edited; and even then it is extremely doubtful whether a coherent account will emerge."[52] However, while his desideratum of a collected edition of the era's texts would not emerge until the twenty-first century,[53] the 1960s saw important work that would transform the study of the era.

A large-scale analysis was begun early in the decade by Kenneth Kitchen (1932–2025), although it would not be completed until 1972, its title popularizing the title "Third Intermediate Period" for the Twenty-first through Twenty-fifth Dynasties. Around the same time, a significant paper was also published on the history and chronology of the period by Klaus Baer* (1930–87).[54] These works incorporated the results of more important detail studies, by Jean Yoyotte* (1927–2009) on the local rulers of the Delta of the ninth–seventh centuries BC,[55] and by Eric Young, which established the reality of Manetho's Twenty-first Dynasty King Osochor.[56] While it seemed likely that he was an Osorkon, and thus the first king with a Libyan name to rule Egypt, this was not verified for another decade and a half. Then Yoyotte employed a much later genealogical text (fig. 14) to finally bring Osorkon the Elder out of the shadows,[57] although distinguishing his monuments from those of Osorkon IV remained a problem into the twenty-first century.[58]

Kitchen's tome[59] comprised a systematic analysis of the material available for the Twenty-first through Twenty-fifth Dynasties, and concluded with a detailed preferred historical outline, whose comprehensive nature led to it being rapidly regarded as the standard work on the period. However, it contained areas where the author differed from other specialists, particularly regarding his identification of Padubast I, Iuput I and II, Shoshenq VI, Osorkon III, Takelot III, and Rudamun all as members of a single line ruling from Leontopolis, rather than some of them being Theban monarchs, as argued by Baer[60] and many earlier scholars. Both he and Kitchen nevertheless understood Takelot II as a king at Tanis. This would not be challenged until the 1980s.

Chronological Conflicts

Standing in contrast to Kitchen's new 1973 "standard theory" came two works, published in 1991 and 1995, which proposed radical changes to pre–eighth century chronology.

These had their ultimate roots in even more radical revisions proposed from the 1950s onward by Immanuel Velikovsky (1895–1979).[61] Among other things, these placed the accession of Rameses II in 609 BC and that of Rameses III in 379, made Thutmose III the biblical Shishak in the tenth century, and argued that Shoshenq I was the "Pharaoh So" of the eighth century (and the last, rather than first, of his line). Not only this, but the Twenty-first Dynasty was proclaimed a line of rulers of the Western Desert oases under the late Persians and early Ptolemies. Velikovsky was thus undertaking a wholesale reordering of events, which also placed the Twenty-second through Twenty-fifth Dynasties between the Eighteenth and Nineteenth Dynasties.

Although Velikovsky's conclusions have been universally rejected by scholarship, his idea that the generally accepted chronologies of Egypt (and the broader ancient world) might not be wholly correct inspired the production of less dramatic, but still radical, proposals for lowering dates prior to the seventh century BC. Two particular options, pivoting on a rejection of the traditional identification of Shishak with Shoshenq I, have been put forward. They differ in that one proposes substituting Rameses II,[62] and the other Rameses III,[63] as the prototype for Shishak.

They nevertheless maintain the date for Shishak's campaign as between 932 and 921 BC, on the basis of Assyrian synchronisms (see page 38). This accordingly requires lowering the date of the accession of Rameses II by three centuries, or that of Rameses III by two and a half. Since everything after the beginning of the Twenty-fifth Dynasty is left untouched in both variants, these two/three centuries of time are "soaked up" by overlapping the Twenty-first Dynasty with the late Twentieth Dynasty and the first part of the Twenty-second, and also overlapping/shortening some reigns within the Twentieth through Twenty-fourth Dynasties. One thread in doing this has been to equate the Osorkon who was a contemporary of Pi(ankh)y with Osorkon III, rather than Osorkon IV.[64]

Not unsurprisingly, the reaction to these proposals was distinctly negative,[65] including unpleasant ad hominem remarks by certain scholars.[66] In contrast, while many simply ignored the ideas, a few Egyptologists reacted by engaging with the arguments and testing the assumptions underpinning the "standard" picture. For example, the present writer argued the impossibility of the necessary overlaps of the Twenty-first and Twenty-second Dynasties on the basis of coffin types securely attached to both dynasties,[67] while at the same time proposing a lowering of the date of Rameses II's accession by fifteen years.[68] Proponents of radical revision continue to produce arguments in support of the thesis of a drastic lowering of dates, with a comprehensive discussion, built around the question of the identity of Shishak, taking place in Cambridge, UK, in 2011.[69] However, although now more welcome to publish in mainstream journals than was once the case, those marshalling arguments in favor of a significant lowering and shortening of chronologies still struggle to achieve traction in the wider worlds of Egyptology, Assyriology, and Aegean studies.

Revising the Standard Model(s)

It is not only such radical proposals that have come up against deep scrutiny. As already noted, Kitchen had insisted that Takelot II was a Tanite king, and that Padubast I, Iuput I, Shoshenq VI, Osorkon III, Takelot III, Rudamun, and Iuput II were all members of a Leontopolis-based single group of monarchs. However, by the second half of the 1980s, new doubts were being expressed by Jeffrey and Patricia Spencer over whether any of these latter kings, other than Iuput II, really belonged to the Delta, and suggested that they might indeed comprise a Theban line.[70] Then, in 1989, David Aston took the further step of not only firmly placing them at Thebes, but also taking Takelot II out of the Tanite line and placing him also at Thebes.[71] This, of course, essentially reverted to the old Daressy–Hall reconstruction, albeit buttressed by a far greater accumulation of data. This included a demonstration two years earlier that the Takelot buried in NRT-I was not Takelot II after all, but actually Takelot I. This removed the only substantive link between Takelot II and the north.[72] This new reconstruction, revisited by Aston in 2009,[73] had various implications for the interpretation of the data surviving from ninth–eighth century Thebes. Aston's proposal rapidly gained wide support, but was vigorously opposed by Kitchen.[74] It should be noted, however, that a significant range of opinions continue to exist on a wide range of issues, in particular detailed chronology, and also how useful (or not) Manetho's lists and numbered dynasties might be in elucidating the problems of the royal succession(s) of the tenth through seventh centuries.

A revision to the core royal succession came in 1993, when it was demonstrated that the second king buried in NRT-V was not, as had been assumed by Montet, Shoshenq I as a reburial, but a hitherto unrecognized and wholly separate Shoshenq IV, who shared the earlier king's prenomen, but whose nomen contained epithets of the kind introduced only under Osorkon II.[75] He then took his place between Shoshenq III's Year 39 (his last attested) and the accession of Pamiu I, shown by Serapeum data to have occurred fourteen years later (pages 82–83). This fitted well with the minimum of ten regnal years guaranteed by a stela of Shoshenq IV, also now reallocated from Shoshenq I.

The question of the "Libyan-ness" of the Libyan pharaohs had been a matter for discussion since these rulers' ethnic identity was first identified: whether they should be judged as "foreigners," or "Egyptians" with a foreign background. Now, as already noted, from the 1980s onward it began to be understood that the fissiparous tendencies of the ninth and eighth centuries might be explained by underlying Libyan political concepts.[76] In 1994, Karl Jansen-Winkeln, early in his series of fundamental contributions to the study of first-millennium BC history, produced a paper that argued that, although no Libyan titles appeared among them, the royal and high-priestly families of the Twenty-first Dynasty were actually Libyans, and that their careers should be seen in such a light (cf. pages 13–14, above).[77] The debate on the matter continues, with an extensive discussion of the issues published by Frédéric Payraudeau in 2014, who concluded that "Libyan-ness" may have been overemphasized, and continuity of traditions minimized, in analyzing the complex situations found during the Third Intermediate Period.[78]

In October 2007, a conference was held at Leiden University in the Netherlands to discuss the Third Intermediate Period, which was attended by all the key specialists in the era, with the papers published two years later.[79] The year 2007 also saw the publication of the first volume of the long-desired digest of inscriptions of the Third Intermediate and Late Periods.[80] The work of Jansen-Winkeln, this came two decades after his first major reference work on the period, a collection of biographical texts of the period.[81] A full range of relevant texts were thus now conveniently available to researchers, although the volumes' organization reflected the compiler's particular views as to matters of chronology and identification.

The Libyan pharaohs are accordingly now far less obscure than they had appeared to many earlier generations of Egyptologists. Nevertheless, there remain many areas of continued debate, with a number of alternative—and generally mutually exclusive—historical and chronological reconstructions in existence. New discoveries may yet resolve some of these disputes, but may also exacerbate matters, emphasizing that ancient Egyptian history remains a network of "working hypotheses," liable to adjustment at any time.

Chronology of Ancient Egypt

LE = Lower Egypt only; UE = Upper Egypt.
Only kings mentioned in this book are included.
All dates are more or less uncertain prior to 690 BC.
Parentheses around a name and date indicate a co-ruler.

Early Dynastic Period

Dynasty 1		3050–2800 BC
Dynasty 2		2800–2660

Old Kingdom

Dynasty 3		2660–2600
Dynasty 4		2600–2470
Dynasty 5		2470–2360
Dynasty 6		2360–2200
Pepy II	2270–2200	

First Intermediate Period

Dynasties 7/8		2200–2100
Dynasties 9/10 (LE)		2100–2000
Dynasty 11a (UE)		2080–2010

Middle Kingdom

Dynasty 11b		2010–1943
Dynasty 12		1943–1760
Amenemhat I	1943–1913	
Senwosret I	1923–1878	
Senwosret III	1838–1797	
Amenemhat III	1825–1777	
Amenemhat IV	1777–1769	
Dynasty 13		1765–1650

Second Intermediate Period

Dynasty 14 (LE)		1700–1650
Dynasty 15 (LE)		1650–1525
Dynasty 16 (UE)		1660–1585
Dynasty 17 (UE)		1585–1530
Kamose	1534–1530	

New Kingdom

Dynasty 18		1530–1278
Amenhotep I	1506–1486	
Thutmose I	1486–1471	
Thutmose II	1471–1468	
Thutmose III	1468–1415	
(Hatshepsut	1462–1447)	
Amenhotep II	1415–1386	
Amenhotep III	1377–1337	
Akhenaten	1337–1321	
(Neferneferuaten	1321–1318)	
Tutankhamun	1321–1312	
Horemheb	1308–1278	
Dynasty 19		1278–1176
Sethy I	1276–1265	
Rameses II	1265–1200	
Merenptah	1200–1190	
Sethy II	1190–1185	
Amenmeses	1189–1186	
Tawosret	1178–1176	

Dynasty 20		1176–1078
Rameses III	1173–1142	
Rameses IV	1142–1136	
Rameses V	1136–1132	
Rameses VI	1132–1125	
Rameses IX	1116–1098	
Rameses X	1098–1095	
Rameses XI	1110–1078	

Third Intermediate Period

Dynasty 21		1078–941
Herihor (UE)	1078–1065	
Nesibanebjedet I (LE)	1078–1053	
Amenemnesut (UE?)	1065–1049	
Panedjem I (UE)	1063–1041	
Pasebkhanut I	1049–999	
Amenemopet	1001–992	
Osorkon the Elder	992–985	
Siamun	985–967	
Pasebkhanut II	967–941	

Dynasty 22		
Shoshenq I	943–922	
Osorkon I	922–888	
Takelot I	888–872	
(Shoshenq IIa	?)	
Osorkon II	872–831	
Shoshenq III	831–791	
Shoshenq IV	791–779	
Pamiu I	779–773	
Shoshenq V	773–736	
Osorkon IV	736–716+	
Pamiu II		
Gemenefkhonsubak		
Padubast III	–666	

(Thebes)		850–755
Horsieset I	–840?	
Takelot II	834–810	
Padubast I	824–800	
Shoshenq VI	800–794	
Osorkon III	791–762	
Takelot III	768–755	
(Herakleopolis)		
Peftjauawybast	fl. 730	
(Hermopolis)		
Nimlot	fl. 730	
Thutemhat		
(South Delta)		
Iuput I		
Padubast II		
Iuput II	fl. 730	
Dynasty 24 (LE)		728–712
Tefnakhte	728–718	
Bakenrenef	718–712	
Dynasty 25		755–656
Kashta	755–750	
Pi(ankh)y	750–713	
Shabataka	713–705	
Shabaka	705–690	
Taharqa	690–664	
Tanutamun	664–656+	

Saite Period

Dynasty 26		672–525
Nekau I (LE)	672–664	
Psamtik I	664–610	
Wahibre	589–570	
Ahmose II	570–526	
Psamtik III	526–525	

Late Period

Dynasty 27 (Persians)		525–404
Dynasty 28		404–398
Dynasty 29		398–379
Dynasty 30		379–340
Dynasty 31 (Persians)		340–332

Hellenistic Period

Dynasty of Macedonia		332–310
Dynasty of Ptolemy		310–30
Ptolemy I	310–282	
Ptolemy II	284–246	

Roman Period

30 BC–AD 395

Notes

Notes to Preface

1 Ritner 2009a.

Notes to Abbreviations and Conventions

1 Broekman, Demarée, and Kaper 2008.

Notes to Introduction

1 For overviews of the nature of the area, its populations, and interactions with Egypt down to the end of the New Kingdom, see Bates 1914; Kitchen 1990; O'Connor 1990; Snape 2003; Hulin 2020; the following narrative is based on these sources.

2 Manassa 2003.

3 Manassa 2003: 25–27.

4 On the wars of Rameses III, see Dodson 2019a: 31–46.

5 For an overview, see Cline 2021.

6 pTurin 2071+1960 (Kitchen 1968–90: VI, 633–44).

Notes to Chapter 1

1 Dodson 2019a: 54–55, 74–81.

2 See Dodson 2019b: 3–7.

3 Dodson 2019b: 9–13.

4 For a detailed discussion of events, see Dodson 2019b: 14–24; this reconstruction is rather different from the "traditional" scenario enshrined in Kitchen 1996.

5 Cf. Dodson 2019b: 20.

6 It was later held by Nesikhonsu A, wife of the later High Priest Panedjem II, but clearly only in some honorary way, perhaps to do with the ownership of certain revenues. There is also a much later example of its use by the Vizier Pamiu i during the reign of Takelot III (see p. 92).

7 The account given is based on the discussion in Dodson 2019b: 24–38; a range of other reconstructions of the period exist.

8 Uphill 1984.

9 The Report of Wenamun (pPushkin 120—Gardiner 1932: 60–76; Korostovtsev 1960; Ritner 2009a: 87–99[18]); while the extant manuscript of this work seems to be a few decades later than the events recounted, there seems to be little doubt that it is fundamentally a genuine report,

and not a complete work of fiction (for summary of debate, see Winand 2011).

10 Kitchen 1996: 250–51, followed by others, regards his kingship as wholly nominal, and restricted to the last years of Rameses XI.

11 While the world record number of children borne by a single woman is 69, this included numerous multiple births, in a total of 27 confinements.

12 For a useful overview of the question of the features of "Libyan" rule, see Broekman 2010b.

13 As first argued in Jansen-Winkeln 1994, and seconded by others.

14 E.g., Ōhshiro 2020, arguing that Pasebkhanut I possessed a silver coffin as a result of being a Libyan, whose remote descendants today prefer silver to gold.

15 Cairo CG61025 (Cooney 2024: 293–303).

16 On the problem of Amenemnesut, see Dodson 2019b: 35, 47–49, 59.

17 On III *prt* 6 of Year 15, the restoration of the mummy of Rameses II had been ordered by the High Priest Panedjem I, but on Year 16, IV *prt* 11 an order was issued by the High Priest "Masaharta son of king Panedjem" to renew the burial of Amenhotep I (Porter and Moss 1960–64: 659).

18 For Third Intermediate Period material from the area between the Fayyum and Hermopolis, see Meffre 2015.

19 This is derived from a document in which an unnamed brother of a certain Masaharta petitions the local god for his cure. Unfortunately, one cannot be certain that the High Priest of the name is involved, nor the date of the petition (pStrasbourg 21—Jansen-Winkeln 2007–23: I, 205–206; Ritner 2009a: 122–23).

20 Known only from the now lost coffin of his son [...]re: see Kitchen 1996: 424–25.

21 Louvre C.256 (Porter and Moss 1972: 294; Jansen-Winkeln 2007–23: I, 72–74[6.1]; Ritner 2009a: 124–29[28]).

22 Dodson 2019b: 56–57.

23 On the basis of a pair of bow caps inscribed jointly for Amenemnesut and Pasebkhanut I (Cairo JE85886—Montet 1951: pl. lxxii).

24 Stela Louvre IM2846 (Jansen-Winkeln 2007–23: II, 271–72[28.12]; Meffre 2015: 104–108).

25 Collected in Kruchten 1989.

26 Jansen Winkeln 2007–23: I, 111[8.1]; Ritner 2009a: 411–12[107].

27 Meffre 2015: 29–34.

28 See Bonhême 1987 for a compilation of royal names of the Third Intermediate Period.

29 A few authors did attempt an up-numbering of the previously acknowledged Osorkons, but this was soon abandoned in view of the resulting confusion.

30 Expanded on the basis of the title of his son Nimlot A; that the full version reads "Mashwesh" is guaranteed by a number of later documents (cf. p. 167).

31 It could *just about* be made to work if each generation reproduced in their early teens, and Isetemkheb A gave birth to Menkheperre in her early forties.

32 Payraudeau 2023a.

33 See Dodson 2009b; cf. Payraudeau 2008: 302–304; Jansen-Winkeln 2016: 87–91.

34 Although it is not impossible that Pasebkhanut III might have transitioned to kingship as Pasebkhanut II, with yet another Pasebkhanut (IV) following him as High Priest, accounting for the Abydos graffito and some other data.

35 Jansen-Winkeln 2007–23: I, 162[10.10–11]; Payraudeau 2008.

36 Cairo JE66285 (Jansen-Winkeln 2007–23: I, 159–62[10.7]; Ritner 2009a:

166–72[41]); although no date survives, the stela most probably dates to the reign of Pasebkhanut II.

37 For a discussion of this, and Shoshenq B's career, see Fujii 2024.

38 For a discussion and references, see Dodson 2019b: 80.

39 Association Française d'Action Artistique 1987: 136–37[19]; Aston 2009b: 51; a scarab of Siamun was also found in the chamber (Jansen-Winkeln 2007–23: I, 113[19.10]; some of the unattributed thirteen canopic jars in the room are also likely to be associated with their burials (cf. Dodson 1994: 85–86; Aston 2009b: 53–54). On the shabtis found at Tanis, see Broekman 2019.

40 Jansen-Winkeln 2007–23: II, 58[13.33]; the dedicator's prenomen, Hedjkheperre, is corruptly written with a *m3ʿt*-feather in lieu of the *ḥḏ*-sign. This has been used to argue that the Shoshenq involved is actually an otherwise unattested physical son of Pasebkhanut II (Broekman 2000), while Jansen-Winkeln (1995: 147–48) suggested that the name belonged to Shoshenq Q, grandson of Pasebkhanut II.

41 Dodson 1993a; Jansen-Winkeln 2007–23: II, 37[12.51]; Manniche 2011: 70–86.

Notes to Chapter 2

1 On the question, see Sagrillo 2009.

2 Kruchten 1989: 49–50, pl. 3, 18.

3 E.g., Kitchen 1996: 288.

4 There is no real evidence for the date of Iuput's appointment as High Priest, other than it must have been before Year 10 of Shoshenq I, in which he is named on a bandage from a mummy in TT320 (Jansen-Winkeln 2007–23: II, 30–31[12.42]). He then remained in office until at least his father's Year 21 (Jansen-Winkeln 2007–23: II, 20–22[12.27]).

5 On a block at Bubastis (Jansen-Winkeln 2007–23: II, 75[15.1]; Lange 2010) and an ostracon from Abydos (Louvre E31886—Jansen-Winkeln 2007–23: II, 75[15.2]).

6 NMS A.1967.2 (Jansen-Winkeln 2007–23: II, 26–27[12.31]).

7 On whose monuments, see Meffre 2015: 63–65, 287–88.

8 Cairo JE37966; Vienna ÄS5791; BM EA14594–5 (Jansen-Winkeln 2007–23: II, 84–85[17.13]).

9 Cairo CG42221 (Jansen-Winkeln 2007–23: II, 243–45[25.51]).

10 BM EA26811 (Jansen-Winkeln 2007–23: II, 27[12.34]).

11 Known from her mummy, cartonnage, and coffin (Louvre Abu Dhabi LAD 2014.023.001). Its provenance is unclear, but the mention of the pyramid of Pepy II in its texts suggests that the princess was buried in the Memphite necropolis, although the design of the cartonnage suggests manufacture at Thebes.

12 For detailed studies of the officials and priesthoods at Memphis and Thebes during the Twenty-second Dynasty, see respectively Jurman 2020 and Payraudeau 2014.

13 On the basis of their placement in the genealogy on Cairo statue CG42218 (Jansen-Winkeln 2007–23: III, 509–10[52.288]). Cf. Broekman 2010a: 137–38, reaffirming the dating of CG42218 prior to the Twenty-fifth Dynasty.

14 Broekman 2010a: 129.

15 There has been much debate on the chronology of the various deposits in the tomb. For a recent discussion, see Aston 2021.

16 Montet 1951: 9–18.
17 Porter and Moss 1974–81: 845; Jansen-Winkeln 2007–23: I, 70[4.134].
18 Porter and Moss 1974–81: 17–19.
19 Jansen-Winkeln 2007–23: I, 99[7.23–29].
20 JansenWinkeln 2007–23: I, 114[9.13], 150–56[9.43–54].
21 Jansen-Winkeln 2007–23: II, 1–2[12.1–7], 4[12.13–14], 410[45.1].
22 Jansen-Winkeln 2007–23: II, 2–3[8–10], 32–36[12.43–48].
23 Jansen-Winkeln 2007–23: II, 3[12.12].
24 Cairo JE39410 (Jansen-Winkeln 2007–23: II, 4–7[12.15]; Meffre 2015: 48–62).
25 Porter and Moss 1934: 124; Arnold 1999: 33; Jansen-Winkeln 2007–23: II, 7–10[12.16]; Ritner 2009a: 220–27[53]; Meffre 2015: 34–48.
26 Porter and Moss 1937: 213; Jansen-Winkeln 2007–23: II, 20–22[12.27]; Ritner 2009a: 187–93[47].
27 Jansen-Winkeln 2007–23: II, 16–19[12.21]; Ritner 2009a: 193–200[48A–C].
28 Porter and Moss 1972: 21–22; Broekman 1988; Cole 2023.
29 Jansen-Winkeln 2007–23: II, 11–16[12.20]; Ritner 2009a: 200–13[48D–E].
30 E.g., Aḥituv 1984; Kitchen 1996: 432–47, 587; Wilson 2005.
31 I Kings 14: 25–26; a longer version is given at II Chronicles 12: 2–9. Shishak is also mentioned slightly earlier, during the reign of Solomon: "Solomon sought therefore to kill Jeroboam. And Jeroboam arose, and fled into Egypt, unto Shishak king of Egypt, and was in Egypt until the death of Solomon" (I Kings 11: 40). Jeroboam went on to found the kingdom of Israel as a rival to Judah.
32 Sagrillo 2015.
33 For a full discussion, see Dodson 2023a.
34 Jerusalem I.3554 (Porter and Moss 1952: 381; Jansen-Winkeln 2007–23: II, 26[12.29]; Ritner 2009a: 218–19[51]); the stratigraphic origin of this piece is somewhat problematic, and it has been suggested that it may derive from a layer conventionally dated to the ninth century. Chapman 2009 argues that the piece (found on a spoil heap) must originally have come from Stratum VA, indicating the erection of the stela in Stratum VB, suggesting secondary or even tertiary deposition. Cf. Broekman 2011: 70–71.
35 Cairo TR 3/12/24/1=JE59635 (Jansen-Winkeln 2007–23: II 10–11[12.19]; Ritner 2009a: 215–18[50]).
36 A similar conclusion is reached by BenDor Evian 2011a in her analysis of the Bubastite Portal tableau.
37 On concerns prior to this point, see Dodson 2019b: 181–85.
38 Laato 2015: 7–13, 25–49, 62–63.
39 In Ashmolean stela 1894.107a (Jansen-Winkeln 2007–23: II, 23–26[28]; Ritner 2009a: 173–78[43]).
40 Krauss 2006b: 411–12.
41 Heidelberg 1970-8.9, 562-4, 562-1 and in situ (Feucht 1981).
42 Fitzwilliam E.8.1896; although found in the Twenty-second Dynasty necropolis around the Ramesseum at Thebes, it seems to have been made in the north (Jansen-Winkeln 2007–23: II, 101[17.27]; Ritner 2009a: 227–28[54]; Taylor 2009: 398, 415, pl. xiv).
43 Ben-Dor Evian 2011b.
44 Saghieh 1983; Kilani 2019.
45 For his report, see Ch. 1 n.9.
46 Berlin VA3361, formerly in the Loytved Collection (Aimé-Giron 1926: 1–5; Porter and Moss 1952: 388; Jansen-Winkeln 2007–23: II, 26[12.30]; Ritner 2009a: 219–20[52]; Lemaire 2006).

47 Jansen-Winkeln 2007–23: I, 162[10.9].

48 Jansen-Winkeln 2007–23: I, 182–83[11.10]; Ritner 2009a: 163–66[40].

49 Jansen-Winkeln 2007–23: II, 55[13.25].

50 Cairo CG42193–4; BM EA8 (Jansen-Winkeln 2007–23: II, 57[30–32]).

51 Jansen-Winkeln 2007–23: II, 62[13.42]; Ritner 2009a: 60[9/Text 34].

52 Cartouches were only ever used for kings until the end of the Twelfth Dynasty, when we find Amenemhat III's daughter Neferuptah granted one—potentially as female heir to the throne. Cartouches then become increasingly usual for kings' wives during the Second Intermediate Period and then normal from the New Kingdom onward. A few royal sons and daughters also employ cartouches around this time, and into the first half of the Eighteenth Dynasty, but no Rameside royal sons are known to have used a cartouche.

53 On whom see Dodson 2009a.

54 II Chronicles 14: 9–15.

55 Cf. Kitchen 1996: 309 n.371.

56 Louvre AO9502 (Jansen-Winkeln 2007–23: II, 54–55[13.21]; Ritner 2009a: 233–34[57]).

57 Jansen-Winkeln 2007–23: II, 52–54[13.17–19]; Ritner 2009a: 229–32[56], 258[61].

58 Goyon and Traunecker 1982.

59 Broekman 2010a: 128.

60 Cairo CG884, Berlin ÄM22461, Louvre E25479, etc. (Jansen-Winkeln 2007–23: II, 89–93[17.10–14) and mentions by descendants: cf. Broekman 2010a: 130–31.

61 Cairo CG884; cf. Broekman 2010a: 130.

62 Broekman 2010a: 130–31.

63 Petrie UC14496 (Jansen-Winkeln 2007–23: II, 59[13.34]; Ritner 2009a: 261–62[63]); Broekman 2010a: 139.

64 Known from the monuments of various descendants (cf. Kitchen 1996: 217–20; Broekman 2010a: 139–40).

65 Jansen-Winkeln 2007–23: II, 61–68[13.39–46].

66 Meffre 2015: 74–80.

67 Meffre 2015: 69–73.

68 Arnold 1999: 36; Jansen-Winkeln 2007–23: II, 38–49[13.4–9]; Ritner 2009a: 237–58[59–60].

69 Jansen-Winkeln 2007–23: II, 49–52[13.11–13]; Ritner 2009a: 235–37[58]; Meffre 2015: 65–68, 81.

70 The genealogical succession is set out in stela Louvre IM3429 from the Serapeum (Jansen-Winkeln 2007–23: II, 394[44.27]; cf. Jurman 2020).

71 Of the God's Father Nakhtefmut E from the Ramesseum (Fitzwilliam E.64.1896—Jansen-Winkeln 2007–23: II, 69–70[13.49]; Aston 2009b: 239; Ritner 2009a: 262–64[64]). A Year 3 on another bandage has generally been attributed to a co-regent—but is more likely to be an old piece from Osorkon's own reign, or that of Takelot I. Another mummy including Osorkon's name incorporated bandages with dates of Years 11, 12, and 23 (of the *waab* priest of Amun, Khonsumakheru, Hamburg C3835–9—Jansen-Winkeln 2007–23: II, 70[50]), the latter also arguing against a reign as short as fifteen years. For other burials datable to Osorkon I's reign, see Jansen-Winkeln 2007–23: II, 69[13.48], 70–72[13.51–55].

72 Cf. Kitchen 1996: 110–11, although his third point becomes invalid under our view that Shoshenq Q and King Shoshenq IIa were separate people.

73 This would argue against Payraudeau's suggestion (2014: 46–47) that Horsieset I might have been king in Thebes while Takelot I was reigning in the north.

74 See Cole 2023 for the volatility of Inundation levels during the Third Intermediate Period.

75 Pushkin I.1.a.5000(4154) (Jansen-Winkeln 2007–23: II, 81[16.10]); Manchester 1785, private collection (Price 2024).

76 BM EA1224 (Jansen-Winkeln 2007–23: II, 81–81[16.9]; Ritner 2009a: 278–80[70]).

77 Cairo JE31882 [the "stela de l'apenage"] (Jansen-Winkeln 2007–23: II, 77–80[16.8]; Ritner 2009a: 271–78[69]).

78 Cairo CG42215 (Jansen-Winkeln 2007–23: II, 240[25.46]).

79 Pectoral Petrie UC13124 (Jansen-Winkeln 2007–23: II, 230[25.23]; Ritner 2009a: 280–81[71]).

80 Iuwlot also had an Egyptian-named daughter, Djedisetesankh i (Cairo CG42215—Jansen-Winkeln 2007–23: II, 240–41[25.46]).

81 Louvre SN82 (Jansen-Winkeln 2007–23: II, 82[16.18]; Jurman 2020: 592–95[D-071]).

82 Cf. Malinine, Posener, and Vercoutter 1968: 18–19; Jurman 2020: 596–98[D-072a–b]; if so, a stela fragment now in Alexandria (Jansen-Winkeln 2007–23: II, 82[19]), dated to a nameless Year 14, may belong to this putative burial.

83 Cairo JE86161 (Jansen-Winkeln 2007–23: II, 82[16.17]).

84 Copenhagen Nationalmuseet 332; Berlin ÄM8437+Aberdeen 1337=1551; Cairo JE31653 (Jansen-Winkeln 2007–23: II: 82–83[16.20–22]).

85 Kitchen's special pleading (1996: 119–20, 545) that the brevity and/or nonindependence of the putative reign of the former Shoshenq Q meant that to his descendants he was "high priest par excellence" does not convince.

86 Gardiner 1961: 448; Jacquet-Gordon 1975: 359; Edwards 1982: 549; Broekman 2006–2007; 2018.

87 Cf. Sagrillo 2009: 356.

88 Cf. Aston 2009a: 21.

89 Derry 1939: 550.

90 Aston 2009a: 21.

91 With the *ḥḏ* White Crown confused with the *m3ʿt* feather, perhaps via a hieratic draft.

92 Jansen-Winkeln 2007–23: II, 118–19[18.29]).

93 Prior to the Nineteenth Dynasty, there had only been a handful of duplicate prenomina, nearly all of these involving Neferkare, the prenomen of the long-reigned Pepy II, and thus holding the same allure as that of Rameses II for his less prominent successors.

94 Meffre 2015: 81–83.

95 Cf. Graefe 1975.

96 Jansen-Winkeln 2007–23: II, 113[18.13].

97 Cairo JE45327 (Jansen-Winkeln 2007–23: II, 131–33[18.69]; Ritner 2009a: 344–47[80]; Meffre 2015: 83–87).

98 Perez Die 2009.

99 Cf. Sagrillo 2009.

100 Jansen-Winkeln 2007–23: II: 123–24[18.41–45], 184–86[22.15–18]. No documents confirm his status as eldest son; for a discussion, see Lenzo, Meffre, and Payraudeau 2023: 173–79.

101 Jansen-Winkeln 2007–23: II, 123[18.41]; 129–30[18.63].

102 Cairo JE28582 (Jansen-Winkeln 2007–23: II, 117[18.22]).

103 Arnold 1999: 38–39.

104 Jansen-Winkeln 2007–23: II, 108[18.1–2].

105 Jansen-Winkeln 2007–23: II, 110[18.4].

106 Jansen-Winkeln 2007–23: II, 112–16, 477[18.13–20a]); Ritner 2009a: 291–344[78–79]; Lange 2009.

107 BM EA1146 (Jansen-Winkeln 2007–23: II, 116–7[18.21]).
108 Jansen-Winkeln 2007–23: II, 118–19[18.29]; Ritner 2009a: 288–90[76].
109 Jansen-Winkeln 2007–23: II, 133[18.70–72].
110 Jansen-Winkeln 2007–23: II, 133–51[18.73–83]; Ritner 2009a: 51–52.
111 Jansen-Winkeln 2007–23: II, 119–20[18.30–32].
112 Jurman 2006b.
113 Cf. Aston 1989: 151–52.
114 Jansen-Winkeln 2007–23: II, 120–21[18.33].
115 Jansen-Winkeln 2007–23: II, 121[18.35]; Ritner 2009a: 288[75].
116 Jansen-Winkeln 2007–23: II, 121[34].
117 For memorials of Nimlot, see Meffre 2015: 92–95.
118 Jansen-Winkeln 2007–23: II, 154–59[19.1–8]; for a discussion of Horsieset and his status, cf. Payraudeau 2014: 52–54.
119 JansenWinkeln 1995: 129–32.
120 Jansen-Winkeln 2007–23: II, 135–39[18.75].
121 JansenWinkeln 1995: 135–36.
122 Jansen-Winkeln 2007–23: II, 225[25.8, end].
123 JansenWinkeln 2006: 241 n.64.
124 Jansen-Winkeln 2007–23: II, 156, 25[25.10]; Aston 2009b: 111.
125 Known from statues of her descendants (Cairo CG42210 and CG42211—Jansen-Winkeln 2007–23: II, 234[25.36], 323[30.7]).
126 Known from a fragment of coffin from Abydos (UPMAA E16186—Jansen-Winkeln 2007–23: II, 226[25.12]).
127 Jansen-Winkeln 2007–23: II, 155–56[19.6].
128 Jansen-Winkeln 2007–23: II, 154[19.1].
129 Jansen-Winkeln 2007–23: II, 226–28[25.13–17]; for her tomb at the Ramesseum (PF1147), see Lurson 2018: 199–204.
130 The damage to [Pa?]du[bast?]'s name seems to have been due purely to wear and tear.
131 Hölscher 1954: 10.
132 Jansen-Winkeln 2007–23: II, 119–20[18.32].
133 Cairo CG42208 (Jansen-Winkeln 2007–23: II, 141–44[18.78]).
134 Cf. Broekman 2010a: 140–41, 146–47 on whether the Osorkon named on Cairo statue JE91720 is to be taken as Osorkon II or as Osorkon III.

Notes to Chapter 3

1 Louvre IM3090 (Jansen-Winkeln 2007–23: II, 129–30[18.63]).
2 Jansen-Winkeln 2007–23: II, 118[18.28].
3 For a summary of these debates, see Ritner 2009b; cf. also Lange 2008.
4 Cf. Ritner's point (2009b: 336–37) regarding the way in which Pedieset A passed on his Egyptian pontifical title to his son, while retaining his Libyan one, and wearing a Libyan feather on his principal monuments: cf. p. 80, below.
5 Unlike the Twenty-first Dynasty, Manetho is of no real help for the Twenty-second: see pp. 159–61.
6 Jansen-Winkeln 2007–23: II, 160[20.2].
7 Elephantine Museum (Jansen-Winkeln 2007–23: II, 172[20.15]).
8 Stela Turin C1468+Vatican 329 (Jansen-Winkeln 2007–23: II, 229[25.21]).
9 Stone fragment Stockholm MM32010 (Jansen-Winkeln 2007–23: II, 229[25.20]).
10 Named in Karnak Priestly Annals 7=Cairo JE36493 and stela Cairo TR 11/9/21/17 (Jansen-Winkeln 2007–23: II, 203[22.38], 22526[25.11])

11 Stela Cairo JE36195 (Jansen-Winkeln 2007–23: II, 161[20.6]; Ritner 2009a: 379–80[84]).

12 Named on the coffins of their daughter and grandson (Berlin ÄM20132-6—Jansen-Winkeln 2007–23: II, 390–91[44.19–20]; Aston 2009b: 250). Isetweret's mother was named Tabakhtenaskhet (A), perhaps the same woman buried in the high-priestly cemetery at Memphis (Aston 2009b: 81).

13 Statue Cairo CG42211 (Jansen-Winkeln 2007–23: II, 320–23[30.7]); cf. Broekman 2010a: 141.

14 Jansen-Winkeln 2007–23: II, 161–68[20.7], 186–96[22.21]; Ritner 2009a: 34877[82]; Broekman 2008; Meffre 2015: 109–13.

15 Louvre E3336=C258 (Jansen-Winkeln 2007–23: II, 168–69[20.10]; Ritner 2009a: 377–79[83]). Year 11 also saw an entry in the Karnak Priestly Annals (Jansen-Winkeln 2007–23: II, 168 [20.9]; Ritner 2009a: 59).

16 Jansen-Winkeln 2007–23: II, 182–83[22.11]; Ritner 2009a: 37.

17 Cf. Krauss 2006a: 377. The wording is unclear: what does appear certain, however, is that no "normal" eclipse is being reported in the text, as has sometimes been proposed (cf. Kitchen 1996: 181–82).

18 Jansen-Winkeln 2007–23: II, 208[23.2]; Ritner 2009a: 37.

19 Jansen-Winkeln 2007–23: II, 212–13[23.15]; Ritner 2009a: 48–49.

20 Jansen-Winkeln 2007–23: II, 208[23.1]; Ritner 2009a: 413[108].

21 Jansen-Winkeln 2007–23: II, 213[23.16]; Ritner 2009a: 49.

22 Jansen-Winkeln 2007–23: II, 250–51[25.57]; Ritner 2009a: 380–82[85].

23 Jansen-Winkeln 2007–23: II, 174, 208[23.3]; Ritner 2009a: 38.

24 Jansen-Winkeln 2007–23: II, 173[21.3–4].

25 Jansen-Winkeln 2007–23: II, 370[39.3].

26 For a discussion of the issues surrounding the date of the death of Shoshenq D, see Lenzo, Meffre, and Payraudeau 2023: 188.

27 Petrie UC14661; Cairo JE36728 (Jansen-Winkeln 2007–23: II, 196[22.22]; III, 371–72[52.43].

28 Stela Cairo JE45610 (Jansen-Winkeln 2007–23: II, 196–97[22.23]; Ritner 2009a: 38586[87]).

29 Stela Louvre E20905; the king's cartouches have been erased (Jansen-Winkeln 2007–23: II, 197–98[22.25]).

30 Berlin ÄM7344 (Jansen-Winkeln 2007–23: II, 201[22.30]).

31 Cairo CG9430 (Jansen-Winkeln 2007–23: II, 415[45.33]).

32 Jansen-Winkeln 2007–23: II, 175[22.1–2]; Ritner 2009a: 390–92[90].

33 Arnold 1999: 40.

34 Jansen-Winkeln 2007–23: II, 179–82[22.6–10].

35 Jansen-Winkeln 2007–23: II, 196–203[22.23–34]; Ritner 2009a: 383–85[86–88].

36 Jansen-Winkeln 2007–23: II, 203[22.36].

37 Jansen-Winkeln 2007–23: II, 185–86[22.19]; Ritner 2009a: 388–90[89].

38 A quarter century appears to be the maximum possible lifespan of a bull, while the gap between burials is approximately four decades. From Apis XXIX onward, however, an essentially unbroken series of bulls stretches into the Late Period.

39 Ritner 2009b: 336–37.

40 Jansen-Winkeln 2007–23: II, 219–20[24.1–6]; Ritner 2009a: 39, 57.

41 Jansen-Winkeln 2007–23: II, 220[24.7]; cf. Aston 1989: 151–52.

42 Ritner 1999.

43 Cairo CG41035 (Jansen-Winkeln 2007–23: III, 357[52.18], who makes her the

granddaughter of Takelot III, rather than II, as here).

44 Cairo JE36439 (Jansen-Winkeln 2007–23: II, 203–204[22.38]; Ritner 2009a: 52–54.

45 Brooklyn 67.118 (Jansen-Winkeln 2007–23: II, 198–99[22.26]; Ritner 2009a: 386–88[88]).

46 Pushkin I.1.a.5647 (Jansen-Winkeln 2007–23: II, 202–203[22.34]).

47 Cairo TR 11/1/25/13 (Jansen-Winkeln 2007–23: II, 200[22.28]).

48 Louvre IM3697, 3736, 4205, 3441 (Jansen-Winkeln 2007–23: II, 261–63, 265–67[27.5–6, 9–10]; Ritner 2009a: 394–400[9497]).

49 Jansen-Winkeln 2007–23: II, 256–58[26.1–8]; Ritner 2009a: 392–93[91–92].

50 Hermitage 5630 (Jansen-Winkeln 2007–23: II, 257[26.6]; Ritner 2009a: 393[92]).

51 Jansen-Winkeln 2007–23: II, 273–74[28.16], where it is assigned to Shoshenq V on the basis of the epithet "-netjerheqwaset" (cf. below p. 84—there is no prenomen on the stela); however, as noted above, there seems to be at least one example of this epithet being used by Shoshenq IV.

52 Reused in the Bab el-Nasr at Cairo (Jansen-Winkeln 2007–23: II, 259–61[27.3]).

53 Jansen-Winkeln 2007–23: II, 259[27.1]; Ritner 2009a: 394[93].

54 Cairo TR 2/2/21/13 (Jansen-Winkeln 2007–23: II, 267[27.13]; Ritner 2009a: 402–403[100]).

55 Louvre IM3697, 3736 (Jansen-Winkeln 2007–23: II, 261–63[27.5–6]; Ritner 2009a: 394–98[94–95]).

56 A shabti of Peftajauwybast is in Cairo (Jansen-Winkeln 2007–23: II, 156[22.20]).

57 Louvre IM4205, 3441, 3083, NN (Jansen-Winkeln 2007–23: II, 265–67[27.9–12]; Ritner 2009a: 398–400[96–97]).

58 Louvre E20368, E.11139 (Jansen-Winkeln 2007–23: II, 263–65[27.7–8]; Ritner 2009a: 401–402[99]).

59 Cf. Aston 2009b: 14–15.

60 Cf. von Beckerath 1995; Muhs 1998.

61 Jansen-Winkeln 2007–23: II, 209–12[23.10–14]; an unprovenanced statuette also bears the name (Jansen-Winkeln 2007–23: II, 209[23.8]).

62 And so not as late as required by Kahn 2006's suggestion that he was a successor of Osorkon IV at Tanis.

63 Leahy 1990: 186–90.

64 Jansen-Winkeln 2007–23: II, 211[12].

65 Kahn 2006: 28–32, seconded by Aston 2009b: 15–16.

66 Cf. the objections to making Padubast I and II the same person pointed out in Kahn 2006 and Aston 2009a.

67 Originally regarded as belonging to Shoshenq I, the presence of an epithet in the nomen (Jansen-Winkeln 2007–23: II, 332[32.1]) means that the king in question must be post–Osorkon II. He has been placed as a successor of Rudamun by Aston (2009b), but an abbreviated writing of the name of Shoshenq IV may be a better solution.

68 From Tihna el-Gebel (Jansen-Winkeln 2007–23: II, 296[29.9]; Ritner 2009a: 421–23[111]; Meffre 2015: 121–23; cf. Ōhshiro 1999).

69 Jansen-Winkeln 2007–23: II, 293[29.1–3]; Ritner 2009a: 39.

70 And even then there are doubts: see Obsomer 1995: 35–145.

71 Dodson 2014.

72 Jansen-Winkeln 2007–23: II, 295[29.8], 315[30.3]; Meffre 2015: 118.

73 Jansen-Winkeln 2007–23: II, 297[29.11].

74 Jansen-Winkeln 2007–23: II, 331[31.4].

75 Jansen-Winkeln 2007–23: II, 295[29.8].

76 MFA 94.321 (D'Auria et al. 1988: 171–72[123]).

77 Jansen-Winkeln 2007–23: II, 393[44.23].

78 Jansen-Winkeln 2007–23: II, 294, 297[29.5, 11–13].

79 Jansen-Winkeln 2007–23: II, 314–18[30.3], 366[36.1], 385[44.1]; III, 259[51.2], 263[51.16], 269[51.17], 334[51.128], 335[51.129], 568[51.6a].

80 Cf. Jansen-Winkeln 2007–23: I, 81[6.25].

81 Cf. Jansen-Winkeln 2007–23: II, 226–28[25.13–16].

82 She is first attested under Horsieset I, around half a century previously, and if appointed in her youth could easily have lived this long (cf. the long lives of many later God's Wives, by their status free from the perils of childbearing).

83 Jansen-Winkeln 2007–23: II, 301–11[29.15–30].

84 Broekman 2010a: 141.

85 Jansen-Winkeln 2007–23: II, 293[29.1], 313[30.1]; Ritner 2009a: 39–40.

86 Jansen-Winkeln 2007–23: II, 298–301[29.14]; Ritner 2009a: 415–21[111]; Bickel 2009.

87 Meffre 2015: 118–21.

88 Jansen-Winkeln 2007–23: II, 313–19[30.3]; Ayad 2009.

89 It is possible that Takelot III had an alternate Horus name, (*nb-mꜥt-ḫrw*, "Possessor of truth of voice"), and an alternate Nebti name, (*ḥkn-m-m3ꜥt*, "He who has rejoiced at Maat"). Both of these are found in the chapel of Osiris-Heqadjet, although generally attributed to Rudamun (Jurman 2006a: 78–85; Payraudeau 2009: 299–301).

90 Jansen-Winkeln 2007–23: II, 313[30.2].

91 Jansen-Winkeln 2007–23: II, 329[30.14]; Kaper 2009: 150–53; the protagonist, the Chief of the Shamin, Nesthuty, was still in office in Year 23 of Pi(ankh)y (Payraudeau 2009: 291–96).

92 This date/name combination lies adjacent to a similar pair linking a Year 12 with the God's Wife Amenirdis I (Jansen-Winkeln 2007–23: II, 355[44.1]), and was long regarded as a single double-dated inscription, providing a synchronism between an Egyptian king (the Shepenwepet date) and a Nubian king (the Amenirdis date—e.g., Kitchen 1996: 543–44, proposing Piye/Iuput II. Piye/Takelot III and Piye/Rudamun have also been put forward). However, the two pairs have now been shown to be almost certainly independent (see Jurman 2006a: 86–91).

93 Jansen-Winkeln 2007–23: II, 393[44.24]; III, 359[52.21].

94 Jansen-Winkeln 2007–23: II, 319[30.4].

95 Cf. Aston and Taylor 1990.

96 Bruyère 1957: 16–18.

97 Jansen-Winkeln 2007–23: III, 357–58[52.19], 362–63[52.26].

98 Jansen-Winkeln 2007–23: III, 357–58[52.19].

99 Jansen-Winkeln 2007–23: III, 355-57[52.17].

100 BM EA74892 (Aston and Taylor 1990: 135–36).

101 Jansen-Winkeln 2007–23: III, 208[48.150], 355[52.16].

102 BM EA22913 (Jansen-Winkeln 2007–23: II, 398–99[44.38]).

103 Payraudeau 2009: 297–99.

104 Jansen-Winkeln 2007–23: II, 320–26[30.7–8].

105 Jansen-Winkeln 2007–23: II, 319–20[30.5], 328[30.13].

106 Turin C1632 (Jansen-Winkeln 2007–23: III, 408[52.132]).

107 Cairo JE37163 (De Meulenaere 1978).
108 Coffins Cairo CG41035 and formerly Berlin NN (Jansen-Winkeln 2007–23: III, 357[52.18], 393[44.23]).
109 Jansen-Winkeln 2007–23: II, 330–31[31.3].
110 Jansen-Winkeln 2007–23: II, 385[44.3].
111 Jansen-Winkeln 2007–23: II, 382–83[42].
112 Raue 2010.
113 Stela Louvre C100 (Jansen-Winkeln 2007–23: II, 382–83[42.2]; Rondot 2022: 100–101[48]).
114 As explicitly stated in Serapeum stela Louvre IM3049 (Jansen-Winkeln 2007–23: II, 280–81[28.26]).
115 Jansen-Winkeln 2007–23: II, 268–69[28.1].
116 Montet 1966: 57–61.
117 Montet 1966: 45–56.
118 Jurman 2009: 129–32.
119 Jansen-Winkeln 2007–23: II, 179[22.5]; Jurman 2009: 128.
120 De Meulenaere 1985.
121 Cf. Jurman 2009: 128–29.
122 Jansen-Winkeln 2007–23: II, 272–78[28.13–23], 291–92[28.47].
123 Jansen-Winkeln 2007–23: II, 280–83[28.26–31].
124 Jansen-Winkeln 2007–23: II, 271–72[28.12], 283–91[28.32–46].
125 Jansen-Winkeln 2007–23: II, 269–70[28.3–8].
126 Brooklyn 67.119 (Jansen-Winkeln 2007–23: II, 274[28.18]).
127 Cairo JE30972 (Jansen-Winkeln 2007–23: II, 276–77[28.21]).
128 IFAO 14456 (Jansen-Winkeln 2007–23: II, 275–76[28.20]).
129 Louvre IM3078 (Jansen-Winkeln 2007–23: II, 286–87[28.37]).
130 Jansen-Winkeln 2007–23: II, 270[28.9–10]; Ritner 2009a: 435–36[123–24].
131 Florence 1777 (Jansen-Winkeln 2007–23: II, 270–71[28.11]).
132 Location uncertain (Jansen-Winkeln 2007–23: II, 273[28.15]; Ritner 2009a: 437–38[126]).
133 Formerly King Faruq Collection (Jansen-Winkeln 2007–23: II, 272–73[28.14]; Ritner 2009a: 436–37[125]).
134 Cf. Kitchen 1996: 355.

Notes to Chapter 4

1 For detail of much of the material in this chapter, see Dodson 2023b.
2 Jansen-Winkeln 2007–23: II, 336[34.1, 4].
3 The reading of whose name continues to be a matter for debate.
4 From Cairo stela JE48862+47086–89 (Jansen-Winkeln 2007–23: II, 337–50[35.1]; Ritner 2009a: 464–92[144]; Meffre 2015: 143–50); all data and quotations in the immediately following text come from this document.
5 Indeed, Morkot and James suggest (2009) that the two Peftjauawybasts were one and the same; however, this would require a radical change in the chronology of the period (see pages 179–81).
6 Cf. Aston 2009a: 18.
7 Mentioned on statue Pushkin I.1.a.5736=4491 and fragments of her own coffin and that of her son (Jansen-Winkeln 2007–23: II, 334–35[33.6]).
8 Cairo JE45948 and TR 11/9/21/14 (Jansen-Winkeln 2007–23: II, 333–34[33.4–5]; Ritner 2009a: 424–26[113]; Meffre 2015: 125–30).
9 MFA 06.2408 (gold) and 1977.16 (bronze—Jansen-Winkeln 2007–23: II, 333[33.1–2]; Ritner 2009a: 423–24[112]).
10 Jansen-Winkeln 2007–23: II, 366[36.1–2].
11 Cf. Payraudeau 2015.
12 See Kitchen 1996: 366 n.710.
13 Brissaud 2010; Payraudeau and Meffre 2016: 290–94.

14 Louvre E7167 (Jansen-Winkeln 2007–23: II, 369[38.3]); the attribution of this piece to Osorkon IV is on the basis that the mothers of the four earlier Kings Osorkon are known to have been named other than Tadibast.

15 The nomina are respectively from the Tanis blocks and the Louvre aegis.

16 E.g., Goyon 1987: 37, who calls a relief from the same group a "true portrait of Djoser." A trial piece clearly of the same date, MMA 11.150.30, was long catalogued as a Third Dynasty piece (Winlock 1917), and then as a fake until recognized for what it really was.

17 Firth and Quibell 1935: 5, 34–35, pl. 15, 16.

18 Cf. Firth and Quibell 1935: passim.

19 II Kings 17: 4.

20 Sargon's Annals and Display Inscriptions at Khorsabad d (Frame 2021: 57–58[53–57]).

21 Botta and Flandin 1849–50: II, pl. 87.

22 Cf. Kahn 2001: 12.

23 Sargon's Annals; prism Berlin VA8424 (Frame 2021: 267[ii ´ 8 ´–11 ´]).

24 Meffre and Payraudeau 2019; Jansen-Winkeln 2007–23: III, 256[50.17].

25 Jansen-Winkeln 2007–23: III, 252–54[50.11–13].

26 Jansen-Winkeln 2007–23: III, 254–55[50.14–15].

27 Geneva 23473; Cairo JE38261; Brooklyn 59.17 (Jansen-Winkeln 2007–23: III, 370–71[39.4, 1–2]).

28 Jansen-Winkeln 2007–23: II, 367–68[37.1–3]; cf. Spencer and Spencer 1986: 199; Aston 2009a: 20; Meffre 2015: 139–42.

29 It has also been proposed, however, that this King Tefnakhte might be the "Stephinatês" listed by Manetho among slightly later rulers of Sais (see page 118); see Priese 1970: 19–20; Perdu 2002; and the discussion in Kahn 2009.

30 Jansen-Winkeln 2007–23: II, 372–73[40.1–2].

31 Jansen-Winkeln 2007–23: II, 375–81[41.1–2, 11–25].

32 The presence of a Year 2 stela of Shabaka apparently in the same room as the Apis buried under Bakenrenef (Jansen-Winkeln 2007–23: II, 2[46.4]) was long regarded as providing a synchronism between the two kings, but with the recognition that Shabataka was actually the king who displaced Bakenrenef from his throne (see below), this is no longer the case.

33 Diodorus Siculus, 1.45.

34 Diodorus Siculus, 1.65, 79, 94.

35 Tacitus 5.3.

36 Jansen-Winkeln 2007–23: II, 365[41.4–5].

37 On the placement of Shabataka as Pi(ankh)y's successor rather than, as long assumed, Shabaka, see the summary in Dodson 2023b: 170–73.

38 From this point onward, the absolute chronology becomes sufficiently solid to be able to quote specific years, with minimal margins for error.

39 Jansen-Winkeln 2007–23: III, 250[50.1–5].

40 Ray 1974.

41 Jansen-Winkeln 2007–23: III, 251[50.6–9]; the item listed as "UC14869" is a misprint for UC14689.

42 Khorsabad Display Inscriptions (Frame 2021: 147[109b–112a]).

43 For an overview of Kushite interactions with Assyria see Dodson 2023b: 54–55, 64–68, 83–93.

44 Text BM K3082+S2027+K3086 and stela from Zenjirli (Berlin VA2708) (Leichty 2011: 185–86).

45 Rassam Cylinder (Novotny and Jeffers 2018: 34[11.i 110–17]), from which the immediately following quotations derive;

for the date of the invasion, see Kitchen 1996: 392 n.874.

46 Ashurbanipal includes a long list of the potentates involved in his text, but only some names and/or places are firmly identifiable.

47 Nubian Museum stela ex-JE48863 (Jansen-Winkeln 2007–23: III, 236–40 [49.8]).

48 Herodotus, 2.152. This states that Nekau was killed by "Sabacos the Ethiopian," but see Dodson 2023b: 139–40 for the way in which kings of the period were conflated under that name.

Notes to Chapter 5

1 Lull 2002: 59.

2 Montet 1951.

3 MMA 47.60; another jar is in the Aubert Collection in Paris (Dodson 1994: 79, 128, 173[41/1, 41/2]).

4 Aston 2009b: 44, 49–50.

5 Aston 2009b: 51.

6 Berlin ÄM11000 (Dodson 1994: 83–84, 131[44], 179).

7 Pasebkhanut I and Amenemopet had conventional separate canopic jars in a wooden chest (Dodson 1994: 80–82), while Takelot I, Osorkon II, Pimay, and Shoshenq III and IV all had simple jars (fig. 102).

8 Dodson 1994: 51–74.

9 But cf. Sagrillo 2009: 341–42, 349–50.

10 Ullmann 2002: 564–70.

11 Brunton 1939.

12 Dodson 1998.

13 For which, see Taylor 2003; 2009.

14 Dodson 1994: 86–89, 131–34.

15 Derry 1942: 264 (by a slip of the pen attributing them to Pasebkhanut I).

16 Montet 1947: 41–81; Lull 2002: 74–117; Aston 2009b: 54–58.

17 No traces of earlier decoration have been reported.

18 Jansen-Winkeln 2007–23: II, 110[18.5]; Ritner 2009a: 347–48[81].

19 For a detailed analysis of the decoration of NRT-I, see Lull 2002: 77–117.

20 See Lenzo, Meffre, and Payraudeau 2023: 66–110.

21 Montet 1947: 81–82; the design of the piece places it in either the reign of Senwosret III or that of Amenemhat III.

22 Pasenbkhanut I had reused the inner sarcophagus of Merenptah from KV8, and the granite anthropoid coffin of a person of the late Eighteenth Dynasty, while Amenemopet had a Middle Kingdom piece.

23 Dodson 2016: 254–57.

24 von Känel 1987: 57.

25 The nearest parallel is the unique outer sarcophagus of Amenhotep-son-of-Hapu, made under Amenhotep III, five centuries earlier (Dodson and Griffin 2024).

26 Aston 2009b: 58.

27 Montet 1960: 53–76; Aston 2009b: 59–60.

28 Lull 2002: 135–55.

29 Ryholt 1997: 216–67, 318.

30 See Sagrillo 2011; thefts during the Second World War (page 177) have exacerbated confusion as to what exactly was found.

31 Montet 1960: 87–89; Aston 2009b: 60.

32 Lull 2002: 40.

33 Hölscher 1954: 8–10; Aston 2009b: 261.

34 Jansen-Winkeln 2007–23: II, 294; Ōhshiro 2017.

35 For various anonymous tombs in the area see Hölscher 1954: 16–33.

36 Jansen-Winkeln 2007–23: II, 320[30.6]; the authenticity of these pieces has been questioned, but is reaffirmed in Dodson and Gee 2017; cf. p. 149.

37 Spiegelberg 1927: 28–29.

38 As first suggested by Taylor 1988: 166.

39 Spencer 2001: 19–20; cf. Broekman 2009.

40 Montet 1947: 59–70; Aston 2009b: 55–58.
41 Yoyotte 1987.
42 Gauthier 1921: 21–27; Aston 2009b: 64–65.
43 Kitchen (1996: 130, 351) assessed the tomb as belonging to the mother of Osorkon III, as support for his view that the latter was a Leontopolitan king.
44 Aston 2009b: 238, 241.
45 Amélineau 1899: 14–23; Jansen-Winkeln 2007–23: II, 29[12.37]; Aston 2009b: 142. This tomb is sometimes regarded as a cenotaph, on the basis of a coffin fragment from the Ramesseum naming Iuput (Jansen-Winkeln 2007–23: II, 30[12.41]); however, this is of a type not found until long after Iuput's death and his name probably belonged to the genealogy of a descendant (Taylor 2003: 97; Aston 2009b: 142).
46 Damarany and Cahail 2016; the sarcophagus employed had been usurped from Rameses II (Payraudeau 2023b).
47 Aston 2009b: 141–42.
48 Cairo JE88131 (Aston 2009b: 78–80; Jansen-Winkeln 2007–23: II, 184–85[22.15]; Lenzo, Meffre, and Payraudeau 2023).
49 See Aston 2009b: 80–81; Jurman 2020: 787–806[D-084, D-085], 887–96[D-095].

Notes to Chapter 6

1 Berlin ÄM8182 (Jansen-Winkeln 2007–23: III, 256–57[50.19]).
2 Greco-Roman Museum, Alexandria (Jansen-Winkeln 2007–23: III, 256 [50.18]. It may be noted that the other side of the wall had the alternating cartouches Wahibre and Haaibre (nomen and prenomen of Apries).
3 Herodotus II: 147, 151–53.
4 Based on Polyaenus §7.3 and Pseudo-Aristeas 14 (Sauneron and Yoyotte 1952a: 199–200; 1952b: 131–35; Burstein 1984).
5 Caminos 1964.
6 Cairo SR241 (Jansen-Winkeln 2007–23: IV, 13–14[53.23]; Ritner 2009a: 585–87[174]).
7 Cf. Dodson 2021: 131–36.
8 For discussions of this, see Moret 1903; Hölbl 1981; Janssen 1954; Gill and Vickers 1996; Ridgway 1999; Markiewicz 2008.
9 Lüddeckens 1954.
10 See Waddell 1940 for the standard edition.
11 E.g., Smendes ("Man of Mendes") is a translation of the Egyptian Nesibanebdjedet ("The One of Banebdjedet"—the latter being the god of the city called "Mendes" by the Greeks).
12 It has been suggested that the latter originated in a word for "query," misunderstood as a name (Petrie 1914a). There are certainly clear examples of misunderstood notations for "lacuna" transmogrifying into kings' names in the Nineteenth Dynasty king lists covering the Second and Third Dynasties (Dodson 2021: 47, 63–64).
13 "Armais" (Horemheb) is said also to be called Danaus, founder of Argos, "Ramesses" (Rameses II) is equated with Aegyptus, and "Thuôris" (Tawosret) said to be "who in Homer is called Polybus, husband [sic!] of Alcandra, in whose reign Troy was taken."
14 Kitchen 1996: 455–61; Ryholt 2004.

Notes to Chapter 7

1 Champollion 1824: 203–206.
2 Champollion 1824–26: II, 119–22, based on stela Turin C1468+Vatican 255288–90 (Malek 2007–12: 332[803-060-400]).
3 For clarity, throughout this chapter all kings are referred to by their modern ordinals (cf. p. xii), unless written in quotation marks.

4 Champollion 1824–26: II, pl. v.
5 Champollion 1909: 161–62, pl. v.
6 Müller 1887.
7 On this tomb and its date, see Dodson 2019b: 81.
8 Wilkinson 1828: 98, pl. ii.
9 Rosellini 1832–33: II, 261.
10 Wilkinson 1837: 135–38.
11 Wilkinson 1837: 136–37.
12 Wilkinson 1837: 135.
13 Leemans 1838: 109–15.
14 Without *s3-b3stt*.
15 With *s3-b3stt*.
16 With a prenomen "Sesheskheperre-setepenamun," based on a corruptly written prenomen of Osorkon I on a scarab.
17 Bunsen 1845: 128–37; 1854: 586–95.
18 Mariette 1855: 95.
19 Lepsius 1856; 1858a.
20 Lepsius 1858b: pl. xlv[389].
21 Brugsch 1879: 216.
22 Gauthier 1914a: 198–204.
23 Birch 1850: 165–70.
24 Mariette 1855: 97, 100.
25 Lepsius 1858a: 21–25.
26 Brugsch 1879: 193–205.
27 Maspero 1880: 112–15.
28 Rougé 1873–74: 87.
29 Müller 1921, following on from a paper in 1908.
30 Brugsch 1891: 365.
31 Renouf 1890–91.
32 Revillout 1903: 168–79.
33 Petrie 1905: 229–32.
34 Naville 1891: 46–47.
35 Breasted 1905: 526–33.
36 Legrain 1896a; 1896b.
37 Breasted 1906–1907: IV, 339–43[693–98], 403–404[794].
38 Kruchten 1989.
39 Daressy 1913.
40 Petrie 1914b.
41 Hall 1925.
42 Gauthier 1914a; 1914b: 361.
43 Ranke 1926.
44 Montet 1939: 535 (author's translation).
45 Brunton 1939: 541–43.
46 Lenzo, Meffre, and Payraudeau 2023; see also Jurman 2020: 685–786[D-083].
47 Montet 1966.
48 Meffre and Payraudeau 2018.
49 Epigraphic Survey 1954.
50 Caminos 1958.
51 Caminos 1952.
52 Gardiner 1961: 333–34.
53 Jansen-Winkeln 2007–23.
54 Baer 1973.
55 Yoyotte 1961.
56 Young 1963: 100–101.
57 Yoyotte 1976–77.
58 Cf. Payraudeau 2000.
59 Which would go through three editions up to Kitchen 1996.
60 Baer 1973.
61 Velikovsky 1952; 1960; 1977; 1978; unpublished material at https://varchive.org/.
62 Rohl 1995.
63 James 1991.
64 E.g., Porter 2011.
65 E.g., Kitchen 1991a.
66 E.g., Kitchen 1991b, dubbing the authors of James 1991 as "sons of Velikovsky." For their rejoinder, see James and Morkot 1991.
67 Dodson 1996.
68 Dodson 2019b: 181–89.
69 The proceedings being published in James and van der Veen 2015.
70 Spencer and Spencer 1986.
71 Aston 1989.
72 Jansen-Winkeln 1987; this work also confirmed Takelot's prenomen.
73 Aston 2009a.
74 Kitchen 1996: xxiii–xxv; 2009: 167–76; cf.

Aston 2009a: 2.

75 Dodson 1993b, building on initial observations in Rohl 1986: 17–18, 21, n.2; 1989/90: 66–67.

76 Leahy 1985; Ritner 2009b.

77 Jansen-Winkeln 1994.

78 Payraudeau 2014: 279–94.

79 Broekman, Demarée, and Kaper 2009.

80 Jansen-Winkeln 2007–23.

81 Jansen-Winkeln 1985.

Bibliography

Abbreviations for Periodicals

ASAE	*Annales du Service des Antiquités de l'Égypte*
BIFAO	*Bulletin de l'Institut Français d'Archéologie Orientale du Caire*
BiOr	*Bibliotheca Orientalis*
BMMA	*Bulletin of the Metropolitan Museum of Art*
BSFE	*Bulletin de la Societé Française d'Egyptologie*
BSFFT	*Bulletin de la Société française des fouilles de Tanis*
CRAIBL	*Comptes rendus de l'Académie des Inscriptions et Belles-Lettres*
EgArch	*Egyptian Archaeology: Bulletin of the Egypt Exploration Society*
GM	*Göttinger Miszellen*
JARCE	*Journal of the American Research Center in Egypt*
JEA	*Journal of Egyptian Archaeology*
JEgH	*Journal of Egyptian History*
JNES	*Journal of Near Eastern Studies*
JSSEA	*Journal of the Society for the Study of Egyptian Antiquities*
Kmt	*Kmt: A Modern Journal of Ancient Egypt*
MDAIK	*Mitteilungen des Deutschen Archäologischen Instituts, Kairo*
OLZ	Orientalische Literaturzeitung
PEQ	*Palestine Exploration Quarterly*
PSBA	*Proceedings of the Society of Biblical Archaeology*
RdE	*Revue d'Egyptologie*
RecTrav	*Recueil de travaux rélatifs à la philologie et à l'archéologie égyptiennes et assyriennes*
SAK	*Studien zur altägyptschen Kultur*
TLS	*Times Literary Supplement*
VA	*Varia Aegyptiaca*
ZÄS	*Zeitschrift für Ägyptische Sprache und Altertumskunde*
ZDMG	*Zeitschrift der Deutschen Morgenländischen Gesellschaft*

List of Works Cited

Aḥituv, S. 1984. *Canaanite Toponyms in Ancient Egyptian Documents*. Jerusalem: Magnes Press.

Aimé-Giron, N. 1926. "Note sur les inscriptions de Aḥiram." *BIFAO* 26: 1–13.

Amélineau, E. 1899. *Les nouvelles fouilles d'Abydos 1895–1896: Compte rendu in extenso des fouilles, description des monuments et objets découverts*. Paris: Ernest Leroux.

Arnold, D. 1999. *Temples of the Last Pharaohs*. New York: Oxford University Press.

Association Française d'Action Artistique. 1987. *Tanis: L'or des pharaons*. Paris: Ministère des Affaires Étrangères/Association Française d'Action Artistique.

Aston, D.A. 1989. "Takeloth II—A King of the 'Theban Twenty-third Dynasty'?" *JEA* 75: 139–53.

———. 2009a. "Takeloth II, a King of the Herakleopolitan/Theban Twenty-third Dynasty Revisited: The Chronology of Dynasties 22 and 23." In *The Libyan Period in Egypt: Historical and Cultural Studies into the 21st–24th Dynasties. Proceedings of a conference at Leiden University, 25–27 October 2007*, edited by G.P.F. Broekman, R.J. Demarée, and O.E. Kaper, 1–28. Leiden: Nederlands Instituut voor het Nabije Oosten; Leuven: Peeters.

———. 2009b. *Burial Assemblages of Dynasty 21–25: Chronology—Typology—Developments*. Vienna: Verlag der Österreichischen Akademie der Wissenschaften.

———. 2021. "The Royal Cache: A History of TT 320." In *Bab el-Gasus in Context: Rediscovering the Tomb of the Priests of Amun*, edited by R. Sousa, A. Amenta, and K.M. Cooney, 31–68. Rome: "L'Erma" di Bretschneider.

Aston, D.A., and J.H. Taylor. 1990. "The Family of Takeloth III and the 'Theban' Twenty-third Dynasty." In *Libya and Egypt, c. 1300–750* BC, edited by A. Leahy, 131–54. London: Centre of Near and Middle Eastern Studies, School of Oriental and African Studies, University of London, and the Society for Libyan Studies.

Ayad, M.F. 2009. "The Transition from Libyan to Nubian Rule: The Role of the God's Wife of Amun." In *The Libyan Period in Egypt: Historical and Cultural Studies into the 21st–24th Dynasties. Proceedings of a conference at Leiden University, 25–27 October 2007*, edited by G.P.F. Broekman, R.J. Demarée, and O.E. Kaper, 29–49. Leiden: Nederlands Instituut voor het Nabije Oosten; Leuven: Peeters.

Baer, K. 1973. "The Libyan and Nubian Kings of Egypt: Notes on the Chronology of Dynasties XXII to XXVI." *JNES* 32: 4–25.

Bates, O. 1914. *The Eastern Libyans: An Essay*. London: Macmillan.

Ben-Dor Evian, S. 2011a. "Shishak's Karnak Relief: More than Just Name-rings." In *Egypt, Canaan and Israel: History, Imperialism, Ideology and Literature, Culture and History of the Ancient Near East*, edited by S. Bar, D. Kahn, and J.J. Shirley, 11–22. Leiden: Brill.

———. 2011b. "Egypt and the Levant in the Iron Age I–IIA: The Ceramic Evidence." *Tel Aviv* 38: 94–119.

Bickel, S. 2009. "The Inundation Inscription in Luxor Temple." In *The Libyan Period in Egypt: Historical and Cultural Studies into the 21st–24th Dynasties. Proceedings of a conference at Leiden University, 25–27 October 2007*, edited by G.P.F. Broekman, R.J. Demarée, and O.E. Kaper, 51–55. Leiden: Nederlands Instituut voor het Nabije Oosten; Leuven: Peeters.

Bierbrier. 2019. *Who Was Who in Egyptology*. 5th ed. London: Egypt Exploration Society.

Birch, S. 1850. "Observations on Two Egyptian Cartouches and Some Other Ivory Ornaments, Found at Nimroud." *Transactions of the Royal Society of Literature of the United Kingdom*, series 2, III: 151–77.

Bonhême, M.-A. 1987. *Les noms royaux dans l'Égypte de la Troisième Période Intermédiaire*. Cairo: Institut français d'archéologie orientale.

Botta, P.E., and E. Flandin. 1849–50. *Monument de Ninive*. 2 vols. Paris: Imprimerie Nationale.

Breasted, J.H. 1905. *A History of Egypt: From the Earliest Times to the Persian Conquest*. New York: Charles Scribner's Sons.

———. 1906–1907. *Ancient Records of Egypt: Historical Documents from the Earliest Times to the Persian Conquest*. 5 vols. Chicago, London, and Leipzig: University of Chicago Press.

Brissaud, P. 2010. "Mission française des fouilles de Tanis: campagne d'automne 2010." *BSFFT* 24: 5–32.

Broekman, G.P.F. 1988. "The Nile Level Records of the Twenty-second and Twenty-third Dynasties in Karnak: A Reconsideration of the Chronological Order." *JEA* 88: 161–78.

———. 2000. "Shoshenq Maäkheperre and Shoshenq Heqakheperre: Contemplations on the Question of Which of Them (If One of the Two) Was Identical with the High Priest of Amun, Shoshenq Son of King Osorkon I." *GM* 176: 39–46.

———. 2006–2007. "On the Identity of King Shoshenq Buried in the Vestibule of the Tomb of Psusennes I in Tanis (NRT III)." *GM* 211: 11–20; 212: 9–28.

———. 2008. "The Chronicle of Prince Osorkon and Its Historical Context." *JEgH* 1: 209–34.

———. 2009. "Falcon Headed Coffins and Cartonnages." *JEA* 95: 67–81.

———. 2010a. "The Leading Theban Priests of Amun and Their Families under Libyan Rule." *JEA* 96: 125–48.

———. 2010b. "Libyan Rule over Egypt: The Influence of the Tribal Background of the Ruling Class on Political Structures and Developments during the Libyan Period in Egypt." *SAK* 39: 86–99.

———. 2011. "The Egyptian Chronology from the Start of the Twenty-second until the End of the Twenty-fifth Dynasty: Facts, Suppositions and Arguments." *JEgH* 4: 41–81.

———. 2018. "On the Identity of King Shoshenq Heqakheperre, Buried in Royal Tomb NRT III in Tanis: A Reconsideration." *GM* 254: 25–36.

———. 2019. "Royal Shabtis from Tanis." *GM* 257: 17–24.

Broekman, G.P.F., R.J. Demarée, and O.E. Kaper. 2008. "The Numbering of the Kings Called Shoshenq." *GM* 216: 9.

Broekman, G.P.F., R.J. Demarée, and O.E. Kaper, eds. 2009. *The Libyan Period in Egypt: Historical and Cultural Studies into the 21th–24th Dynasties. Proceedings of a conference at Leiden University, 25–27 October 2007*. Leiden: Nederlands Instituut voor het Nabije Oosten; Leuven: Peeters.

Brugsch, H. 1879. *A History of Egypt under the Pharaohs, derived entirely from the monuments*. Translated by H.D. Seymour, edited by P. Smith. London: John Murray.

———. 1891. *A History of Egypt under the Pharaohs*. Translated by M. Brodrick. London: John Murray.

Brunton, G. 1939. "Some Notes on the Burial of Shashanq HeqakheperRe'." *ASAE* 39: 541–47.

Bruyère, B. 1957. "Une nouvelle famille de prêtres de Montou trouvée par Baraize à Deir el Bahri." *ASAE* 54: 11–33.

Bunsen, C.C.J. von. 1845. *Aegyptens Stelle in der Weltgeschichte* III. *Das mittlere und neue Reich*. Hamburg: Friedrich Perthes.

———. 1854. *Egypt's Place in Universal History* II. *Researches into the Chronology and History of the Old, Middle and New Empires*. Translated by C.H. Cottrell. London: Longman, Brown, Green, and Longmans.

Burstein, S.M. 1984. "Psamtek I and the End of Nubian Domination in Egypt." *JSSEA* 14: 31–34.

Caminos, R. 1952. "Gebel es-Silsilah No. 100." *JEA* 38: 46–61.

———. 1958. *The Chronicle of Prince Osorkon*. Rome: Pontificium Institutum Biblicum.

———. 1964. "The Nitocris Adoption Stela." *JEA* 50: 71–101.

Champollion, J.-F. 1824. *Précis du système hiéroglyphique des anciens Égyptiens, ou recherches sur les élémens premiers de cette écriture sacrée, sur leurs diverses combinaisons, et sur les rapports de ce système avec les autres méthodes graphiques égyptiennes*. 2 vols. Paris: Treuttel et Würtz.

———. 1824–26. *Lettres à M. le duc de Blacas d'Aulps, Premier Gentilhomme de la Chambre, Pair de France, etc., relatives au Musée Royal Égyptien de Turin*. 2 vols. Paris: Didot.

———. 1909. *Lettres de Champollion le Jeune*. Edited by H. Hartleben. Paris: Ernest Leroux.

Chapman, R.P. 2009. "Putting Sheshonq I in His Place." *PEQ* 141/1: 3–17.

Cline, E.H. 2021. *1177 B.C.: The Year Civilization Collapsed*. 2nd ed. Princeton: Princeton University Press.

Cole, E.M. 2023. "A Quantitative Analysis of the Third Intermediate Period Nile Level Records from the Karnak 'Quay' and Their Implications." *Claroscuro* 22/2: 1–23. DOI: https://doi.org/10.35305/cl.vi22.137

Cooney, K. 2024. *Recycling for Death: Coffin Reuse in Ancient Egypt and the Theban Royal Caches*. Cairo: American University in Cairo Press.

Damarany, A., and K.M. Cahail. 2016. "The Sarcophagus of the High Priest of Amun, Menkheperre, from the Coptic Monastery of Apa Moses at Abydos." *MDAIK* 72: 11–30.

Daressy, G. 1913. "Notes sur les XXIIe, XXIIIe et XXIVe dynasties." *RecTrav* 35: 129–50.

D'Auria, S., P. Lacovara, and C.H. Roehrig. 1988. *Mummies and Magic: The Funerary Arts of Ancient Egypt*. Boston: Museum of Fine Arts.

De Meulenaere, J. 1978. "La statuette JE 37163 du Musée du Caire." *SAK* 6: 63–68.

———. 1985. "Les grands-prêtres de Ptah à l'époque saïto-perse." In *Mélanges offerts à Jean Vercoutter*, edited by F. Geus and F. Thill, 263–66. Paris: Éditions Recherche sur les civilisations.

Derry, D.E. 1939. "Note on the Remains of Shashanq." *ASAE* 39: 549–51.

———. 1942. "Mummification. II.—Methods Practiced at Different Periods." *ASAE* 41: 240–69.

Dodson, A. 1993a. "Psusennes II and Shoshenq I." *JEA* 79: 267–68.

———. 1993b. "A New King Shoshenq Confirmed?" *GM* 137: 53–58.

———. 1994. *The Canopic Equipment of the Kings of Egypt*. London and New York: Kegan Paul International.

———. 1996. "Coffin Development: A Problem for the New Chronology." In *A Test of Time: The London Debate*, edited by M. Rowland, 23–26. Basingstoke: Institute for the Study of Interdisciplinary Sciences.

———. 1998. "A Funerary Mask in Durham and Mummy Adornment in the Late Second Intermediate Period and Early Eighteenth Dynasty." *JEA* 84: 93–99.

———. 2009a. "The Priest of Amun Iuput and his Distinguished Ancestors." *JEA* 95: 51–66.

———. 2009b. "The Transition between the 21st and 22nd Dynasties Revisited." In *The Libyan Period in Egypt: Historical and Cultural Studies into the 21st–24th Dynasties. Proceedings of a conference at Leiden University, 25–27 October 2007*, edited by G.P.F. Broekman, R.J. Demarée, and O.E. Kaper, 103–12. Leiden: Nederlands Instituut voor het Nabije Oosten; Leuven: Peeters.

———. 2014. "The Coregency Conundrum." *Kmt* 25/2: 28–35.

———. 2016. "Sarcophagi." In *The Oxford*

Handbook of the Valley of the Kings, edited by R.H. Wilkinson and K. Weeks, 245–59. Oxford: Oxford University Press.

———. 2019a. *Rameses III, King of Egypt: His Life and Afterlife*. Cairo: American University in Cairo Press.

———. 2019b. *Afterglow of Empire: Egypt from the Fall of the New Kingdom to the Saite Renaissance*. 2nd ed. Cairo: American University in Cairo Press.

———. 2021. *The First Pharaohs: Their Lives and Afterlives*. Cairo: American University in Cairo Press.

———. 2023a. "The Palestinian Campaign(s) of Shoshenq I." In *Weseretkau "Mighty of Kas": Papers in Memory of Cathleen A. Keller*, edited by C. Redmount and D. Kiser-Go, 295–305. Columbus, GA: Lockwood Press.

———. 2023b. *The Nubian Pharaohs of Egypt: Their Lives and Afterlives*. Cairo: American University in Cairo Press.

Dodson, A., and J. Gee. 2017. "The Authenticity of the Canopic Jars of a King Takelot in Leiden." *GM* 253: 67–75.

Dodson, A., and K. Griffin. 2024. "The Sarcophagus and Stone Coffin of Amenhotep-son-of-Hapu." In *From Objects to Histories: Studies in Honour of John H. Taylor*, edited by N. Strudwick and D.A. Aston, 130–45. Wallasey: Abercromby Press.

Edwards, I.E.S. 1982. "Egypt: From the Twenty-second to the Twenty-fourth Dynasty." In *Cambridge Ancient History*, 3/1: *The Prehistory of the Balkans, the Middle East and the Aegean World, Tenth to Eighth Centuries* B.C., edited by J. Boardman, I.E.S. Edwards, N.G.L. Hammond, and E. Sollberger, 534–77. Cambridge: Cambridge University Press.

Epigraphic Survey. 1930. *Medinet Habu* I. *Earlier Historical Records of Ramses III*. Chicago: University of Chicago Press.

———. 1932. *Medinet Habu* II. *The Later Historical Records of Ramses III*. Chicago: University of Chicago Press.

———. 1954. *Reliefs and Inscriptions at Karnak III. The Bubastite Portal*. Chicago: University of Chicago Press.

———. 1979. *The Temple of Khonsu I. Scenes of King Herihor in the Court*. Chicago: Oriental Institute.

Fazzini, R. 1997. "Several Objects, and Some Aspects of the Art of the Third Intermediate Period." In *Chief of Seers: Egyptian Studies in Memory of Cyril Aldred*, edited by E. Goring, N. Reeves, and J. Ruffle, 113–37. London: Kegan Paul International.

Feucht, E. 1981. "Ein Relief Scheschonqs I. beim Erschlagen der Feinde aus El-Hibe." *SAK* 9: 105–17.

Firth, C.M., and J.E. Quibell. 1935. *The Step Pyramid*. 2 vols. Cairo: Imprimerie de l'Institut français d'archéologie orientale.

Frame, G. 2021. *The Royal Inscriptions of Sargon II, King of Assyria (721–705* BC*)*. Winona Lake, IN: Eisenbrauns.

Fujii, N. 2024. "A Study on the Rise of Sheshonq B, Later King Sheshonq I of the 22nd Dynasty." *Orient* 59: 71–77.

Gardiner, A.H. 1932. *Late-Egyptian Stories*. Brussels: Fondation égyptologique Reine Élisabeth.

———. 1961. *Egypt of the Pharaohs: An Introduction*. Oxford: Clarendon Press.

Gauthier, H. 1914a. "Les rois Chéchanq." *BIFAO* 11: 197–216.

———. 1914b. *Le Livre des rois d'Égypte* III. Cairo: Institut français d'archéologie orientale.

———. 1921. "À travers la Basse-Égypte." *ASAE* 21: 17–39, 197–213.

Gill, D., and M. Vickers. 1996. "Bocchoris the Wise and Absolute Chronology." *Römische Mitteilungen* 103: 1–9.

Goyon, G. 1987. *La découverte des trésors de Tanis: Aventures archéologiques en Égypte*. Paris: Perséa.

Goyon, J.-C., and C. Traunecker. 1982. "La chapelle de Thot et d'Amon au sud-ouest du Lac Sacré." In *Cahiers de Karnak* 7: 355–66. Paris: Éditions Recherche sur les Civilisations.

Graefe, E. 1975. "Der libysche Stammesname *p(j)d(j)/pjt* im spätzeitlichen Onomastikon." *Enchoria* 5: 13–17.

Hall, H.R.H. 1925. "The Eclipse of Egypt." In *The Cambridge Ancient History* 3: *The Assyrian Empire*, edited by J.B. Bury, S.A. Cook, and F.E. Adcock, 251–69. Cambridge: Cambridge University Press.

Hölbl, G. 1981. "Die Aegyptiaca des griechischen, italischen und westphönikischen Raumes aus der Zeit des Pharao Bocchoris (718/17–712 v. Chr.)." *Grazer Beiträge* 10: 1–20.

Hölscher, U. 1954. *The Excavation of Medinet Habu V. The Post-Ramessid Remains*. Chicago: Chicago University Press.

Hulin, L. 2020. "The Libyans." In *The Oxford Handbook of Egyptology*, edited by E. Shaw and E. Bloxam, 493–513. Oxford: Oxford University Press.

Jacquet-Gordon, C. 1975. Review of 1973 edition of Kitchen 1996. *BiOr* 32: 358–60.

James, P. 1991. *Centuries of Darkness: A Challenge to the Conventional Chronology of Old World Archaeology*. London: Jonathan Cape.

James, P., and R. Morkot. 1991. "'Centuries of Darkness.'" *TLS* 4601: 15.

James, P., and P.G. van der Veen, eds. 2015. *Solomon and Shishak: Current Perspectives from Archaeology, Epigraphy, History and Chronology. Proceedings of the Third BICANE Colloquium held at Sidney Sussex College, Cambridge, 26–27 March, 2011*. Oxford: Archaeopress.

Jansen-Winkeln, K. 1985. *Ägyptische Biographien der 22. und 23. Dynastie*. Wiesbaden: Otto Harrassowitz.

———. 1987. "Thronname und Begräbnis Takeloths I." *VA* 3: 253–58.

———. 1994. "Der Beginn der libyschen Herrschaft in Ägypten." *Biblische Notizen* 71: 78–97.

———. 1995. "Historische Probleme der 3. Zwischenzeit." *JEA* 81: 129–49.

———. 2006. "Third Intermediate Period." In *Ancient Egyptian Chronology*, edited by E. Hornung, R. Krauss, and D.A. Warburton, 234–65. Leiden: Brill.

———. 2007–23. *Inschriften der Spätzeit*. 5 vols. Wiesbaden: Harrassowitz.

———. 2016. "Beiträge zur Geschichte der 21. Dynastie." *JEA* 102: 73–96.

Janssen, J.M.A. 1954. "Over farao Bocchoris." In *Varia Historica aangeboden aan Professor Doctor A. W. Byvanck ter gelegenheid van zijn zeventigste verjaardag door de Historische Kring te Leiden*, 17–29. Assen: Van Gorcum.

Jurman, C. 2006a. "Die Namen des Rudjamun in der Kapelle des Osiris-Hekadjet: Bemerkungen zu Titulaturen der 3. Zwischenzeit und dem Wadi Gasus-Graffito." *GM* 210: 69–91.

———. 2006b. "The Osiris Chapels of the Third Intermediate Period and the Late Period at Karnak: Some Aspects of Their Religious and Historical Significance." In *Aegyptus et Pannonia* III: *Acta symposii anno 2004*, edited by H. Győry, 107–30. Budapest: MEBT-ÓEB.

———. 2009. "From the Libyan Dynasties to the Kushites in Memphis: Historical Problems and Cultural Issues." In *The Libyan Period in Egypt: Historical and Cultural Studies into the 21th–24th Dynasties. Proceedings of a conference at Leiden University, 25–27 October 2007*, edited by G.P.F. Broekman, R.J. Demarée, and O.E. Kaper, 113–38. Leiden: Nederlands Instituut voor het Nabije Oosten; Leuven: Peeters.

———. 2020. *Memphis in der Dritten Zwischenzeit: eine Studie zur (Selbst-) Repräsentation von Eliten in der 21. und 22. Dynastie*. 2 vols. Hamburg: Widmaier.

Kahn, D. 2001. "The Inscription of Sargon II at Tang-i Var and the Chronology of Dynasty 25." *Orientalia* 70: 1–18.

———. 2006. "A Problem of Pedubasts?" *Antiguo Oriente* 4: 21–40.

———. 2009. "The Transition from Libyan to Nubian Rule in Egypt: Revisiting the Reign of Tefnakht." In *The Libyan Period in Egypt: Historical and Cultural Studies into the 21st–24th Dynasties. Proceedings of a conference at Leiden University, 25–27 October 2007*, edited by G.P.F. Broekman, R.J. Demarée, and O.E. Kaper, 139–48. Leiden: Nederlands Instituut voor het Nabije Oosten; Leuven: Peeters.

Kaper, O. 2009. "Epigraphic Evidence from the Dahleh Oasis in the Libyan Period." In *The Libyan Period in Egypt: Historical and Cultural Studies into the 21st–24th Dynasties. Proceedings of a conference at Leiden University, 25–27 October 2007*, edited by G.P.F. Broekman, R.J. Demarée, and O.E. Kaper, 149–59. Leiden: Nederlands Instituut voor het Nabije Oosten; Leuven: Peeters.

Kilani, M. 2019. *Byblos in the Late Bronze Age: Interactions between the Levantine and Egyptian Worlds*. Leiden: Brill.

Kitchen, K.A. 1968–90. *Ramesside Inscriptions: Historical and Biographical*. 8 vols. Oxford: Blackwell.

———. 1990. "The Arrival of the Libyans in Late New Kingdom Egypt." In *Libya and Egypt, c 1300–750 BC*, edited by A. Leahy, 15–27. London: Centre of Near and Middle Eastern Studies, School of Oriental and African Studies, University of London, and the Society for Libyan Studies.

———. 1991a. "Egyptian Chronology: Problem or Solution?" *Cambridge Archaeological Journal* 1: 235–39.

———. 1991b. "Blind Dating." *TLS* 4598: 21.

———. 1996. *The Third Intermediate Period in Egypt (1100–650 B.C.)*. 3rd ed. Warminster: Aris and Phillips.

———. 2009. "The Third Intermediate Period in Egypt: An Overview of Fact and Fiction." In *The Libyan Period in Egypt: Historical and Cultural Studies into the 21st–24th Dynasties. Proceedings of a conference at Leiden University, 25–27 October 2007*, edited by G.P.F. Broekman, R.J. Demarée, and O.E. Kaper, 161–202. Leiden: Nederlands Instituut voor het Nabije Oosten; Leuven: Peeters.

Korostovtsev, M.A. 1960. *Путешествие Ун–Амуна в Библ*. Moscow: Academy of Sciences.

Krauss, R. 2006a. "Dates Relating to a Seasonal Phenomena." In *Ancient Egyptian Chronology*, edited by E. Hornung, R. Krauss, and D.A. Warburton, 369–79. Leiden: Brill.

———. 2006b. "Lunar Dates." In *Ancient Egyptian Chronology*, edited by E. Hornung, R. Krauss, and D.A. Warburton, 395–431. Leiden: Brill.

Kruchten, J.-M. 1989. *Les annales des prêtres de Karnak (XXI–XXIIImes dynasties) et autres textes contemporains relatifs à l'initiation des prêtres d'Amon*. Leuven: Departement Oriëntalistiek.

Laato, A. 2015. *Guide to Biblical Chronology*. Sheffield: Phoenix Press.

Lange, E. 2008. "Legitimation und Herrschaft in der Libyerzeit: Eine neue Inschrift Osorkons I. aus Bubastis (Tell Basta)." *ZÄS* 135: 131–41.

———. 2009. "The Sed-Festival Reliefs of Osorkon II at Bubastis: New Investigations." In *The Libyan Period in Egypt: Historical and Cultural Studies into the 21st–24th Dynasties. Proceedings of a conference at Leiden University, 25–27 October 2007*, edited by G.P.F. Broekman, R.J. Demarée, and O.E. Kaper, 203–18. Leiden: Nederlands Instituut voor het Nabije Oosten; Leuven: Peeters.

———. 2010. "King Shoshenqs at Bubastis." *EgArch* 37: 19–20.

Leahy, A. 1985. "The Libyan Period in Egypt: An Essay in Interpretation." *Libyan Studies* 16: 51–65.

———. 1990. "The Twenty-third Dynasty." In *Libya and Egypt, c 1300–750* BC, edited by A. Leahy, 177–200. London: Centre of Near and Middle Eastern Studies, School of Oriental and African Studies, University of London; Society for Libyan Studies.

Leemans, C. 1838. *Lettre à M. François Salvolini sur les monumens égyptiens portant des légendes royales dans les musées d'antiquités de Leide, de Londres et dans quelques collections particulières en Angleterre*. Leiden: Hazenberg.

Legrain, G. 1896a. "Textes gravés sur le quai de Karnak." *ZÄS* 34: 111–18.

———. 1896b. "Les crues du Nil depuis Sheshonq Ier jusqu'à Psametik." *ZÄS* 34: 119–21.

———. 1914a. "Au pylône d'Harmhabi à Karnak (X[e] pylône)." *ASAE* 14: 13–44.

———. 1914b. *Statues et statuettes des rois et particuliers*, 3. Cairo: Institut français d'archéologie orientale.

Leichty, E. 2011. *The Royal Inscriptions of Esarhaddon, King of Assyria (680–669* BC*)*. Winona Lake, IN: Eisenbrauns.

Lemaire, A. 2006. "La datation des rois de Byblos Abibaal et Élibaal et les relations entre l'Égypte et le Levant au Xe s. av. notre ère." *CRAIBL* 150: 1697–1716.

Lenzo, G., R. Meffre, and F. Payraudeau. 2023. *La tombe memphite du prince héritier Chéchonq et son mobilier funéraire*. Cairo: Institut français d'archéologie orientale.

Lepsius, C.R. 1849–59. *Denkmaeler aus Aegypten und Aethiopien*. 6 vols. Berlin and Leipzig: Nicolaische Buchandlung.

———. 1856. "Über die XXII. ägyptische Königsdynastie: nebst einigen Bemerkungen zu der XXVI. und anderen Dynastieen des Neuen Reichs." *Abhandlungen der Königlichen Akademie der Wissenschaften zu Berlin, hist.-philol. Kl.* 1856: 259–320.

———. 1858a. *The XXII. Egyptian Royal Dynasty: with some remarks on XXVI. and other dynasties of the New Kingdom*. Translated by W. Bell. London: Trübner.

———. 1858b. *Königsbuch der alten Ägypter*. 2 vols. Berlin: Bessersche Buchhandlung.

Lüddeckens, E. 1954. "Herodot und Ägypten." *ZDMG* 104: 330–46.

Lull, J. 2002. *Las tumbas reales egipcias del Tercer Período Intermedio (dinastías XXI–XXV)*. Oxford: Archaeopress.

Lurson, B. 2018. "From the Foundations to the Excavation: A Stratigraphy-based History of the Temple of Tuya." *In Thebes in the First Millennium* BC*: Art and Archaeology of the Kushite Period and Beyond*, edited by E. Pischikova, J. Budka, and K. Griffin, 193–213. London: Golden House Publications.

Malek, J. 2007–12. *Topographical Bibliography of Ancient Egyptian Hieroglyphic Texts, Reliefs and Paintings* 8, nos. 3–4, *Objects of Provenance Unknown, Stelae*. Oxford: Griffith Institute.

Malinine, M., G. Posener, and J. Vercoutter. 1968. *Catalogue des stèles du Sérapéum de Memphis*, 1. Paris: Imprimerie Nationale.

Manassa, C. 2003. *The Great Karnak Inscription of Merenptah: Grand Strategy in the 13th Century* BC. New Haven: Yale Egyptological Seminar.

Manniche, L. 2011. *Lost Ramessid and Post-Ramessid Private Tombs in the Theban Necropolis.* Copenhagen: Museum Tusculanum Press.

Mariette, A. 1855. "Renseignements sur les soixante-quatre Apis trouvés dans les souterrains du Sérapéum." *Bulletin archéologique de l'Athénaeum français* 1: 45–50, 53–58, 66–68, 85–90, 93–100.

———. 1857. *Le Sérapeum de Memphis découvert et décrit par Aug. Mariette. Ouvrage dédié à S. A. I. Mgr. le Prince Napoléon et publié sous les auspices de S. E. M. Achille Fould, ministre d'état*. Paris: Gide.

Markiewicz, T. 2008. "Bocchoris the Lawgiver—or Was He Really?" *JEgH* 1: 309–30.

Maspero, G. 1880. Review of Brugsch 1879. *Revue critique d'histoire et litterature* 2: 105–17.

Meffre, R. 2015. *D'Héracléopolis à Hermopolis: la Moyenne Égypte durant la Troisième Période intermédiaire (XXIe–XXIVe dynasties)*. Paris: Presses de l'Université Paris–Sorbonne.

Meffre, R., and F. Payraudeau. 2018. "Enquête épigraphique, stylistique et historique sur les blocs du lac sacré de Mout à Tanis: Commentaires à propos d'un ouvrage récemment paru." *BSFE* 199: 128–43.

———. 2019. "Un nouveau roi à la fin de l'époque libyenne: Pami II." *RdE* 69: 147–57.

Montet, P. 1939. "Découverte d'une nécropole royale à Tanis." *ASAE* 39: 529–39.

———. 1942. "La nécropole des rois Tanites." *Kêmi* 9: 1–96.

———. 1947. *La nécropole royale de Tanis I: Les constructions et le tombeau de Osorkon II à Tanis*. Paris: n.p.

———. 1951. *La nécropole royale de Tanis II: Les constructions et le tombeau de Psousennes à Tanis*. Paris: n.p.

———. 1960. *La nécropole royale de Tanis III: Les constructions et le tombeau de Chéchanq III à Tanis*. Paris: n.p.

———. 1966. *Le lac sacré de Tanis*. Paris: Imprimerie Nationale.

Moret, A. 1903. *De Bocchori rege*. Paris: Leroux.

Morkot, R., and P. James. 2009. "Peftjauawybast, King of Nen-nesut: Genealogy, Art History, and the Chronology of Late Libyan Egypt." *Antiguo Oriente* 7: 13–55.

Muhs, B. 1998. "Partisan Royal Epithets in the Late Third Intermediate Period and the Dynastic Affiliations of Pedubast I and Iuput II." *JEA* 84: 220–23.

Müller, W.M. 1887. "The Supposed Name of Judah in the List of Shoshenq." *PSBA* 10: 81–86.

———. 1908. "Königsnamen der 22. ägyptischen Dynastie." *OLZ* 11: 361–63.

———. 1921. "Aegyptisch-Libysches." *OLZ* 24: 193–97.

Naville, E. 1891. *Bubastis (1887–1889)*. London: Egypt Exploration Fund.

———. 1892. *The Festival Hall of Osorkon II in the Great Temple of Bubastis (1887–1889)*. London: Egypt Exploration Fund.

Novotny, J., and J. Jeffers. 2018–23. *The Royal Inscriptions of Ashurbanipal (668–631 BC), Aššur-etel-ilāni (630–627 BC), and Sîn-šarra-iškun (626–612 BC), Kings of Assyria*. 2 vols. Winona Lake, IN: Eisenbrauns.

Obsomer, C. 1995. *Sésostris Ier: étude chronologique et historique du règne*. Brussels: Conaissance de l'Egypte Ancienne.

O'Conner, D. 1990. "The Nature of Tjemhu (Libyan) Society in the Later New Kingdom." In *Libya and Egypt, c 1300–750 BC*, edited by A. Leahy, 29–113. London: Centre of Near and Middle Eastern Studies, School of Oriental and African Studies, University of London, and the Society for Libyan Studies.

Ōhshiro, M. 1999. "The Identity of Osorkon III: The Revival of an Old Theory (Prince Osorkon = Osorkon III)." 古代オリエント博物館紀要 [*Bulletin of the Ancient Orient Museum*] 20: 33–49.

———. 2020. "Why Did King Psusennes I Own a Silver Coffin?" *GM* 262: 185–90.

———. 2017. "Searching for the Tomb of the Theban King Osorkon III." In *A True Scribe of Abydos: Essays on First Millennium Egypt in Honour of Anthony Leahy*, edited by C. Jurman, B. Bader, and D.A. Aston, 299–317. Leuven: Peeters.

Payraudeau, F. 2000. "Remarques sur l'identité du premier et du dernier Osorkon." *GM* 178: 175–80.

———. 2008. "Des nouvelles annales sacerdotales des règnes de Siamon, Psousennès II et Osorkon Ier." *BIFAO* 108: 293–308.

———. 2009. "Takeloth III: Considerations on Old and New Documents." In *The Libyan Period in Egypt: Historical and Cultural Studies into the 21st–24th Dynasties. Proceedings of a conference at Leiden University, 25–27 October 2007*, edited by G.P.F. Broekman, R.J. Demarée, and O.E. Kaper, 291–302. Leiden: Nederlands Instituut voor het Nabije Oosten; Leuven: Peeters.

———. 2014. *Administration, société et pouvoir à Thèbes sous la XXIIe dynastie bubastite*. 2 vols. Cairo: Institut français d'archéologie orientale.

———. 2015. "La situation politique de Tanis sous la XXVe dynastie." In *Proceedings of the Tenth International Congress of Egyptologists, University of the Aegean, Rhodes, 22–29 May 2008*, edited by P. Kousoulis and N. Lazaridis, 849–60. Louvain: Peeters.

———. 2023a. "Une stèle inédite du chef des Ma Nimlot à Karnak." *BSFE* 208: 61–75.

———. 2023b. "Le sarcophage de Ramsès II remployé à Abydos!" *RdE* 73: 103–15.

Payraudeau, F., and R. Meffre. 2016. "Varia tanitica I: Vestiges royaux." *BIFAO* 116: 273–302.

Perdu, O. 2002. "De Stéphinates à Necho ou les débuts de la XXVIe Dynastie." *CRAIBL* 2002: 1215–44.

Perez Die, M.C. 2009. "The Third Intermediate Period Necropolis at Herakleopolis Magna." In *The Libyan Period in Egypt: Historical and Cultural Studies into the 21st–24th Dynasties. Proceedings of a conference at Leiden University, 25–27 October 2007*, edited by G.P.F. Broekman, R.J. Demarée, and O.E. Kaper, 301–26. Leiden: Nederlands Instituut voor het Nabije Oosten; Leuven: Peeters.

Petrie, W.M.F. 1905. *A History of Egypt III*. London: Methuen.

———. 1914a. "The Mysterious Zêt." *Ancient Egypt* A: 32.

———. 1914b. Review of Daressy 1913. *Ancient Egypt* A: 39–40.

Porter, B., and R.B. Moss. 1934. *Topographical Bibliography of Ancient Egyptian Hieroglyphic Texts, Reliefs and Paintings* IV. *Lower and Middle Egypt*. Oxford: Clarendon Press.

———. 1937. *Topographical Bibliography of Ancient Egyptian Hieroglyphic Texts, Reliefs and Paintings* V. *Upper Egypt: Sites*. Oxford: Clarendon Press.

———. 1952. *Topographical Bibliography of Ancient Egyptian Hieroglyphic Texts, Reliefs and Paintings* VII. *Nubia, Deserts, and Outside Egypt*. Oxford: Clarendon Press.

———. 1960–64. *Topographical Bibliography of Ancient Egyptian Hieroglyphic Texts, Reliefs and Painting*, I. *The Theban Necropolis*. 2nd ed. Oxford: Clarendon Press.

———. 1972. *Topographical Bibliography of Ancient Egyptian Hieroglyphic Texts, Reliefs and Paintings* II. *Theban Temples*. 2nd ed. Oxford: Clarendon Press.

———. 1974–81. *Topographical Bibliography of Ancient Egyptian Hieroglyphic Texts, Reliefs and Paintings* III. *Memphis*. 2nd ed. by J. Málek. Oxford: Clarendon Press/Griffith Institute.

Porter, R.M. 2011. "Osorkon III of Tanis: The Contemporary of Piye?" *GM* 230: 111–12.

Price, C. 2024. "Two Baboons of Iuwlot." In *From Objects to Histories: Studies in Honour of John H. Taylor*, edited by N. Strudwick and D.A. Aston, 469–75. Wallasey: Abercromby Press.

Priese, K.-H. 1970. "Der Beginn der Kuschitischen Herrschaft." *ZÄS* 98: 16–32.

Ranke, H. 1926. *Koptische Friedhöfe bei Karâra und der Amontempel Scheschonks I bei El Hibe: Bericht über die badischen Grabungen in Ägypten in den Wintern 1913 und 1914*. Berlin and Leipzig: Walter de Gruyter.

Raue, D. 2010. "Third Intermediate Period: King Ini on Elephantine." *ASAE* 84: 352–53.

Ray, J.D. 1974. "Pharaoh Nechepso." *JEA* 60: 255–56.

Renouf, P. Le P. 1890–91. "Who Were the Libyans?" *PSBA* 13: 599–603.

Revillout, E. 1903. *Précis du droit égyptien comparé aux autres droits de l'antiquité*. Paris: Giard & Brière.

Ridgway, D. 1999. "The Rehabilitation of Bocchoris: Notes and Queries from Italy." *JEA* 85: 143–52.

Ritner, R.K. 1999. "An Oblique Reference to the Expelled High Priest Osorkon?" In *Gold of Praise: Studies on Ancient Egypt in Honor of Edward F. Wente*, edited by E. Teeter and J.A. Larson, 351–60. Chicago: Oriental Institute of the University of Chicago.

———. 2009a. *The Libyan Anarchy: Inscriptions from Egypt's Third Intermediate Period*. Atlanta: Society of Biblical Literature.

———. 2009b. "Fragmentation and Re-integration in the Third Intermediate Period." In *The Libyan Period in Egypt: Historical and Cultural Studies into the 21st–24th Dynasties. Proceedings of a conference at Leiden University, 25–27 October 2007*, edited by G.P.F. Broekman, R.J. Demarée, and O.E. Kaper, 327–40. Leiden: Nederlands Instituut voor het Nabije Oosten; Leuven: Peeters.

Rohl, D.M. 1986. "Forum: David Rohl Replies." *Chronology and Catastrophism Workshop* 1986/1: 17–23.

———. 1989–90. "The Early Third Intermediate Period: Some Chronological Considerations." *Journal of the Ancient Chronology Forum* 3: 45–70.

———. 1995. *A Test of Time I. The Bible: From Myth to History*. London: Century.

Rondot, V., ed. 2022. *Pharaon des Deux Terres: l'épopée africaine des rois de Napata*. Paris: Louvre éditions/éditions El Viso.

Rosellini, I. 1832–33. *I monumenti dell'Egitto e della Nubia: disegnati dalla Spedizione Scientifico-Letteraria Toscana in Egitto I. Monumenti Storici*. 2 vols. Pisa: Niccolò Capurro.

Rougé, E. de. 1873–74. "Étude sur quelques monuments du règne de Tahraka." *Mélanges d'archéologie égyptienne et assyrienne* 1: 11–23, 85–89.

Ryholt, K.S.B. 1997. *The Political Situation in Egypt during the Second Intermediate Period, c. 1800–1550* B.C. Copenhagen: Museum Tusculanum Press.

———. 2004. "The Assyrian Invasion of Egypt in Egyptian Literary Tradition." In *Assyria and Beyond: Studies Presented to Mogens Trolle Larsen*, edited by J.G. Dercksen, 384–511. Leiden: Nederlands Instituut voor het Nabije Oosten.

Saghieh, M. 1983. *Byblos in the Third Millennium* B.C.*: A Reconstruction of the Stratigraphy and a Study of the Cultural Connections*. Warminster: Aris & Phillips.

Sagrillo, T.L. 2009. "The Geographic Origins of the 'Bubastite' Dynasty." In *The Libyan Period in Egypt: Historical and Cultural Studies into the 21st–24th Dynasties. Proceedings of a conference at Leiden University, 25–27 October 2007*, edited by G.P.F. Broekman, R.J. Demarée, and O.E. Kaper, 341–59. Leiden: Nederlands Instituut voor het Nabije Oosten; Leuven: Peeters.

———. 2011. "The Heart Scarab of King Shoshenq III (Brooklyn Museum 61.10)." *JEA* 97: 240–46.

———. 2015. "Shoshenq I and Biblical Šîšaq: A Philological Defense of Their Traditional Equation." In *Solomon and Shishak: Current Perspectives from Archaeology, Epigraphy, History and Chronology*, edited by P. James and P.G. van der Veen, 61–81. Oxford: Archaeopress.

Sauneron, S., and J. Yoyotte. 1952a. "La campagne nubienne de Psammétique II et sa signification historique." *BIFAO* 50: 157–207.

———. 1952b. "Sur la politique palestinienne des rois saïtes." *Vetus Testamentum* 2: 131–36.

Snape, S. 2003. "The Emergence of Libya on the Horizon of Egypt." In *Mysterious Lands*, edited by D. O'Connor and S. Quirke, 93–106. London: UCL Press.

Spencer, A.J. 2001. "An Elite Cemetery at Tell el-Balamun." *EgArch* 18: 18–20.

Spencer, P.A., and A.J. Spencer. 1986. "Notes on Late Libyan Egypt." *JEA* 72: 198–201.

Spiegelberg, W. 1927. "Die Falkenbezeichnung des Verstorbenen in der Spätzeit." *ZÄS* 62: 27–34.

Stern, L. 1883. "Die XXII. manethonische Dynastie." *ZÄS* 21: 15–26.

Taylor, J.H. 1988. "The Development of Cartonnage Cases." In *Mummies and Magic: The Funerary Arts of Ancient Egypt*, edited by S. D'Auria, P. Lacovara, and C.H Roehrig, 166–67. Boston: Museum of Fine Arts.

———. 2003. "Theban Coffins from the Twenty-second to the Twenty-sixth Dynasty." In *The Theban Necropolis: Past, Present and Future*, edited by N. Strudwick and J.H. Taylor, 95–121. London: British Museum Press.

———. 2009. "Coffins as Evidence for a 'North–South Divide' in the 22nd–25th Dynasties." In *The Libyan Period in Egypt: Historical and Cultural Studies into the 21st–24th Dynasties. Proceedings of a conference at Leiden University, 25–27 October 2007*, edited by G.P.F. Broekman, R.J. Demarée, and O.E. Kaper, 375–415. Leiden: Nederlands Instituut voor het Nabije Oosten; Leuven: Peeters.

Ullmann, M. 2002. *Die Häuser der Millionen von Jahren: eine Untersuchung zu Königskult und Tempeltypologie in Ägypten*. Wiesbaden: Harrassowitz.

Uphill, E.P. 1984. *The Temples of Per Ramesses*. Warminster: Aris & Phillips.

Velikovsky, I. 1952. *Ages in Chaos: From the Exodus to King Akhnaton*. New York: Doubleday.

———. 1960. *Oedipus and Akhnaton*. New York: Doubleday.

———. 1977. *Peoples of the Sea*. New York: Doubleday.

———. 1978. *Ramses II and His Time*. New York: Doubleday.

von Beckerath, J. 1995. "Beiträge zur Geschichte der Libyerzeit, 3. Die Könige namens Pedubaste." *GM* 147: 9–13.

von Känel, F. 1987. "Notes épigraphiques." *Cahiers de Tanis* 1: 45–60.

Waddell, W.G. 1940. *Manetho*. Cambridge, MA: Harvard University Press; London: William Heinmann.

Wilkinson, J.G. 1828. *Materia hieroglyphica: containing the Egyptian pantheon, and the succession of the pharaohs, from the earliest times to the conquest by Alexander, and other hieroglyphical subjects; with plates, and notes explanatory of the same*. Malta: Government Press.

———. 1837. *Manners and Customs of the Ancient Egyptians*. 3 vols. London: John Murray.

Wilson, K.A. 2005. *The Campaign of Pharaoh Shoshenq I into Palestine*. Tübingen: Mohr Siebeck.

Winand, J. 2011. "The *Report of Wenamun*: A Journey in Ancient Egyptian Literature." In *Ramesside Studies in Honour of K. A. Kitchen*, edited by M. Collier and S. Snape, 541–59. Bolton: Rutherford Press.

Winlock, H.E. 1917. "Bas-reliefs from the Egyptian Delta." *BMMA* 12: 64–67.

Young, E. 1963. "Some Notes on the Chronology and Genealogy of the Twenty-first Dynasty." *JARCE* 2: 99–112.

Yoyotte, J. 1961. "Les principautés du Delta au temps de l'anarchie libyenne." In *Mélanges Maspero* 1/4: 121–81. Cairo: Institut français d'archéologie orientale.

———. 1976–77. "'Osorkon fils de

Mehytouskhé,' un pharaon oublié." *BSFE* 77–78: 39–54.

———. 1987. "La datation de la cuve et du couvercle du prince Hornakht." In *Cahiers de Tanis* 1, edited by P. Brissaud, 121–27. Paris: Editions Recherche sur les Civilisations.

Sources of Images

All images by author unless otherwise stated.

1. Lepsius 1849–59: III, pl. 136
2. Bottom left: Epigraphic Survey 1930: pl. 19
   Bottom right: Epigraphic Survey 1932: pl. 72
6. Top: Richard Sellicks
9. Bottom: Epigraphic Survey 1979: pl. 26.
14. Lepsius 1849–59: III, pl. 258c
15. b. Kruchten 1989: pl. 17
    d. Kruchten 1989: pl. 18
17. Bodleian Library, Oxford.
19. Tell Basta-Project, courtesy Eva Lange-Athinodorou
21. Right: Lonneke Delpeut
23. Bottom left, bottom right: Salima Ikram
24. Middle upper: Salima Ikram
    Middle lower and bottom: Robert Ajtai & Steffen Fuchs, © Ägyptische Sammlung, Universität Heidelberg.
26. Bottom: Steve Harvey
27. Bottom: Dyan Hilton. Inset: Caminos 1952: pl x–xiii.
30. a. Author's collection
    b. Peter van der Veen
34. c. Legrain 1914b: pl. ii
35. Oriental Museum, Durham
37. Bottom: Dyan Hilton
38. Metropolitan Museum of Art, New York
48. Naville 1892: frontispiece

54. Musée du Louvre
55. Hölscher 1954: pl. 10b.
59. Epigraphic Survey 1954: pl. 16-22
61. Inset: Legrain 1914a: 14
63. Bottom: †Martin Davies
64. Musée du Louvre
66. Brooklyn Museum
67. Trustees of the British Museum
68. Musée du Louvre
69. Left: Michael Martin via Wikimedia Commons
70. Centre franco-égyptien d'Étude des Temples de Karnak
73. Left: Museo Egizio, Turin; right: Musée du Louvre, Paris
74. Top right: Fazzini 1997: 137, fig. 4, courtesy Egyptian Museum
    Bottom right: Montet 1966: pl. xlvii[29]
75. Musée du Louvre
77. Museum of Fine Arts, Boston
80. a–b. Mission français des fouilles de Tanis/Christelle Desbordes
    c. Montet 1966: pl. lxxviii[243]
    d. Montet 1966: pl. lxxvii[242]
81. Musée du Louvre
82. Top: David Moyer
    Bottom: Firth and Quibell 1935: pl. 15–16.
84. Top: Montet 1966: pl. lxxiii[230]
85a. Brooklyn Museum
86. Top: Mariette 1857: pl. 34. Bottom: Musée du Louvre
88. Petrie Museum
94. Adapted from Montet 1947: pl. vii
95. Adapted from Montet 1947: pl. viii, viiibis
96. Marco Pinfari
97. Adapted from Montet 1947: pl. xxiv–xxxviii
98. Montet 1947: pl. xxvi
99. Marco Pinfari
100. Top: Marco Pinfari
    Bottom: Dyan Hilton
101. Montet 1947: pl. xlvii

102. a–e. Montet 1942: pl iii
f–h. Montet 1960: pl. xlix
i–j. Montet 1947: pl. liv
103. Top: Montet 1947: pl. lvi
Bottom: Montet 1947: pl lv
104. Bottom: Montet 1947: 39
105. Montet 1947: pl. xxx
107. Adapted from Montet 1960: pl. xxvii.
108. Montet 1960: pl. xxix-xxxiii
109. Marco Pinfari
110. Brooklyn Museum
112. Bottom: Hölscher 1954: fig. 9
113. Hölscher 1954: pl. 9, 10c
117. Salima Ikram
118. Top: Amélineau 1899: frontispiece
120. Adapted from Lenzo, Meffre, and Payraudeau 2023: 14
122. Sailko via Wikimedia Commons
123. Musée du Louvre
124. Egypt Exploration Society
125. Egypt Exploration Society
126. Goyon 1987: 61.
127. Goyon 1987: 99.
128. Montet 1939: pl. xcii
129. Left: Montet 1951: pl. xxi
Center and right: Goyon 1987: 123
130. Montet 1947: pl. xv

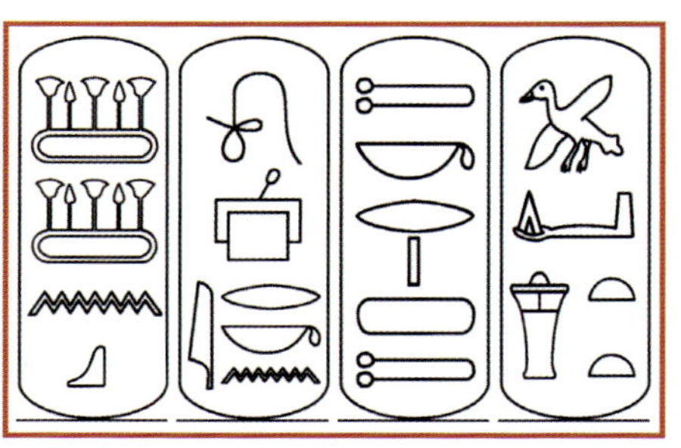

Index

Kings' names are capitalized.